Architecting Microsoft Azure Solutions – Exam Guide 70-535

A complete guide to passing the 70-535 Architecting
Microsoft Azure Solutions exam

Sjoukje Zaal

BIRMINGHAM - MUMBAI

Architecting Microsoft Azure Solutions – Exam Guide 70-535

Commissioning Editor: Vijin Boricha
Acquisition Editor: Rahul Nair
Content Development Editor: Ron Mathew
Technical Editor: Aditya Khadye
Copy Editors: Dipti Mankame, Safis Editing
Project Coordinator: Judie Jose
Proofreader: Safis Editing
Indexer: Tejal Daruwale Soni
Graphics: Tom Scaria
Production Coordinator: Shantanu Zagade

First published: April 2018

Production reference: 1250418

Published by Packt Publishing Ltd.
Livery Place
35 Livery Street
Birmingham
B3 2PB, UK.

ISBN 978-1-78899-173-5

www.packtpub.com

`mapt.io`

Mapt is an online digital library that gives you full access to over 5,000 books and videos, as well as industry leading tools to help you plan your personal development and advance your career. For more information, please visit our website.

Why subscribe?

- Spend less time learning and more time coding with practical eBooks and Videos from over 4,000 industry professionals

- Improve your learning with Skill Plans built especially for you

- Get a free eBook or video every month

- Mapt is fully searchable

- Copy and paste, print, and bookmark content

PacktPub.com

Did you know that Packt offers eBook versions of every book published, with PDF and ePub files available? You can upgrade to the eBook version at `www.PacktPub.com` and as a print book customer, you are entitled to a discount on the eBook copy. Get in touch with us at `service@packtpub.com` for more details.

At `www.PacktPub.com`, you can also read a collection of free technical articles, sign up for a range of free newsletters, and receive exclusive discounts and offers on Packt books and eBooks.

Foreword

It's such an amazing time to be a software architect. We live in a time where there is an infinite number of virtual machines available at our fingertips. The rise of software-based networking allows us to model and create complex networks, firewalls, DMZs, and more in minutes, whereas in the past, it might take months or more even to conceive of such networks!

However, with these new tools come new complexities. There is a huge cafeteria of choices, and it can become extremely overwhelming for even the savviest of architects. Fortunately, Sjoukje Zaal has written the book you're reading right now, as a light to guide you through Architecting Microsoft Azure Solutions! She will walk you through all the exam objectives and enable you to pass 70-535, but more importantly, she'll make you a better software architect.

By the time you're done, you'll understand the full stack, from virtual machines and infrastructure as a service to designing and configuring compute-intensive applications. You'll move up the stack to designing web applications and implementing serverless systems, including microservices.

We will connect these applications and look at how to create robust networking implementations, then connect to data implementations and secure them. We'll explore artificial intelligence and the IoT, and tie it all together with monitoring and alerting strategies.

There's a ton of information out there, and I'm thrilled that someone as experienced as Sjoukje has written such a complex book on the topic! I hope you appreciate her attention to detail and technical insights as much as I do!

We're looking forward to seeing what you build with Azure, and wish you the best of luck in passing the 70-535 exam. You're on your way to architecting *your own* Microsoft Azure Solutions!

Scott Hanselman
@shanselman
Principal Program Manager - .NET and Azure Web Tools

Contributors

About the author

Sjoukje Zaal is a Microsoft Azure MVP and a Microsoft Principal Expert with over 15 years of experience providing architecture, development, consultancy, and design expertise in Microsoft-related technologies. She works at Ordina, a System Integrator in the Netherlands. She is an MCSE Cloud Platform and Infrastructure, MCSD Azure Solutions Architect-, MCSE Productivity-, and MCSD App Builder- certified professional.

Sjoukje is active in the Microsoft Community as a cofounder of SP&C NL and the Mixed Reality User Group, a writer, public speaker, and on MSDN/TechNet.

About the reviewers

Chervine Bhiwoo is a Microsoft MVP, Solutions Architect, and software developer from Mauritius.

He discovered the world of programming at the age of 15, and since then has not been able to stop learning more about it. Today, he uses this knowledge to design and build software solutions that helps to solve business problems and make people's lives easier.

Chervine also actively contributes to several technical communities, both online and offline.

Stephane Eyskens is a freelance consultant who works as a pure DevOps Architect between infrastructure, development, and security teams. He turned to Microsoft technologies about 15 years ago. Having a background as a .NET and SharePoint architect, he quickly focused on Azure. He specializes in security, cloud and hybrid architectures.

Stephane holds a Bachelor's Degree in Computer Sciences, a Master's Degree in ICT Sciences and is also a graduate of Solvay Business School.

Packt is searching for authors like you

If you're interested in becoming an author for Packt, please visit authors.packtpub.com and apply today. We have worked with thousands of developers and tech professionals, just like you, to help them share their insight with the global tech community. You can make a general application, apply for a specific hot topic that we are recruiting an author for, or submit your own idea.

Table of Contents

Preface   1

Chapter 1: Working with Azure Virtual Machines   7
  Technical requirements   8
  Designing solutions for virtual machines   8
  Virtual machine series and sizes   9
    Available VM series and sizes   9
  Availability Sets   10
  Fault domains and update domains   11
  Managed Disks   13
  Creating highly available virtual machines   13
    Creating highly available virtual machines from the Azure Portal   13
    Creating highly available virtual machines from PowerShell   18
  VM Scale Sets   21
    Creating a VM Scale Set from the Azure Portal   22
    Accessing your VM Scale Sets   24
    VM Scale Set templates   24
  Disaster recovery   25
    Backup and recovery   25
    Replication   26
  Summary   27
  Questions   27
  Further reading   28

Chapter 2: Configuring Compute-Intensive Applications   29
  High-performance compute virtual machines   29
  Microsoft HPC Pack   30
    Cloud-native HPC solutions   31
    Hybrid HPC architecture   32
  Azure Batch   34
    Creating an Azure Batch service   35
    Stateless components   39
    Containers on Azure Batch   41
  Summary   41
  Questions   41
  Further reading   42

Chapter 3: Designing Web Applications   43
  Technical requirements   44

Azure Web Apps 44
App Service plans 45
  The App Service Environment (ASE) 49
    Creating an ASE 50
Web Apps for Containers 53
  Getting started with Web App for Containers 54
Designing Web Apps for high availability, scalability, and performance 58
  High availability and performance 58
    Using a CDN 58
    Using Redis Cache 59
    Using Azure Traffic Manager 61
  Scalability 62
    Scaling out 63
    Scaling up 65
Designing and securing custom Web APIs 66
  Designing your Web API 66
  Securing your Web API 72
Summary 73
Questions 73
Further reading 74

Chapter 4: Implementing Serverless and Microservices 75
Technical requirements 76
Event-driven actions using Azure Functions 76
  Consumption App Service plan 78
  Designing application solutions using Azure Functions 78
  Durable Functions 87
Workflow-driven applications using Logic Apps 87
  Designing application solutions using Logic Apps 89
Designing for serverless computing using Azure Container Instances 97
  Creating containers 97
  Container orchestrations 98
Azure Service Fabric 99
  Life cycle management 101
API Management 102
  API Gateway 102
  API Management portal 102
  Developer portal 103
Cloud-native deployments versus migrating assets 103
Summary 105
Questions 105
Further reading 106

Chapter 5: Robust Networking Implementations   107
  Technical requirements   108
  Azure Virtual Network   108
    IP addresses   109
      Public IP address   110
      Private IP address   111
      Creating a public IP address   111
    DNS   112
    Creating a VNet with two subnets   113
  Azure Load Balancer   117
    Probes   119
  Azure Traffic Manager   119
  Azure Application Gateway   120
  External connectivity for Azure Virtual Networks   122
    Azure VPN   122
      Site-to-site VPN   123
      VNet-to-VNet VPN   124
      Point-to-site VPN   124
      ExpressRoute   125
  Network security strategies   126
    DMZ   127
    Network Security Groups   127
      Creating a NSG   128
    User Defined Routes   132
      Creating User Defined Routes   133
    Virtual network service tunneling   137
    Web Application Firewall   138
  Summary   139
  Questions   139
  Further reading   140

Chapter 6: Connecting Hybrid Applications   141
  Azure Relay service   142
    Hybrid connections   143
    WCF Relays   144
  Azure Data Management Gateway for Data Factory   144
  Azure On-premises Data Gateway   145
  Azure App Service Hybrid Connections   146
  Azure App Service Virtual Network Integration   148
  Azure AD Application Proxy   150
  Joining VMs to domains   151
    Enabling Azure AD Domain Services   151
    Adding the VM to the managed domain   156
  Summary   157
  Questions   157

Further reading — 158

Chapter 7: Using Storage Solutions — 159
  Technical requirements — 160
  Azure Storage and replication types — 160
    Storage account types — 160
      General-purpose v1 (GPv1) — 160
      Blob storage — 161
      General-purpose v2 (GPv2) — 161
    Storage replication types — 161
      Locally Redundant Storage — 162
      Zone Redundant Storage — 162
      Geo-redundant Storage — 162
  Azure Blob Storage — 162
    Access tiers — 163
      Hot — 163
      Cool — 163
      Archive — 163
  Azure Table Storage — 164
    Creating a storage account — 164
    Uploading data to Azure Table Storage — 165
  Azure Queue Storage — 168
  Azure File Storage — 169
  Azure Disk Storage — 169
    Standard Disk Storage — 169
    Premium Disk Storage — 170
    Unmanaged versus Managed Disks — 170
  StorSimple — 170
    StorSimple Virtual Array — 170
    StorSimple 8000 Series — 171
  Cosmos DB Storage — 173
  Azure Search — 175
  Summary — 177
  Questions — 177
  Further reading — 178

Chapter 8: Scalable Data Implementations — 179
  Technical requirements — 180
  Azure Data Catalog — 180
  Azure Data Factory — 181
  Azure SQL Data Warehouse — 182
  Azure Data Lake — 183
    Azure Data Lake Store — 184
    Azure Data Lake Analytics — 185
      Analyzing your data using Data Lake Analytics — 185

Azure HDInsight	191
Azure Analysis Services	192
Azure SQL Database	193
SQL Server Stretch Database	194
High availability	194
Active geo-replication	194
Failover groups	194
Configuring active geo-replication and failover groups	195
Backup and recovery	200
Azure Database for MySQL	202
Azure Database for PostgreSQL	203
Summary	204
Questions	205
Further reading	205
Chapter 9: Securing Your Resources	207
Technical requirements	207
Azure Active Directory	207
Microsoft Graph	209
Azure AD Connect	209
Azure Active Directory password hash synchronization	211
Azure Active Directory pass-through authentication	211
Active Directory Federation Services	212
Multi-Factor Authentication	212
Enabling MFA in the Azure Portal	213
Enabling MFA in Office 365	214
Azure Active Directory Business to Business	215
Azure Active Directory Business to Consumer	216
Leveraging Azure AD B2C in your application	217
Summary	231
Questions	232
Further reading	232
Chapter 10: Securing Your Data	235
Technical requirements	235
Azure Key Vault	236
Creating an Azure Key Vault in the Azure Portal	236
Azure Key Vault secrets in ARM templates	243
Azure Storage Service Encryption	244
Azure Disk Encryption	246
Azure SQL Database Security	247
Azure Active Directory Managed Service Identity	248
Summary	250
Questions	250

Further reading	251
Chapter 11: Governance and Policies	253
Technical requirements	254
Azure Role-Based Access Control	254
Built-in Roles	256
Custom Roles	256
Creating a Custom Role	257
Azure Resource Policies	258
Azure AD Privileged Identity Management	259
Azure AD Identity Protection	260
Azure Security Center	262
Advanced Threat Detection	264
Azure Endpoint Protection	264
Operations Management Suite - Security and Compliance	268
Summary	270
Questions	271
Further reading	271
Chapter 12: Artificial Intelligence, IoT, and Media Services	273
Technical requirements	274
Azure Cognitive Services	274
Available services and APIs	274
Using the Computer Vision API	277
Azure Bot Service	282
Creating a Bot from the Azure Portal	283
Azure Machine Learning	289
Azure IoT Hub	291
Azure Event Hub	292
Azure IoT Edge	294
Azure Stream Analytics	294
Azure Time Series Insights	295
Azure Media Services	297
Azure Media Analytics	298
Using the Azure Media Analytics Indexer	298
Summary	304
Questions	304
Further reading	305
Chapter 13: Implementing Messaging Solutions	307
Technical requirements	307
Azure Queue Storage	308
Azure Service Bus	308
Azure Event Grid	310

Routing Events with Azure Event Grid   311
Notification Hubs   320
Designing an effective messaging architecture   321
Summary   322
Questions   322
Further reading   323

Chapter 14: Application Monitoring and Alerting Strategies   325
Azure Log Analytics   326
Creating a Log Analytics Workspace   326
Azure Monitor   332
Application Insights   335
Azure Service Health   337
Azure Advisor   338
Address Recommendation from Azure Advisor   338
Azure Network Watcher   341
Summary   343
Questions   343
Further reading   344

Chapter 15: Exploring Operations Automation Strategies   345
Designing an Operations Automation Strategy   345
Azure PowerShell   346
Desired State Configuration   346
Azure Automation   347
Creating an Azure Automation Runbook   348
Chef   353
Puppet   353
Azure Event Grid   354
Azure Logic Apps   355
Visual Studio Team Services   355
Designing an autoscaling strategy   356
Summary   357
Questions   358
Further reading   358

Appendix A – Assessments   361
Appendix B – Mock Test Questions   367
Appendix C – Mock Test Answers   383
Other Books You May Enjoy   391
Index   395

Preface

Azure is an ever-evolving platform. It offers an environment on the cutting edge of technology that suits different industry requirements. New capabilities and features are coming out fast, which makes it difficult to stay up to date. This book will give you a complete overview of all the current features and capabilities that Azure has to offer, and is a complete guide to preparing for the 70-535 exam.

This book will cover all the exam objectives. It will start with designing compute infrastructures, where you will learn about designing solutions with virtual machines, web applications, serverless and microservices, high-performance computing (HPC), and other compute-intensive applications. You will learn how to design effective networking implementations using Azure Virtual Networks and how to design connectivity for hybrid applications. You will learn about designing data implementations using different data services, relational database storage, and NoSQL storage. You will also learn how to keep your solutions and applications secure and how and when to use the different platform services in Azure, such as platforms and services for IoT and artificial intelligence. Finally, you will learn about all the monitoring capabilities and solutions that Azure has to offer.

Each chapter will conclude with a *Further reading* section, which is a very important part of the book as well, because it will give you extra and sometimes crucial information for passing the 70-535 exam. As the questions of the exam will change slightly over time and this book will become outdated soon, the further reading section will be the place that will provide you with all the updates.

Who this book is for

This book targets experienced developers and architects who want to pass the Exam 70-535: Architecting Microsoft Azure Solutions and broaden their knowledge of Azure from an architecture perspective

What this book covers

Chapter 1, *Working with Azure Virtual Machines*, will cover how to design solutions using Azure virtual machines. This includes designing VM deployments using availability sets, fault and update domains, and backup and recovery.

Chapter 2, *Configuring Compute-Intensive Applications*, covers how to design HPC and other compute-intensive applications using Azure Services, such as Azure Batch.

Chapter 3, *Designing Web Applications*, will cover how to design web applications and custom web APIs, how design for business continuity, scalability and performance, and more.

Chapter 4, *Implementing Serverless and Microservices*, will teach you how to design serverless and microservice-based solutions. This chapter will cover Azure Service Fabric, Azure Functions, Logic Apps, and more.

Chapter 5, *Robust Networking Implementations*, will cover all the networking features and capabilities that Azure has to offer and how to design effective networking solutions.

Chapter 6, *Connecting Hybrid Applications*, will teach you how to design connectivity to on-premises data from Azure applications using Azure Data Management Gateway for Data Factory, Azure On-Premises Data Gateway, and more.

Chapter 7, *Using Storage Solutions*, will cover how to design storage solutions using Azure Blob Storage, blob tiers, Azure Files, disks, and StorSimple. It will cover NoSQL and CosmosDB.

Chapter 8, *Scalable Data Implementations*, will cover how to design solutions using Azure Data Services. This includes determining when to use Data Catalog, Azure Data Factory, SQL Data Warehouse, Azure Data Lake Analytics, Azure Analysis Services, and Azure HDInsight.

Chapter 9, *Securing Your Resources*, covers how to secure your Azure resources and applications using Azure Active Directory, multi-factor authentication, and more.

Chapter 10, *Securing Your Data*, will cover data security solutions and capabilities, such as Azure Key Vault, Azure Storage Encryption, and Azure Disk Encryption.

Chapter 11, *Governance and Policies*, will cover designing a mechanism of governance and policies for administering Azure resources, such as determining when to use Azure RBAC standard roles and custom roles, when to use Azure resource policies, and more.

Chapter 12, *Artificial Intelligence, IoT, and Media Services*, will discuss the different features and capabilities that Azure has to offer for designing artificial intelligence and IoT solutions. It will also cover how to design solutions using Azure Media Services.

`Chapter 13`, *Implementing Messaging Solutions*, will cover how to design an effective messaging architecture using Azure Storage Queues, Azure Service Bus, Azure Event Hubs, Event Grid, and more.

`Chapter 14`, *Application Monitoring and Alerting Strategies*, will cover how to design an application monitoring and alerting strategy and how to design a platform-monitoring and alerting strategy using the different Microsoft products and services for monitoring Azure platform solutions.

`Chapter 15`, *Exploring Operations Automation Strategies*, will cover different solutions and methods for designing an operations automation strategy and designing an autoscaling strategy.

`Appendix A`, *Assessments*, will contain the answers for all the questions given at the end of each chapter.

`Appendix B`, *Mock Test Questions*, will consist of mock questions for you to test your knowledge. It tries to cover all the topics from the scope of the exam and challenges your understanding of the topics.

`Appendix C`, *Mock Test Answers*, will have the answers to the questions present in `Appendix B`, *Mock Test Questions*.

To get the most out of this book

This book assumes that readers are already familiar with the basics of networking, security, databases, integration, developing and administering applications, and solutions on the Azure platform.

Download the example code files

You can download the example code files for this book from your account at `www.packtpub.com`. If you purchased this book elsewhere, you can visit `www.packtpub.com/support` and register to have the files emailed directly to you.

You can download the code files by following these steps:

1. Log in or register at `www.packtpub.com`.
2. Select the **SUPPORT** tab.
3. Click on **Code Downloads & Errata**.
4. Enter the name of the book in the **Search** box and follow the onscreen instructions.

Once the file is downloaded, please make sure that you unzip or extract the folder using the latest version of:

- WinRAR/7-Zip for Windows
- Zipeg/iZip/UnRarX for Mac
- 7-Zip/PeaZip for Linux

The code bundle for the book is also hosted on GitHub at `https://github.com/PacktPublishing/Architecting-Microsoft-Azure-Solutions-Exam-Guide-70-535`. In case there's an update to the code, it will be updated on the existing GitHub repository.

We also have other code bundles from our rich catalog of books and videos available at `https://github.com/PacktPublishing/`. Check them out!

Download the color images

We also provide a PDF file that has color images of the screenshots/diagrams used in this book. You can download it here: `https://www.packtpub.com/sites/default/files/downloads/ArchitectingMicrosoftAzureSolutionsExamGuide70535_ColorImages.pdf`.

Conventions used

There are a number of text conventions used throughout this book.

`CodeInText`: Indicates code words in text, database table names, folder names, filenames, file extensions, pathnames, dummy URLs, user input, and Twitter handles. Here is an example: "Mount the downloaded `WebStorm-10*.dmg` disk image file as another disk in your system."

A block of code is set as follows:

```
namespace PacktPubToDoAPI.Models
{
    public class TodoItem
    {
        public long Id { get; set; }
        public string Name { get; set; }
        public bool IsComplete { get; set; }
    }
}
```

Any command-line input or output is written as follows:

```
Login-AzureRmAccount
```

Bold: Indicates a new term, an important word, or words that you see onscreen. For example, words in menus or dialog boxes appear in the text like this. Here is an example: "Click on **New** and, on the right-hand side, choose an image (or you can type an image name in the search bar). "

 Warnings or important notes appear like this.

 Tips and tricks appear like this.

Get in touch

Feedback from our readers is always welcome.

General feedback: Email feedback@packtpub.com and mention the book title in the subject of your message. If you have questions about any aspect of this book, please email us at questions@packtpub.com.

Errata: Although we have taken every care to ensure the accuracy of our content, mistakes do happen. If you have found a mistake in this book, we would be grateful if you would report this to us. Please visit www.packtpub.com/submit-errata, selecting your book, clicking on the Errata Submission Form link, and entering the details.

Piracy: If you come across any illegal copies of our works in any form on the Internet, we would be grateful if you would provide us with the location address or website name. Please contact us at copyright@packtpub.com with a link to the material.

If you are interested in becoming an author: If there is a topic that you have expertise in and you are interested in either writing or contributing to a book, please visit authors.packtpub.com.

Reviews

Please leave a review. Once you have read and used this book, why not leave a review on the site that you purchased it from? Potential readers can then see and use your unbiased opinion to make purchase decisions, we at Packt can understand what you think about our products, and our authors can see your feedback on their book. Thank you!

For more information about Packt, please visit packtpub.com.

Working with Azure Virtual Machines

1

This is the first chapter of the book *Architecting Azure Solutions*. This book will cover all the objectives for the 70-535 exam. When relevant, we will provide you with extra information and further guidance on how to design and architect robust, future-proof, and effective solutions on the Azure platform.

This chapter introduces the Microsoft Azure **Virtual Machine** (**VM**) objective. We will cover information about series and sizes. We will also cover how to design VM deployments using Availability Sets, fault domains, and update domains. In addition, we will show you how to create an Availability Set from the Azure Portal, as well as from Azure PowerShell. Finally, we will cover how to design and manage VM Scale Sets from the Azure Portal.

In this chapter, the following topics will be covered:

- Designing solutions for virtual machines
- Virtual machine series and sizes
- Availability Sets
- Fault domains and update domains
- Managed Disks
- Creating highly available VMs
- VM Scale Sets
- Disaster recovery

Technical requirements

This chapter uses the following tools for its examples:

- Azure PowerShell: `https://docs.microsoft.com/en-us/powershell/azure/install-azurerm-ps?view=azurermps-5.6.0viewFallbackFrom=azurermps-5.1.1`

The source code for this chapter can be downloaded here:

- `https://github.com/SjoukjeZaal/AzureArchitectureBook/tree/master/Chapter%201`

Designing solutions for virtual machines

In Azure, you can run both Windows VMs as well as Linux VMs. Virtual machines come in all sorts of sizes and a variety of prices, ranging from VMs with a small amount of memory and processing power for general purposes to large VMs that can be used for GPU-intensive and high-performance computing workloads.

To create a virtual machine, you can choose from a number of predefined images. There are images available for operating systems such as Windows Server or Kali Linux, as well as predefined applications, such as SQL Server images and complete farms, which consist of multiple VMs that can be deployed at once. An example of a farm is a three-tier SharePoint farm.

VMs can be created and managed either from the Azure Portal, PowerShell, or CLI. If you're planning on using PowerShell, please note that there are multiple versions of Azure PowerShell available, and that there is a notable difference between Azure PowerShell, which supports the classic deployment model, and the *new* Azure PowerShell. To install and configure Azure PowerShell, please refer to the beginning of this chapter.

 For the demos in this book, we will be using the Azure PowerShell version that supports the *new* Azure PowerShell. I strongly advise using this version of PowerShell for all your new deployments and solutions. The classic model should only be used for solutions that have already been deployed using this model previously.

Designing the most effective virtual machine solution depends on a few things, such as deciding which size and series to use, deciding if your VMs need high availability, and if your solution will need to scale up and down easily.

Virtual machine series and sizes

There are a lot of different VM sizes available to choose from in Azure. Note that it is important to know what options there are from a design perspective, because choosing the wrong VM size can have a negative impact on the performance of your VM, or your application installed on the VM. Choosing between the different available options will also have a huge effect on the overall costs. For example, if your company or client wants to reduce costs by migrating data centers to Azure, choosing your VMs wisely will either make your project a success or a failure.

Azure VMs are organized into machine series, starting with the A-series, which are VMs mainly used for general purposes. There are also VM sizes that are optimized for compute, memory, storage, and GPU, as well as high-performance compute VMs. All of the available series and sizes are explained in more detail in the following section.

Available VM series and sizes

At the time of writing this book, the following VM series are available:

Sizes	Type	Description
A0-7, Av2, B, D, DS, Dv2, DSv2, Dv3, Dsv3	General purpose	These VMs have a balanced CPU-to-memory ratio and are ideal for testing and development scenarios. They are also suitable for small and medium databases and web servers with low to medium traffic.
F, Fs, Fsv2	Compute optimized	These VMs have a high CPU-to-memory ratio and are suitable for web servers with medium traffic, application servers, and network appliances for nodes in batch processing.
D, DS, Dv2, DSv2, Ev3, Esv3, G, GS, M	Memory optimized	These VMs have a high memory-to-CPU ratio and are suitable for relational database servers, medium to large caches, and in-memory analytics.
Ls	Storage optimized	These VMs have high disk throughput and IO and are suitable for big data, SQL, and NoSQL databases.

NC, NCv2, NCv3, ND, NV	GPU	These VMs are targeted for heavy graphic rendering and video editing, deep learning applications, and machine learning model training. These VMs are available with single or multiple GPUs.
A8-11, H	High-performance compute	These are the fastest VMs available. They offer the most powerful CPU with optional high-throughput network interfaces (RDMA).

 VM machine series are updated constantly. New series, types, and sizes are added and removed frequently. To stay up to date with these changes, you can refer to the following site for Windows VM sizes: `https://docs.microsoft.com/en-us/azure/virtual-machines/windows/sizes`. For Linux VM sizes, you can refer to `https://docs.microsoft.com/en-us/azure/virtual-machines/linux/sizes?toc=%2fazure%2fvirtual-machines%2flinux%2ftoc.json`.

Availability Sets

To create a reliable infrastructure, adding your virtual machines to an Availability Set is key. There are several scenarios that can have an impact on the availability of your Azure Virtual Machines. These are as follows:

- **Unplanned hardware maintenance event**: When hardware is about to fail, Azure fires an unplanned hardware maintenance event. Live migration technology is used, which predicts the failure and then moves the VM, the network connections, memory, and storage to different physical machines without disconnecting the client. When your VM is moved, the performance is reduced for a short time because the VM is paused for 30 seconds. Network connections, memory, and open files are still preserved.

- **Unexpected downtime**: The virtual machine is down when this event occurs because Azure needs to heal your VM inside the same data center. A hardware or physical infrastructure failure often causes this event to happen.

- **Planned hardware maintenance event:** This type of event is a periodic update from Microsoft in Azure to improve the platform. Most of these updates don't have a significant impact on the uptime of VMs, but some of them may require a reboot or restart.

To provide redundancy during these types of events, you can group two or more VMs in an Availability Set. By leveraging Availability Sets, VMs are distributed across multiple isolated hardware nodes in a cluster. This way, Azure can ensure that during an event or failure, only a subset of your VMs is impacted and your overall solution will remain operational and available. This way, the 99.95% Azure SLA can be met.

> For a detailed overview of when and how the SLA applies, you can refer to the following overview: `https://azure.microsoft.com/en-us/support/legal/sla/virtual-machines/v1_6/`.

Fault domains and update domains

When you place your VMs in an Availability Set, Azure guarantees to spread them across fault and update domains. By default, Azure will assign **three fault domains and five update domains** (which can be increased to a maximum of 20) to the Availability Set.

When spreading your VMs over fault domains, your VMs sit over three different racks in the Azure data center. So, in the case of an event or failure on the underlying platform, only one rack gets affected and the other VMs are still accessible.

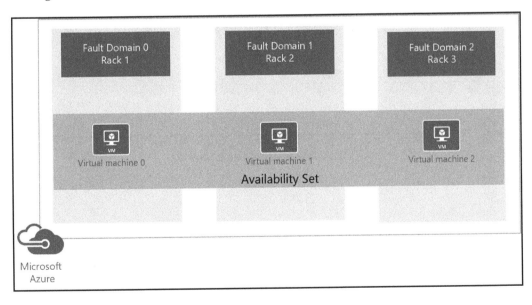

VMs spread over three fault domains

Update domains are useful in the case of an OS or host update. When you spread your VMs across multiple update domains, one domain will be updated and rebooted while the others remain accessible.

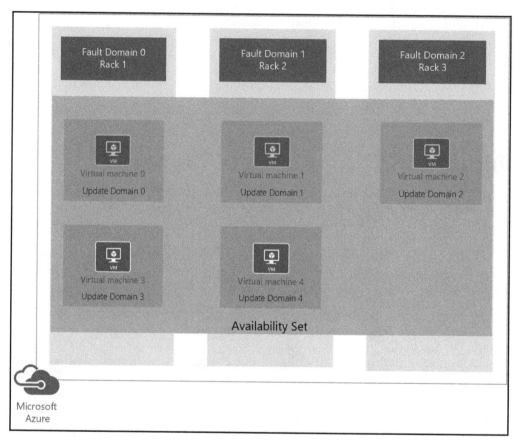

VMs spread over five update domains and three fault domains

Managed Disks

Azure Managed Disks are the default disks selected when you create a VM in the Azure Portal. They handle storage for your virtual machines completely. Previously, you would have to manually create storage accounts to store VM hard disks, and when your VM needed to scale up, you have to add additional storage accounts to make sure you didn't exceed the limit of 20,000 IOPS per account.

With Managed Disks, this burden is now handled for you by Azure. You can now create 10,000 VM disks inside a subscription, which can result in thousands of VMs inside a subscription, without the need to copy disks between storage accounts.

 If you are still using Unmanaged Disks, it is highly recommended that you switch to Managed Disks. To convert your disks from Unmanaged to Managed, refer to the following article: `https://docs.microsoft.com/en-us/azure/virtual-machines/windows/convert-unmanaged-to-managed-disks`.

Creating highly available virtual machines

VMs can only be added to an an Availability Set by creation. When you want to add existing VMs to an Availability Set, this will result in recreating your VMs. This is something to be aware of when designing your solutions.

Creating highly available virtual machines from the Azure Portal

Follow the given steps to create a VM from the Azure Portal:

1. Navigate to the Azure Portal by opening `https://portal.azure.com/`.

2. Click on **New** and, on the right-hand side, choose an image (or you can type an image name in the search bar). For this demo, we have selected the Windows Server 2016 VM image:

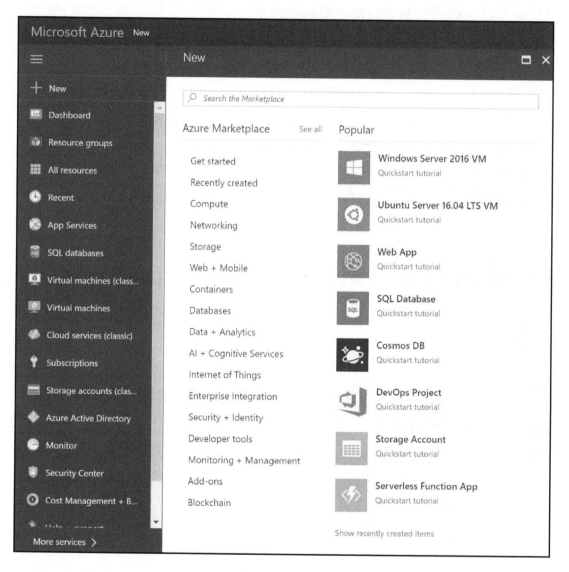

Creating an Azure VM

3. A new blade opens up where you can fill in the basic settings of the VM. Add the following details and click on **OK**:

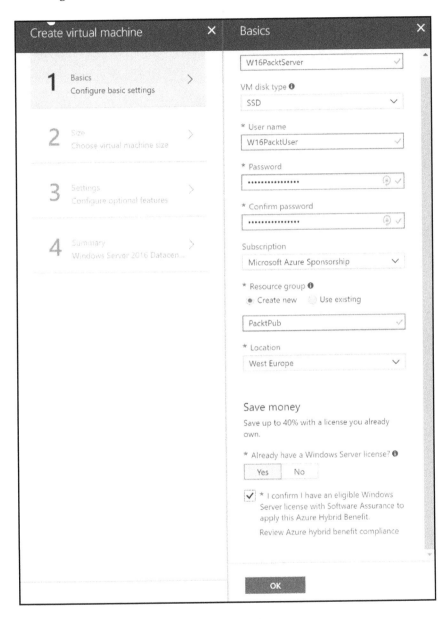

Filling in the basic settings

4. A new blade will open where you can choose the VM type and size. By default, only the recommended VMs are displayed, but you can choose to display all VMs by clicking on **View all** and then clicking on **Select**, as shown in the following screenshot:

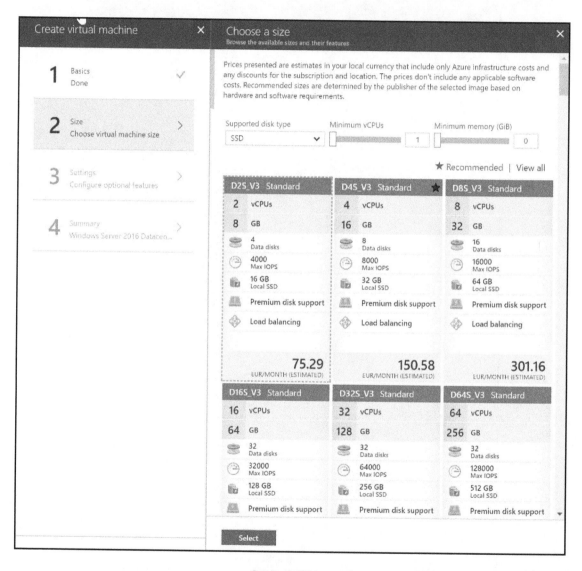

Choosing your VM size

5. A new blade opens up where you can configure additional options. Here, select **Availability set** and then click **Create new**:

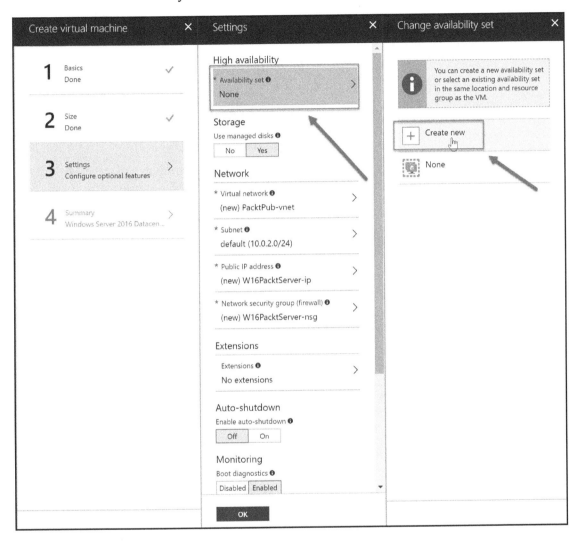

Creating a high Availability Set

6. By default, your VMs are assigned two fault domains and five update domains. Accept the default settings here and click on **OK** twice when prompted.

7. The last blade opens up, which provides a summary with all the settings you've entered. Check the permission box.

8. Click on **Create** and your VM is now created. Next to the **Create** button, you should see a link where you can download the ARM template of this virtual machine.

9. Create the second VM and, instead of creating a new Availability Set, add the second VM to the Availability Set that we have already created using the previous steps.

You can download the ARM template of the configuration of the VM. This template can be used to deploy the second VM as well. There are a lot of templates available on GitHub that have been created by Microsoft and the community: https://azure.microsoft.com/en-us/resources/templates/.

Creating highly available virtual machines from PowerShell

VMs and Availability Sets can be created using PowerShell as well. Besides the traditional PowerShell, you can also use the **Azure Cloud Shell** to create your Availability Set. By using the Azure Cloud Shell, you are basically using PowerShell from inside the browser. Inside the Azure Cloud Shell, Windows users can opt for PowerShell and Linux users can opt for Bash. You can open the Azure Cloud Shell from the Azure Portal, as shown in the following screenshot:

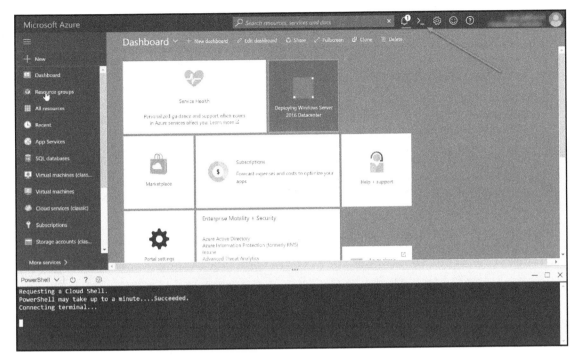

Azure Cloud Shell

To create two VMs and add them to an Availability Set, add the following PowerShell statements to Azure Cloud Shell or Windows PowerShell (note that when using the Azure Cloud Shell, you don't have to log in):

```
Login-AzureRmAccount
```

If necessary, select the right subscription, shown as follows:

```
Select-AzureRmSubscription -SubscriptionId "********-****-****-****-
***********"
```

Create a resource group:

```
New-AzureRmResourceGroup -Name PacktPubPS -Location WestEurope
```

Now, create an Availability Set:

```
New-AzureRmAvailabilitySet -Location WestEurope -Name AvailabilitySet02 -
ResourceGroupName PacktPubPS -Sku Aligned -PlatformFaultDomainCount 2 -
PlatformUpdateDomainCount 2
```

Next, we need to create the two VMs and add them to the Availability Set. This is done by setting the `-AvailabilitySetId` parameter to the ID of the Availability Set. When running this script, you will be prompted for the username and password for your VM, as shown in the following snippet:

```
$availabilitySet = Get-AzureRmAvailabilitySet -ResourceGroupName PacktPubPS
-Name AvailabilitySet02

$cred = Get-Credential -Message "Enter a username and password for the
virtual machine."

$subnetConfig = New-AzureRmVirtualNetworkSubnetConfig -Name PacktSubnet -
AddressPrefix 192.168.1.0/24
$vnet = New-AzureRmVirtualNetwork -ResourceGroupName PacktPubPS -Location
WestEurope -Name PacktVnet -AddressPrefix 192.168.0.0/16 -Subnet
$subnetConfig

$nsgRuleRDP = New-AzureRmNetworkSecurityRuleConfig -Name
PacktNetworkSecurityGroupRuleRDP -Protocol Tcp -Direction Inbound -Priority
1000 -SourceAddressPrefix * -SourcePortRange * -DestinationAddressPrefix *
-DestinationPortRange 3389 -Access Allow

$nsg = New-AzureRmNetworkSecurityGroup -Location WestEurope -Name
PacktSecurityGroup -ResourceGroupName PacktPubPS -SecurityRules $nsgRuleRDP

# Apply the network security group to a subnet
Set-AzureRmVirtualNetworkSubnetConfig -VirtualNetwork $vnet -Name
PacktSubnet -NetworkSecurityGroup $nsg -AddressPrefix 192.168.1.0/24

# Update the virtual network
Set-AzureRmVirtualNetwork -VirtualNetwork $vnet
```

```
for ($i=1; $i -le 2; $i++)
{
 $pip = New-AzureRmPublicIpAddress -ResourceGroupName PacktPubPS -Location
WestEurope -Name "$(Get-Random)" -AllocationMethod Static -
IdleTimeoutInMinutes 4

 $nic = New-AzureRmNetworkInterface -Name PacktNic$i -ResourceGroupName
PacktPubPS -Location WestEurope -SubnetId $vnet.Subnets[0].Id -
PublicIpAddressId $pip.Id -NetworkSecurityGroupId $nsg.Id

 # Specify the availability set
 $vm = New-AzureRmVMConfig -VMName PacktVM$i -VMSize Standard_D2_v3 -
AvailabilitySetId $availabilitySet.Id

 $vm = Set-AzureRmVMOperatingSystem -ComputerName myVM$i -Credential $cred
-VM $vm -Windows -EnableAutoUpdate -ProvisionVMAgent
 $vm = Set-AzureRmVMSourceImage -VM $vm -PublisherName
MicrosoftWindowsServer -Offer WindowsServer -Skus 2016-Datacenter -Version
latest

 $vm = Add-AzureRmVMNetworkInterface -VM $vm -Id $nic.Id
 New-AzureRmVM -ResourceGroupName PacktPubPS -Location WestEurope -VM $vm
}
```

VM Scale Sets

VM Scale Sets are used for deploying multiple VMs at once without the need for manual actions or using scripts. You can then manage them all at once from a single place. VM Scale Sets are typically used to build large-scale infrastructures, where keeping all of your VMs in sync is key. The maintenance of VMs, including keeping them in sync, is handled by Azure.

VM Scale Sets use Availability Sets under the hood. VMs inside a scale set are automatically spread over the fault and update domains by the underlying platform. VM Scale Sets use Azure autoscale by default. You can, however, add or remove instances yourself instead of using autoscale.

When creating a scale set, a couple of artifacts are created for you automatically. As well as the number of VMs you have specified being added to the set, an **Azure Load Balancer** and **Azure Autoscaling** is added, along with a virtual network and a public IP:

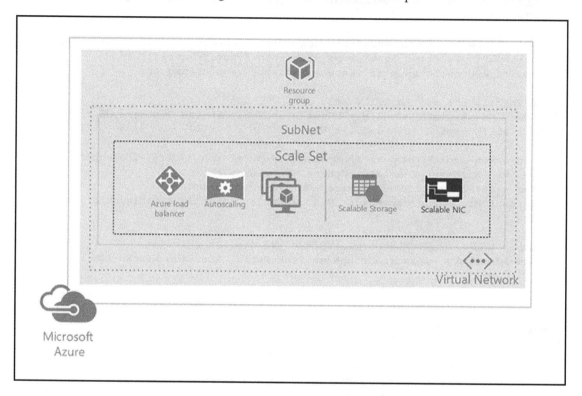

Azure VM Scale Set architecture

Creating a VM Scale Set from the Azure Portal

1. Navigate to the Azure Portal by opening `https://portal.azure.com/`.
2. Click on **New** and type in `Scale` in the search bar. Select **Virtual machine scale set**.
3. In the next screen, click on **Create** and add the following settings before clicking the **Create** button:

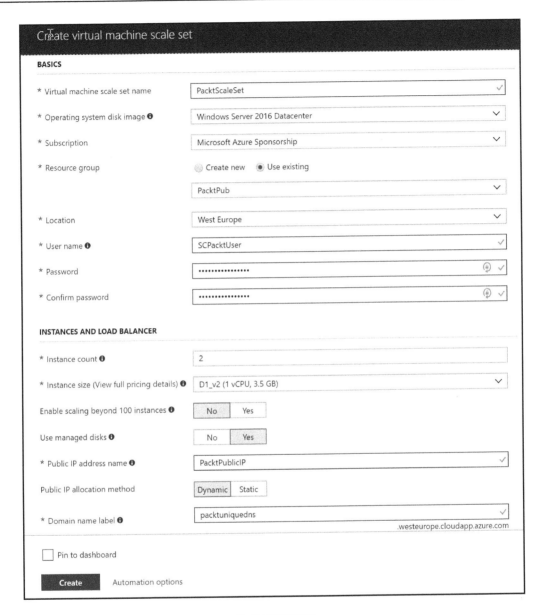

Creating a VM Scale Set

After creation, you can manage the VM Scale Set from the Azure Portal as well as from PowerShell and CLI.

Accessing your VM Scale Sets

There are a number of ways to access your VM Scale Sets; they are as follows:

- **Connect to VM instances using RDP or SSH**: To connect to VM instances using RDP or SSH, you can configure a scale set to automatically assign a public IP address. This option is turned off by default. The VMs are inside a virtual network, making it impossible to connect to them using RDP or SSH.
- **Connect to VM instances using a jumpbox**: You can create a standalone VM inside the same virtual network to act as a jumpbox to connect to another scale set instance in the set. The standalone VM gets a public IP address, which can be connected using RDP or SSH. Once connected to the VM, you can use it to connect to other instances using the internal IP address.
- **Connect to VM instances using NAT rules**: You can also connect to VM instances using NAT rules that are created inside the load balancer. Those NAT rules assign the instances to a different RDP port.
- **Distribute incoming traffic using load balancing:** Incoming traffic can be distributed across VM instances using the round-robin approach. You can use the Azure Load Balancer and the Azure Application Gateway for this, where the former provides layer-4 load balancing rules, and the latter layer-7 load balancing rules.

VM Scale Set templates

You can also deploy VM Scale Sets using ARM templates. ARM templates are a great way to deploy solutions automatically, and you can even embed customization and extensions inside the template. You can, for instance, install an application inside a container and deploy it within the VM instances during the deployment process of your scale set.

There are also ARM templates provided by Microsoft and the community that have already been configured for different architectures; these can be downloaded and deployed to create Azure scale sets, with extensions to manage the scale sets included. Some examples of templates are as follows:

- **Simple deployment of a VM Scale Set of Windows VMs behind a load balancer with NAT rules**: `https://github.com/Azure/azure-quickstart-templates/tree/master/201-vmss-windows-nat`
- **Simple deployment of a VM Scale Set of Linux VMs behind a load balancer with NAT rules**: `https://github.com/Azure/azure-quickstart-templates/tree/master/201-vmss-linux-nat`

- **Simple deployment of a VM Scale Set of Linux VMs with a jumpbox**: `https://
github.com/Azure/azure-quickstart-templates/tree/master/201-vmss-
linux-jumpbox`
- **Windows VM Scale Set with Application Gateway Integration**: `https://
github.com/Azure/azure-quickstart-templates/tree/master/201-vmss-
windows-app-gateway`

Disaster recovery

Business continuity and disaster recovery is still key, even when you are deploying your virtual machines to the cloud. Azure provides two different services for this: the **Azure Backup Service** and the **Azure Site Recovery Service**. Together, they address disaster recovery needs natively in the cloud.

Backup and recovery

Azure uses the Azure Backup Service to back up virtual machines. You can use this service to back up your Azure VMs as well as your on-premises VMs. You can also use it to extend your backup solution in a hybrid configuration or fully replace your on-premises backup solution with Azure Backup. The service can back up files, folders, VMs, applications, workloads, system states, and volumes.

Azure Backup consists of the following backup components:

- **Azure Backup (MARS) agent**: This agent needs to be installed on a Windows Server VM (there is currently no support for Linux) that runs in Azure or resides on your on-premises infrastructure. You can use it to back up VMs, files, folders, and system states.
- **Protection for system center Data Protection Manager (DPM) servers**: You can use Azure Backup for a hybrid setup in conjunction with DPM servers. The DPM server can be deployed inside your on-premises data center or on a virtual machine in Azure. You can use it to store older data in the Azure Recovery Services Vault and use the disks for newer data, for instance.
- **Azure Backup Server**: This component is installed on an on-premises Windows server or a Windows VM in Azure. It offers backup support for Windows and Linux servers and it uses the Azure Recovery Services Vault to store backups.
- **Azure IaaS VM backup**: This consists of an agent that needs to be installed on your Azure VMs. These can be either Linux or Windows VMs. You cannot use this tool to back up your on-premises servers.

When using the Azure Backup Service to back up your VM, most of the work will be in preparing the virtual machines. Your VM must meet the prerequisites before the backup can be initiated to take snapshots from the virtual machines. First, you will need to create a **Recovery Services Vault** in Azure to store the backups. Then, the VM agent needs to be installed on the virtual machine. You also need to check your network connectivity at this point. When all the prerequisites have been met, you can back up your VMs to the Recovery Services Vault. These backups are easily created from the Azure Portal, PowerShell, or CLI. The snapshots are then stored inside the Recovery Services Vault, and from there you can also restore the snapshots. When restoring, you can choose to either restore the whole VM or only individual files or folders.

 The prerequisites for backing up virtual machines are described in detail in the following article: https://docs.microsoft.com/en-us/azure/ backup/backup-azure-arm-vms-prepare.

Replication

Azure Site Recovery Services offers a business continuity and disaster recovery solution from Azure by orchestrating and automating the replication of Azure VMs. It can replicate workloads and applications from a primary to a secondary location so that your VMs or applications are still up and running during a disaster. You can also easily fall back to the primary location when it is up and running again.

Azure Site Recovery Services offers the following features and capabilities:

- **Azure VM, on-premises VM, and workload replication**: You can set up the disaster recovery of Azure VMs from a primary region to a secondary region in Azure. You can replicate on-premises VMs and physical servers to Azure or to a secondary on-premises data center. You can replicate any workload from on-premises Hyper-V and VMware VMs, Windows/Linux physical servers, and Azure VMs.
- **Data resilience**: No application data is intercepted during replication. Data is stored in Azure storage, and during failover the VMs are created using data from Azure storage.
- **Customized recovery plans**: You can create customized recovery plans where you can group VMs together or add custom scripts or tasks.
- **BDCR integration**: You can integrate Azure Recovery Services with other BDCR solutions as well.

- **Network integration**: Azure Recovery Services is integrated with networking features in Azure. You can reserve IP addresses, configure load balancers, and integrate Azure Traffic Manager for network switchovers.
- **Consistent apps**: You can keep applications consistent during failovers using recovery points with application-consistent snapshots. These snapshots can capture disk data, all data in memory, and all transactions in process.

 For more information about all the features that Azure Recovery Services provides, you can refer to `https://docs.microsoft.com/en-us/azure/site-recovery/site-recovery-overview`.

Summary

In this chapter, we covered the virtual machine objective. We covered the different sizes and series that are available from Azure. We also covered Availability Sets, fault and update domains, and how to create them. We also covered Managed Disks and we showed you how to create highly available VMs. We've talked about VM Scale Sets and when to use them, and finally we covered backup and recovery for your virtual machines.

The next chapter will cover compute-intensive applications using Azure services and Azure Batch.

Questions

Answer the following questions to test your knowledge of the information found in this chapter. You can find the answers in the *Assessments* section at the end of this book.

1. Are Azure Managed Disks selected by default when creating a new virtual machine?
    1. Yes
    2. No

2. If you want your virtual machines to be available when failure occurs in the underlying infrastructure, should you use Availability Sets?
    1. Yes
    2. No

3. Are VMs spread over three fault domains, and four update domains when you add them to an Availability Set by default?
    1. Yes
    2. No

Further reading

You can check the following links for more information about the topics covered in this chapter:

- **Managing the availability of Windows virtual machines in Azure**: `https://docs.microsoft.com/en-us/azure/virtual-machines/windows/manage-availability`
- **Example Azure infrastructure walkthrough for Windows VMs**: `https://docs.microsoft.com/en-us/azure/virtual-machines/windows/infrastructure-example`
- **Planned maintenance for virtual machines in Azure**: `https://docs.microsoft.com/en-us/azure/virtual-machines/windows/maintenance-and-updates`
- **Virtual Machine Scale Sets Documentation**: `https://docs.microsoft.com/en-us/azure/virtual-machine-scale-sets/`
- **Using a custom Docker image for Web App for Containers**: `https://docs.microsoft.com/en-us/azure/app-service/containers/tutorial-custom-docker-image`
- **Overview of the features in Azure Backup**: `https://docs.microsoft.com/en-us/azure/backup/backup-introduction-to-azure-backup`
- **Backing up Azure virtual machines to a Recovery Services Vault**: `https://docs.microsoft.com/en-us/azure/backup/backup-azure-arm-vms`
- **Planing your VM backup infrastructure in Azure**: `https://docs.microsoft.com/en-us/azure/backup/backup-azure-vms-introduction`
- **Site recovery**: `https://docs.microsoft.com/en-us/azure/site-recovery/site-recovery-overview`

Configuring Compute-Intensive Applications

2

In the previous chapter, we covered the Azure Virtual Machine (VM) objective. We covered how to design Azure VMs by discussing the available series and sizes. We also covered how to design for high availability and performance using the various features Azure provides.

This chapter introduces the compute-intensive applications objective. It will cover how to design high-performance computing (HPC) and other compute-intensive applications using Azure services, how to determine when to use Azure Batch, and how to design stateless components to accommodate scale and containers with Azure Batch.

The following topics will be covered:

- High-performance compute virtual machines
- Microsoft HPC Pack
- Azure Batch

High-performance compute virtual machines

Azure offers several virtual machine series and sizes that are designed and optimized for compute-intensive tasks. They are also known as compute-intensive instances. At the time of writing this book, Azure offers the A8-A11, the N-series, and the H-series, which all support HPC workloads.

These series and sizes consist of hardware that is designed and optimized for compute-intensive, graphics-intensive, and network-intensive applications. They are best suited for modeling, simulations, and HPC cluster applications:

- The A-series offers RDMA networking, which provides ultra-low-latency and high bandwidth networking.
- The N-series is aimed at graphics-intensive and compute-intensive applications. They consist of different NVIDIA Tesla GPUs that are well suited for deep learning applications, gaming applications, or virtualization.
- The H-series offers virtual machines that are specifically aimed at high performance. They offer fast Intel Xeon processors, SSD-based local storage, and DDR4 memory. These VMs are best suited for HPC workloads, such as batching, modeling, and simulations.

 For more information on the hardware specifications of the N-series virtual machines, you can refer to the following article: `https://docs.microsoft.com/en-us/azure/virtual-machines/windows/sizes-gpu`. For more information about high-performance VMs, you can refer to the following article: `https://docs.microsoft.com/en-us/azure/virtual-machines/windows/sizes-hpc?toc=%2Fazure%2Fvirtual-machines%2Fwindows%2Ftoc.json`.

The Azure Marketplace offers several virtual machine images that are specifically designed for HPC, such as Azure Data Science VMs for Windows and Linux, D3View, and more. You can navigate to the marketplace using the following URL: `https://azuremarketplace.microsoft.com/en-us/marketplace`.

Microsoft HPC Pack

Microsoft provides an HPC Pack for Windows Server 2012, 2016, and Linux machines. This is a free offering and you can use this to create HPC clusters on your on-premises servers and Azure VMs.

You can install HPC Pack on a Windows or Linux Server. These machines will automatically become the head node of the cluster. You can then add additional nodes to the cluster and run a job on it. This job will be distributed across all the available nodes automatically.

It offers the following additional features:

- **Hybrid Cluster**: You can set up hybrid clusters using on-premises servers and Azure VMs
- **HPC Cluster Manager**: A tool for managing, deploying, and configuring HPC clusters
- **PowerShell:** You can use HPC PowerShell to manage, configure, deploy, add, and execute jobs on the cluster

You can use HPC Pack for designing effective cloud-native HPC solutions and hybrid HPC solutions. Both of these are explained in the following sections.

Cloud-native HPC solutions

A cloud-native HPC solution uses HPC virtual machines and can scale up to thousands of instances and compute cores. It uses a head node, several compute nodes, and storage. The following Azure resources can be used to create a cloud-native HPC architecture:

- **HPC head node**: The head node runs in Azure on a Windows or Linux server virtual machine. When you install Azure HPC Pack on this machine, it will become the head node automatically.
- **HPC compute nodes**: The HPC compute nodes are created using A8 and A9 instances. These instances provide RDMA networking, which can be used to achieve high bandwidth and microsecond latencies between the nodes.
- **Virtual Machine Scale Set**: You can place the compute nodes in a **Virtual Machine Scale Set** (**VMSS**) for redundancy and availability. VMs that use RDMA for communicating with each other are placed in the same Availability Set.
- **Virtual network**: All the Azure resources, such as the head node, the compute nodes, and storage layer, are added to an Azure virtual network.
- **Storage**: The disks that are used for all the different nodes are stored inside Azure Blob Storage.

- **ARM templates**: You can use ARM templates to deploy the applications to the nodes.

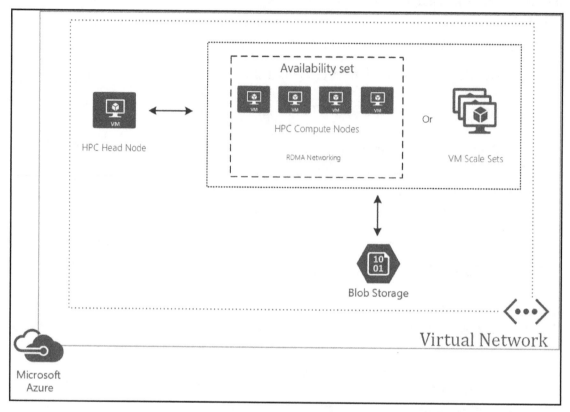

Cloud-native HPC architecture

Hybrid HPC architecture

Hybrid HPC architecture uses some of the building blocks that are used for a cloud-native HPC architecture complemented with the on-premises part. The following Azure resources will be used in this scenario:

- **HPC head node**: The head node runs on your on-premises environment. The head node can be installed on a virtual machine in Azure as well, on a Windows or Linux server virtual machine, and just like the cloud-native architecture, you can install Azure HPC Pack on it and it will become the head node automatically.

- **HPC compute nodes**: The HPC compute nodes in your on-premises environment can be Linux or Windows servers with sufficient compute power. The VMs in Azure are created using A8 and A9 instances and provide RDMA networking.
- **Virtual Machine Scale Sets**: You can place the compute nodes in Azure inside a VMSS for redundancy and availability. VMs that use RDMA for communicating with each other are placed in the same availability set.
- **Virtual network**: The Azure resources, such as the compute nodes and storage layer are added to an Azure virtual network.
- **ExpressRoute**: ExpressRoute offers a secure and reliable connection between your on-premises environment and Azure. These connections don't go over the public internet but use a private connection, which is usually set up between an ExpressRoute broker and Azure.
- **VPN Gateway**: A VPN Gateway offers an endpoint between Azure and your on-premises network and enables secure connectivity and communication between the different nodes in the HPC cluster. This connection uses the public internet.
- **Storage**: The disks that are used for the nodes that are hosted in Azure, are stored inside Azure Blob Storage.

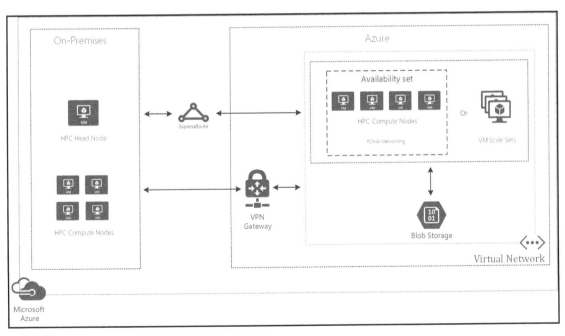

Hybrid HPC architecture

Azure Batch

Azure Batch is a service that helps developers scale their workloads over virtual machines (Windows or Linux) or containers, without the need to manage the infrastructure. With Azure Batch, you can run large-scale, parallel and HPC applications efficiently in the cloud. Batch computing is most commonly used for applications that regularly process, transform, or analyze large volumes of data. Typically, HPC applications that run on Azure Batch include deep learning applications, image rendering applications, media encoding applications, and Monte Carlo simulations. Azure Media Services uses Azure Batch internally for media encoding as well.

The Azure Batch service uses Azure compute as its infrastructure, which means you can use both Windows or Linux VMs to host your applications or workloads. Azure uses the A8/A9 series VMs with RDMA networking internally for the nodes and is fully responsible for creating and managing those virtual machines. Azure adds the nodes to a **pool** inside the Azure Batch account.

Inside the Azure Batch account, a **job** can be created that will run the workload on the pool. Your workload is then added to the Batch **queue** and split up into several tasks, so they can run in parallel. Azure Batch scales those tasks automatically and they can be scheduled as well. Your workloads, which are called **tasks**, are added to the Batch Queue, spread over the managed pool of virtual machines, and can be scaled automatically. Most of these tasks can run completely independent, but for some HPC workloads, it might be necessary for the tasks to communicate with each other. In that case, Azure Batch uses persistent storage to store output data for retrieval by other tasks. By default, Azure Blob Storage is used for this, but you can use other storage types as well. The tasks communicate with each other using a runtime called **Message Passing Interface** (**MPI**) and the outcome of all these different tasks can be consolidated into a single result:

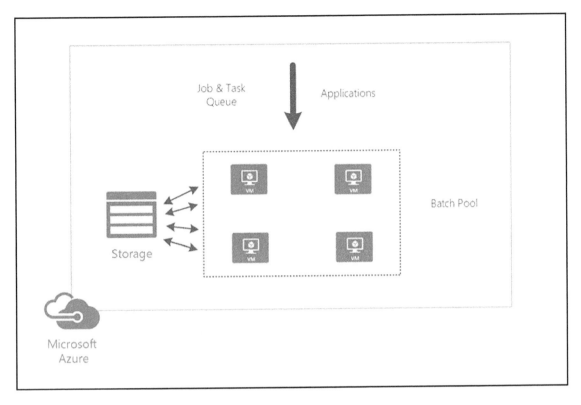

Azure Batch architecture

To automate the creation of Azure Batch processes, Azure Batch uses a JSON template (not to be confused with an ARM template, this one is different). In this template, you can automate the creation of the Batch pool, including the VM sizes, the operating system, and the number of nodes (the number of VMs). You can use Azure CLI for automation as well.

A Batch pool consists of virtual machines that can be created using images from the Azure Marketplace, cloud services (a standard guest image from Azure), custom images (a custom VHD from a storage account), and specific graphic and rendering images.

You can use low priority VMs for Azure Batch. This reduces the costs of VMs significantly. This discount is only available for Azure Batch, for all the VM sizes Azure Batch supports, and in all regions. For more information on these prices, you can refer to the following web page: https://azure.microsoft.com/en-us/pricing/details/batch/.

Creating an Azure Batch service

In this example, we are going to create a Batch pool from the Azure Portal. This will give you some extra information on the different settings for Azure Batch, such as how to start your applications on the pool of VMs.

To create an Azure Batch pool, you can refer to the following steps:

1. The first step is to create an Azure Batch account in the Azure Portal. You can refer to the following article to create one: `https://docs.microsoft.com/en-us/azure/batch/batch-account-create-portal`. I've created an Azure Batch account called **packtpub** in a **Resource group** called **PacktBatchGroup**:

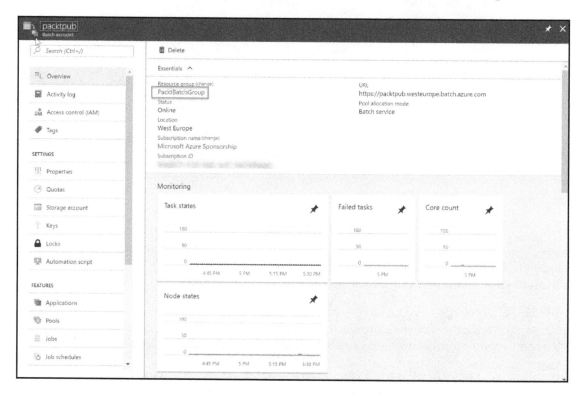

Azure Batch service

2. Next, click on **Pools** in the left-menu and click on **Add**. Add the following values:
    - **Pool ID: packtpool1**
    - **Display name**: PactPool
    - **Image Type**: **Cloud Services (Windows Only)**
    - **Node Size**: Pick **Standard A1**
    - **Scale Mode**: **Auto Scale**
    - **Formula**: "$TargetDedicated=0" (you can refer to the following article about **Automatic Scaling Formulas** for more information: `https://docs.microsoft.com/en-us/azure/batch/batch-automatic-scaling`)
    - **Start Task**: **Disabled** (here, you can provide a command for the startup of executables or other workloads)

Leave the other default values for the rest of the settings.

 For the virtual network settings, you can run your Batch pool inside a VNet. This way, the VMs can communicate with other VMs that are not part of the Batch pool, such as a file server or a license server.

3. Click on **OK**:

Azure Batch pool settings

4. After creating the Batch pool, you can select **Application packages** from the left-hand menu to upload your executables, libraries, or other metadata that is associated with your application. To upload packages, you have to create or link an Azure Storage account. Application packages are uploaded as ZIP files that consist of all the necessary files. Those files are installed on the VMs automatically by Azure:

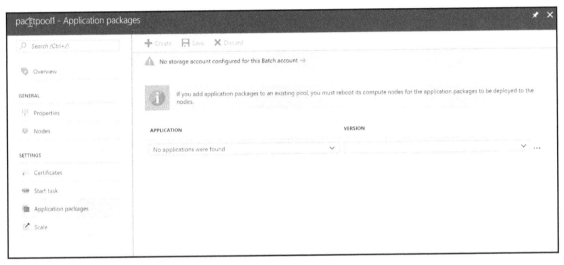

Azure Batch application packages

5. You can also provide the **Start task** properties from the left-hand menu as well.

 This is just one way of creating a Batch service. There are more methods that you can use. You can use Visual Studio, call the Batch API directly, or use CLI or PowerShell.

Stateless components

Azure Batch uses parallel actions to process the workloads. To fully leverage this capability, applications need to be split up into single and stateless tasks, called multi-instance tasks. By default, a Batch task is executed on a single compute node. By enabling multi-instance tasks, the task is executed on multiple compute nodes.

Those multi-instance tasks are submitted to the Batch job and then distributed over the available nodes inside the Batch pool. Azure Batch automatically creates one primary task and several subtasks based on the multi-instance settings. The tasks that run in parallel then use Azure Storage to save and retrieve the data that's used by the different tasks:

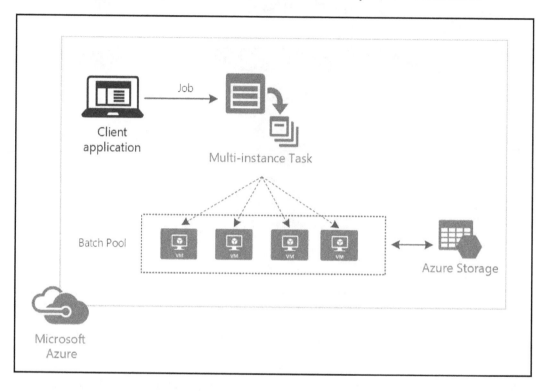

Azure Batch jobs and tasks

Those multi-instance tasks can be created in code using the Batch .NET SDK or the Python SDK.

For more information on creating an Azure Batch Solution using the Batch .NET SDK, you can refer to the following tutorial: `https://docs.microsoft.com/en-us/azure/batch/tutorial-parallel-dotnet`.

Containers on Azure Batch

Azure Batch also supports the deployment of containers. You can use Docker containers or Singularity. Singularity is similar to Docker, but it is primary designed to run on shared HPC clusters in on-premises environments and super computing installations. Singularity does not require root privileges to execute containers. It allows applications to leverage GPUs and specialized networking within the privilege scope of the executing user. This makes Singularity compatible for permissions-constrained HPC environments. Where Docker is originally designed to run Linux containers, Singularity can import Docker images and run Windows containers as well.

Singularity can be run from the Azure Cloud Shell without any installation and can be installed from the Azure Batch Shipyard release. This is an open system for enabling simple, configuration-based container execution on Azure Batch. Any knowledge of the Azure Batch .NET SDK is not needed; only configuration files are used here.

 For more information on containers on Batch Shipyard, you can refer to the following GitHub page: `https://github.com/Azure/batch-shipyard`.

Summary

In this chapter, we have covered the compute-intensive applications objective. We've covered how to design HPC and other compute-intensive applications using Azure services, how to determine when to use Azure Batch, and how to design stateless components to accommodate scale and Containers on Azure Batch.

In the next chapter, we will cover the web application objective.

Questions

Answer the following questions to test your knowledge of the information in this chapter. You can find the answers in the *Assessments* section at the end of this book:

1. You want to create HPC clusters in your on-premises environment. Should you use Azure Batch?
    1. Yes
    2. No

2. For creating high-performance compute VMs, should we use the H-series?
    1. Yes
    2. No

3. To automate the creation of Azure Batch processes, should we use ARM templates?
    1. Yes
    2. No

Further reading

You can check the following links for more information about the topics that are covered in this chapter:

- **High performance compute VM sizes**: https://docs.microsoft.com/en-us/azure/virtual-machines/windows/sizes-hpc?toc=%2Fazure%2Fvirtual-machines%2Fwindows%2Ftoc.json
- **Options with HPC Pack to create and manage a cluster for Windows HPC workloads in Azure**: https://docs.microsoft.com/en-us/azure/virtual-machines/windows/hpcpack-cluster-options
- **Batch Documentation**: https://docs.microsoft.com/en-us/azure/batch/
- **HPC, Batch, and Big Compute solutions using Azure VMs**: https://docs.microsoft.com/en-us/azure/virtual-machines/linux/high-performance-computing
- **Deploy applications to compute nodes with Batch application packages**: https://docs.microsoft.com/en-us/azure/batch/batch-application-packages
- **Solution architecture: On-premises HPC implementation bursting to Azure**: https://azure.microsoft.com/en-us/solutions/architecture/hpc-on-prem-burst/
- **Solution architecture: HPC cluster deployed in the cloud**: https://azure.microsoft.com/en-us/solutions/architecture/hpc-cluster/
- **Solution architecture: Big compute solutions as a service**: https://azure.microsoft.com/en-us/solutions/architecture/hpc-big-compute-saas/

Designing Web Applications 3

In the previous chapter, we covered the compute-intensive application objectives. We covered how to design high-performance computing and other compute-intensive applications.

This chapter introduces the web application's objectives. It will cover information about Azure Web Apps, the different App Service plans that are available, and what the characteristics are for the different App Service plans. You will learn more about designing Web Apps for Containers using Azure Container Services and Docker, how to design Web Apps for high availability, scalability, and performance using Redis Cache, auto-scaling, App Service environments, and more. You will also learn how to design a custom Web API and what Azure offers in terms of securing custom APIs.

The following topics will be covered:

- Azure Web Apps
- App Service plans
- Designing Web Apps for Containers
- Designing Web Apps for high availability, scalability, and performance
- Designing and securing custom Web APIs

Technical requirements

This chapter uses the following tools for the examples:

- Visual Studio 2017: `https://www.visualstudio.com/downloads/`

The source code for this chapter can be downloaded here:

- `https://github.com/SjoukjeZaal/AzureArchitectureBook/tree/master/Chapter%203/`

Azure Web Apps

Azure Web Apps is a part of Azure App Services and it is where you can host your websites and applications in Azure. Using Web Apps, you only pay for the compute resources you use, not for the actual hosting of your site or application. Besides websites and applications, you can also host your Web APIs and your mobile backends inside Azure Web Apps.

You can use a programming language of your choice for developing applications. At the time of writing, Azure Web Apps supports .NET, .NET Core, Java, Ruby, Node.js, PHP, and Python. Those applications are hosted on Windows or Linux virtual machines that are fully managed by Microsoft and can easily be scaled using out-of-the-box features. Besides scaling, you can leverage other Azure features, such as security, load balancing, and insights and analytics. You can also use the DevOps capabilities, such as Continuous Integration and deployment from VSTS, GitHub, Docker Hub, and other resources, SSL certificates, package management, staging environments, and custom domains.

App Service plans

Azure Web Apps are hosted inside App Service plans. Inside the App Service plan, you can configure all the required settings, such as the costs, the compute resources, and in which region you want to deploy your apps. There are different types of App Service plans available in Azure, from free plans where you share all the resources with other customers and that are most suitable for development applications, to paid plans, where you can choose to host your apps on Windows VMs or Linux VMs and can set the available CPU, and more.

Azure offers the following service plan SKUs:

- **Free and Shared**: Your app runs on the same VM as other apps in a shared environment. This environment can also include apps from other customers. Each app has a CPU quota and there is no ability to scale up or out. These App Service plans are most suited for development and test apps or apps with less traffic. There is no SLA support for those two plans. The Shared service plan offers the ability to add custom domains.

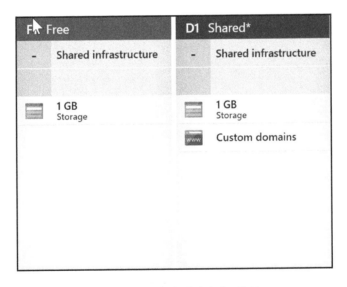

Free and Shared App Service plan in the Azure Portal

- **Basic**: The Basic tier is the first tier, where you can choose between different pricing ranges. It offers three tiers and the available cores and RAM will double for every tier. Apps run on dedicated Linux or Windows VMs and the compute resources are only shared between apps that are deployed inside the same App Service plan. All apps inside the same App Service plan reside in an isolated environment, which supports SSL and custom domains. The Basic tier offers scaling to three instances, but you need to do this manually. This tier is most suitable for development and test environments and applications with less traffic.

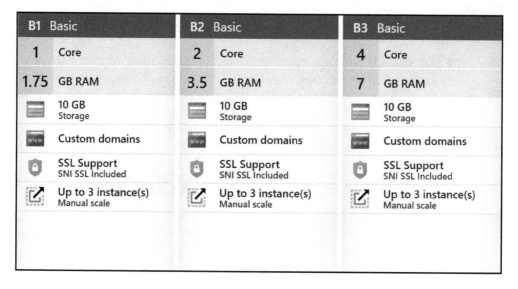

Basic App Service plan in the Azure Portal

- **Standard:** The Standard tier also has three tiers to choose from. It offers custom domains and SSL support, offers autoscale up to ten instances, and offers five deployment slots, which can be used for testing, staging, and production apps. It also provides daily backups and Azure Traffic Manager.

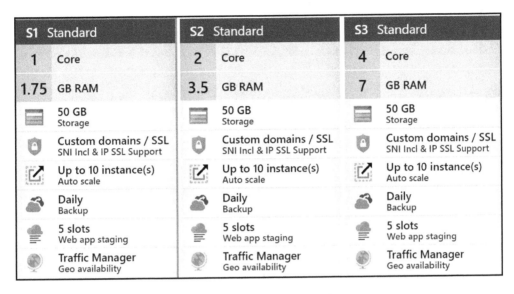

Standard App Service plan in the Azure Portal

- **Premium:** Premium offers two types of tiers, Premium and PremiumV2. They both offer all the features of the Standard tier, but the Premium tier offers extra scale instances and deployment slots. The Premium V2 runs on Dv2-series virtual machines, which offer faster processors and SSD drives and drastically increase the performance of your application.

P1V2 PremiumV2	P2V2 PremiumV2	P3V2 PremiumV2
1 Core	**2** Core	**4** Core
3.5 GB RAM	**7** GB RAM	**14** GB RAM
SSD and faster CPU Dv2 series workers	SSD and faster CPU Dv2 series workers	SSD and faster CPU Dv2 series workers
250 GB Storage	250 GB Storage	250 GB Storage
Custom domains / SSL SNI Incl & IP SSL Support	Custom domains / SSL SNI Incl & IP SSL Support	Custom domains / SSL SNI Incl & IP SSL Support
Up to 20 instance(s) * Subject to availability	Up to 20 instance(s) * Subject to availability	Up to 20 instance(s) * Subject to availability
20 slots Web app staging	20 slots Web app staging	20 slots Web app staging
Traffic Manager Geo availability	Traffic Manager Geo availability	Traffic Manager Geo availability

P1 Premium	P2 Premium	P3 Premium
1 Core	**2** Core	**4** Core
1.75 GB RAM	**3.5** GB RAM	**7** GB RAM
250 GB Storage	250 GB Storage	250 GB Storage
Custom domains / SSL SNI Incl & IP SSL Support	Custom domains / SSL SNI Incl & IP SSL Support	Custom domains / SSL SNI Incl & IP SSL Support
Up to 20 instance(s) * Subject to availability	Up to 20 instance(s) * Subject to availability	Up to 20 instance(s) * Subject to availability
20 slots Web app staging	20 slots Web app staging	20 slots Web app staging
50 times daily Backup	50 times daily Backup	50 times daily Backup
Traffic Manager Geo availability	Traffic Manager Geo availability	Traffic Manager Geo availability

Premium App Service plan in the Azure Portal

- **Isolated**: The Isolated tier offers full isolation for your applications by providing a private environment with dedicated virtual machines and virtual networks. You can also scale up to 100 instances. To create a private environment, App Services uses an **App Service Environment** (**ASE**), which will be covered in the next section. All apps run on Dv2-series virtual machines, so it offers high-performance capabilities. The Isolated App Service plan is most suitable for apps that need complete isolation, because of high security demands for instance, but that want to leverage all the capabilities that Azure Web Apps offer, such as auto-scale and deployment slots.

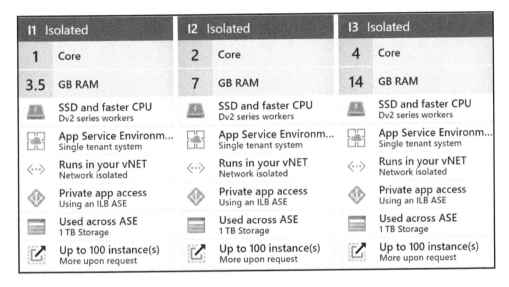

Isolated App Service plan in the Azure Portal

The App Service Environment (ASE)

The ASE is a feature of Azure App Service that provides a fully isolated environment for your Web Apps, mobile apps, API apps, and Azure Functions. An ASE is deployed inside a subnet of the VNet, so this provides full isolation and secure network access. ASEs are most suitable for apps that require high-scale workloads because they can be spread across a single or multiple Azure regions. Because of the network isolation, ASEs are also very suitable for apps with high security requirements.

There can only be one ASE created per Azure subscription and it can host up to 100 instances; from 100 app instances in a single App Service plan to 100 App Service plans with one app instance.

ASEs use frontends and workers where the former are suitable for automatic load balancing of the requests inside the ASE and the latter host the actual Web Apps inside the ASE. They are added automatically by Azure.

> At the time of writing, there are two different versions of ASE, v1 and v2. The difference between the two versions is that v2 automatically adds frontends and workers to the ASE depending on the scale of the App Service plans. In v1, you had to add those roles manually before you could scale out your App Service plan.

Creating an ASE

You can create an Azure ASE from the Azure Portal by taking the following steps:

1. Navigate to the Azure Portal by opening `https://portal.azure.com/`.
2. Click on **New** and type `App Service Environment` in the search bar. Click the **Create** button.
3. A new blade opens up, where you can fill in the basic settings of the VM. Add the following:
   - **Name:** `PacktASE`
   - **Subscription:** Select a subscription here
   - **Resource Group:** `PacktPubASE`

- **Virtual Network/Location**: Azure will automatically create a new virtual network for you. If you want to pick an existing one, you can change the settings by clicking the link.

Creating ASE in the Azure Portal

4. Click on **Create**. Azure will create an ASE, a virtual network, a route table, and a NSG for you.

5. You can now choose this ASE when you create a new Azure App Service plan:

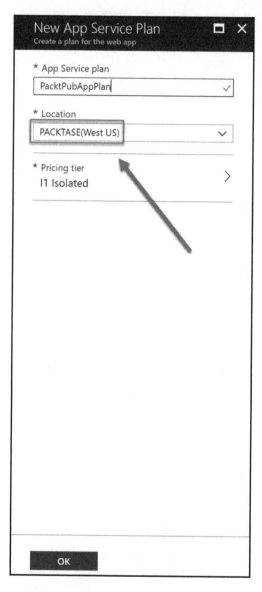

Creating an ASE in the Azure Portal

Please note that the creation of an ASE can be quite expensive, so I strongly advise you to remove this when you are finished with your test.

For more information about Azure ASE, you can refer to the following Microsoft documentation: `https://docs.microsoft.com/en-us/azure/app-service/environment/intro`.

Web Apps for Containers

Web Apps for Containers is part of the Azure App Service on Linux. It lets you easily deploy and scale your own Docker-formatted images on Azure. Docker is based on open standards, which means it can run on all major Linux distributions and Windows Server 2016.

Docker containers are lightweight sandboxes on top of your OS. When your application is deployed inside a Docker container, the app cannot see or access all other applications or processes that are running on the same OS. You can compare this to creating different VMs to host different types of workloads or applications, but without the overhead of the virtualization itself. Docker containers also share the same OS and infrastructure, whereas VMs need to have their own OS installed inside their own infrastructure.

With containers, you share the underlying resources of the Docker host and you build a Docker image that includes everything you need to run the application. You can start with a basic image and then add everything you need.

Docker containers are also extremely portable. You can deploy a Docker container including all the settings, such as configuration settings, a specific runtime, framework, and tooling on a VM with Docker installed. You can then easily move that same container to the Azure App Service on Linux, and the application will still run as expected. This solves the *it works on my machine* problem that (mostly) all developers face. This makes Docker not a virtualization technology, but an application delivery technology.

Docker containers are very suitable for building applications that leverage the microservices architecture, where parts of an application are loosely coupled, and divided into separate services that all collaborate with each other. Each service can then be deployed into a separate container, written in their own programming language, using their own configuration settings. A service can consist of a database, or a Web API, or a mobile backend for instance. You can easily deploy multiple copies of a single application, or database. The only thing to be aware of is that they all share the same OS. If your application needs to run on a different OS, you still have to use a VM.

For more information on Azure App Service on Linux, you can refer to the following website: `https://docs.microsoft.com/en-us/azure/app-service/containers/app-service-linux-intro`.

Microsoft released a sample project, called **Developer Finder**, which is available on GitHub. This will give you an great overview of the possibilities of Docker containers and is a good starting point for developing your own applications using Docker. You can refer to the following site: `https://github.com/azure-app-service/demoapp`.

Getting started with Web App for Containers

Web App for Containers can be created from the Azure Portal. Follow these steps to create a project:

In this example, I'm using the Docker Hub as a repository for images. You can create an account using the following link: `https://hub.docker.com/`.

1. Navigate to the Azure Portal by opening `https://portal.azure.com/`.
2. Click on **New** and in the search bar type `Web App for Containers`. Click on the **Create** button, as shown in the following screenshot:

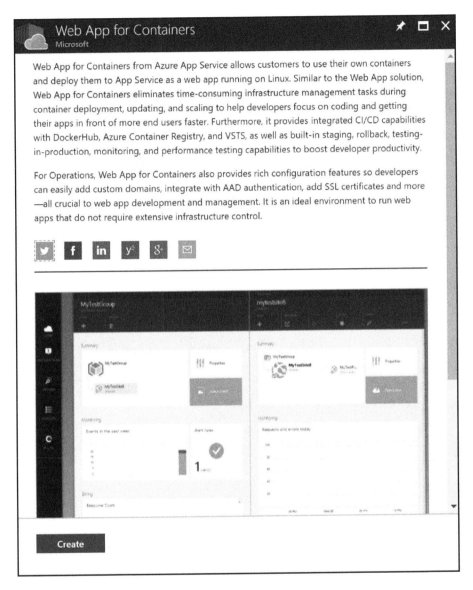

Creating a Web App for Containers project in the Azure Portal

3. A new blade opens up. Add the following values:
    - **App name**: `PacktContainers`.
    - **Subscription**: Select a subscription here.
    - **Resource Group**: This one is automatically filled in when you enter the app name. Leave it as default.

- **App Service plan/Location**: A new App Service plan will automatically be created. If you want to pick an existing one, or change the default settings, you can click on it.

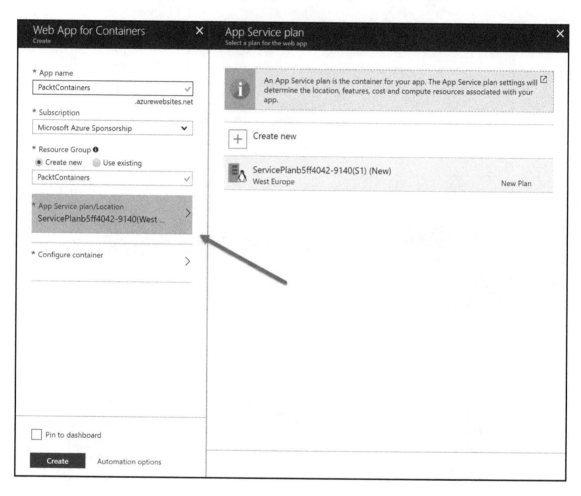

Web App for Containers settings in the Azure Portal

- **Configure container**: This will take you to the actual Docker settings. Here, pick **Docker Hub** as an image source.
- **Image and optional tag**: `mysql`.

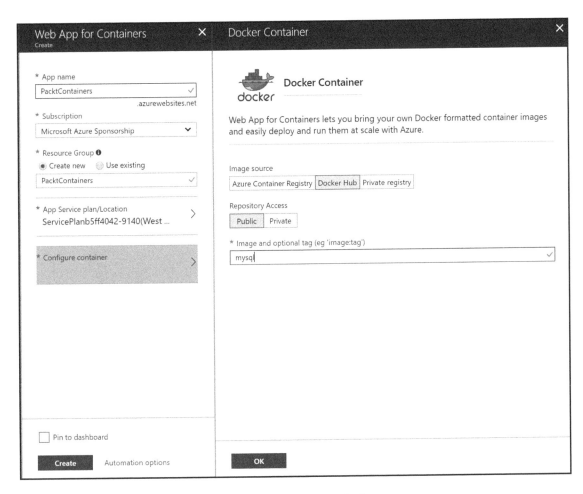

Configuring a container in the Azure Portal

Designing Web Apps for high availability, scalability, and performance

Performance is an important issue to keep in mind when designing Web Apps. Web Apps that are unresponsive or that perform badly will eventually lose all their visitors. They will simply hop on to another site. Azure provides multiple options to make your Web App highly available and scalable, which will result in a better performance to keep your visitors on board.

 Beside the features that Azure offers to design for high availability, scaling, and performance, you can keep certain architecture patterns in mind when architecting your Web App. You can refer to the following article from the Azure Architecture Center for these patterns: `https://docs.microsoft.com/en-us/azure/architecture/patterns/category/performance-scalability`.

High availability and performance

Azure provides several ways to make your Web App perform better and to become highly available. You can use a **Content Delivery Network (CDN)**, a cache, or you can copy your Web App over to multiple regions.

Using a CDN

You can use a CDN to scale your websites globally. By using a CDN, your static content, such as HTML pages, style sheets, client-side scripts, images, documents, and files, are cached in different regions. This way, it takes less time to download the content, because the static content is physically closer to the user, which increases the performance of your Web App.

Azure CDN allows you to use custom domain names to access your content. This can be configured inside the Azure Portal. You can refer to the following article to add a custom domain: `https://docs.microsoft.com/en-us/azure/cdn/cdn-map-content-to-custom-domain`. You can also enable HTTPS for your CDN: `https://docs.microsoft.com/en-us/azure/cdn/cdn-custom-ssl`.

Using Redis Cache

Redis Cache in Azure is based on the popular open-source implementation, Redis Cache. It provides a secure cache from where you can access your data and that runs in an Azure data center. It can be used by different types of applications, including Web Apps, applications inside a virtual machine, or other cloud services. Caches can be shared by all applications that have the appropriate access key.

Azure Redis Cache comes in the following tiers:

- **Basic**: This is a single node cache, ideal for development, test environments, and non-critical workloads. This tier has no SLA.
- **Standard**: Provides a replicated cache. The data is automatically replicated between the two nodes. This tier offers an SLA.
- **Premium:** The Premium tier has all the standard features and, in addition, it provides bigger workloads, better performance, disaster recovery, and enhanced security. It also offers Redis Persistence, which persists data that is stored inside the cache. Snapshots and backups can be created and restored in case of failures. It also offers Redis Cluster, which automatically shares data across multiple Redis nodes, so you can create workloads of bigger memory sizes (greater than 53 GB) and get better performance. It also offers support for Azure Virtual Networks, which gives the ability to isolate your cache by using subnets, access control policies, and more. You can provision an Azure Redis Cache from the Azure Portal using an ARM template.

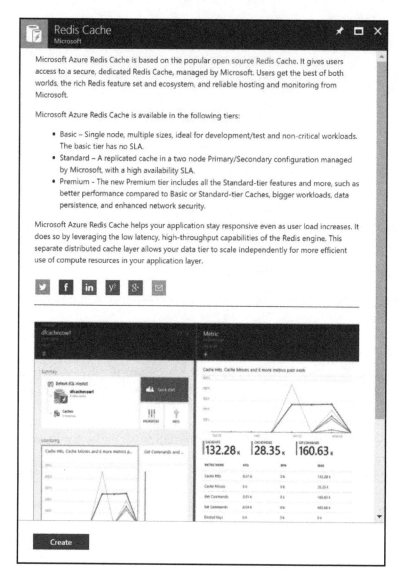

Provisioning Redis Cache from the Azure Portal

You can refer to the following article to download some sample ARM templates for deploying Azure Redis Cache with different types of configuration settings: `https://docs.microsoft.com/en-us/azure/redis-cache/cache-redis-cache-arm-provision`.

Using Azure Traffic Manager

Another way of designing for availability and scalability is copying your Web App over to multiple regions or data centers. Azure uses Azure Traffic Manager to spread the workload. Your Web App can be reached by using a single URL, where Azure Traffic Manager will handle the load and locate the closest geographical region or most suitable region for you at the DNS level.

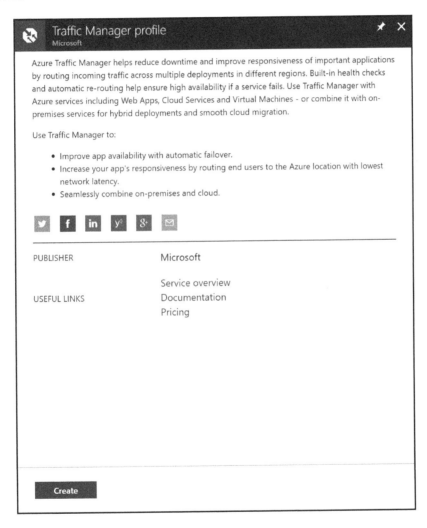

Azure Trafic Manager

When creating an Azure Traffic Manager profile from the Azure Portal, you can choose between four different routing methods:

- **Performance**: Select this method when you have endpoints in different geographical locations and you want end users to use the closest endpoint in terms of the lowest network latency.
- **Weighted**: This method is best suitable for when you want your application to be distributed evenly or according to certain weights, which you define.
- **Priority**: Use this method when you want one endpoint to be the primary endpoint for all traffic, and provide backups in case the primary or the backup endpoints are unavailable.
- **Geographic**: This method is best suitable for scenarios where knowing a user's geographical region and routing them based on that is important. Localization of content can be a reason for choosing this method, for instance. Users are then directed to specific endpoints based on the geographical location where their DNS query comes from.

> Azure Traffic Manager is also discussed in `Chapter 5`, *Robust Networking Implementations*. For more information, you can refer to that chapter.

Scalability

Azure provides the ability to scale your Web Apps. One of the possibilities is to scale out, where you can scale your Web Apps globally. Scaling out means adding nodes to, or removing nodes from, a Web App. This way, the load time is decreased when the Web App is accessed from different locations. The other option is to scale up. Scaling up means adding resources to, or removing resources from, a Web App, such as CPUs or memory. When scaling up, you switch to another pricing tier inside your App Service plan, or pick a different App Service plan.

> For more information about Azure App Service plans, you can refer to the beginning of this chapter.

Scaling out

There are multiple ways to scale out your Web App. You can scale out manually or automatically by using **Azure Autoscale**. To use Autoscale, take the following steps:

1. Under **Settings**, click on **Scale Out (App Service plan)**.
2. In the right-hand side of the screen, you can increase or decrease the **Instance count**. The maximum instance count depends on the App Service plan:

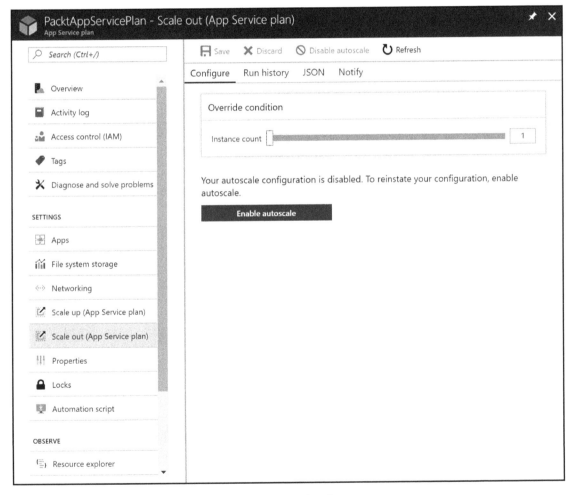

Azure App Service plan scaling

3. Here, you can also turn on autoscale (only for the Standard, Premium, and Isolated App Service plans). You have to name the autoscale set, and add at least one scaling condition. You can choose between scaling based on a metric or a specific instance count. When using scale based on a metric, you need to add a scale rule:

Azure App Service plan auto scaling

 Azure Autoscale lets you configure a lot of settings that are beyond the scope of this book. You can refer to the following URL for more information on Azure Autoscale and the available settings: `https://docs.microsoft.com/en-us/azure/monitoring-and-diagnostics/monitoring-understanding-autoscale-settings`.

Scaling up

You can choose a different pricing tier or App Service plan to scale up your website. This can be done from the App Service plan settings inside the Azure Portal as well, such as when scaling out your Web App.

Navigate to the Azure App Service settings in the Azure Portal and, under **Settings**, click on **Scale Up (App Service plan)**. You can then select a different App Service plan, as shown in the following screenshot:

Azure App Service plan scaling up

Designing and securing custom Web APIs

Custom Web APIs can be created using Visual Studio code or Visual Studio 2017. For creating Web APIs, the following programming languages are available:

- ASP.NET
- ASP.NET Core
- Angular
- React.js

Designing your Web API

This demo will be created using .NET Core Framework 2.0 and Visual Studio 2017. Begin by opening up Visual Studio 2017:

1. Click on **File** | **New** | **Project** and, in the new **Project** window, select **ASP.NET Core Web Application**. Name the project and click on **OK**:
2. A pop-up window opens up where you can select the **Web API** template, select **ASP.NET Core 2.0**, and click on **OK**:

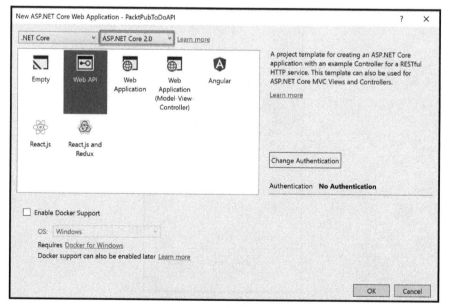

Creating a custom Web API from Visual Studio 2017

3. Add a `Models` folder in the **Solution Explorer**. Right-click your project name and select **Add | New Folder**. Add a `TodoItem` class by right-clicking the `Models` folder and click **Add | Class**.

4. Update the `TodoItem` class with the following code:

```
namespace PacktPubToDoAPI.Models
{
    public class TodoItem
    {
        public long Id { get; set; }
        public string Name { get; set; }
        public bool IsComplete { get; set; }
    }
}
```

5. The next step is to add the database context class that coordinates entity framework functionality. Add a `TodoContext` class inside the `Models` folder and replace it with the following code:

```
using Microsoft.EntityFrameworkCore;
using PacktPubToDoAPI.Models;

namespace PacktPubToDoAPI.Models
{
    public class TodoContext : DbContext
    {
        public TodoContext(DbContextOptions<TodoContext> options)
            : base(options)
        {
        }

        public DbSet<TodoItem> TodoItems { get; set; }

    }
}
```

6. The next step is to register the database context with the dependency injection container. You can do this by replacing the code in the `StartUp.cs` with the following:

```
using Microsoft.AspNetCore.Builder;
using Microsoft.EntityFrameworkCore;
using Microsoft.Extensions.DependencyInjection;
using PacktPubToDoAPI.Models;

namespace PacktPubToDoAPI
```

```
{
    public class Startup
    {
        public void ConfigureServices(IServiceCollection services)
        {
            services.AddDbContext<TodoContext>(opt =>
opt.UseInMemoryDatabase("TodoList"));
            services.AddMvc();
        }

        public void Configure(IApplicationBuilder app)
        {
            app.UseMvc();
        }
    }
}
```

7. In the **Solution Explorer**, right-click the `Controllers` folder and add a controller named `TodoController`. Replace the controller with the following code:

```
using System.Collections.Generic;
using Microsoft.AspNetCore.Mvc;
using PacktPubToDoAPI.Models;
using System.Linq;

namespace PacktPubToDoAPI.Controllers
{
    [Route("api/[controller]")]
    public class TodoController : Controller
    {
        private readonly TodoContext _context;

        public TodoController(TodoContext context)
        {
            _context = context;

            if (_context.TodoItems.Count() == 0)
            {
                _context.TodoItems.Add(new TodoItem { Name =
"Item1" });
                _context.SaveChanges();
            }
        }
    }
}
```

8. This code uses dependency injection in the constructor to inject the `TodoContext` inside the controller. This context is used for the **create**, **read**, **update**, **delete** (**CRUD**) methods on the data. The constructor adds an item to the in-memory database if it is empty.

9. The next step is to implement the CRUD methods. Add the following code to the constructor for the `Get` requests:

```
[HttpGet]
public IEnumerable<TodoItem> GetAll()
{
    return _context.TodoItems.ToList();
}

[HttpGet("{id}", Name = "GetTodo")]
public IActionResult GetById(long id)
{
    var item = _context.TodoItems.FirstOrDefault(t => t.Id == id);
    if (item == null)
    {
      return NotFound();
    }
    return new ObjectResult(item);
}
```

10. Add the following underneath for `Post` requests:

```
[HttpPost]
public IActionResult Create([FromBody] TodoItem item)
{
   if (item == null)
   {
        return BadRequest();
   }

   _context.TodoItems.Add(item);
   _context.SaveChanges();

   return CreatedAtRoute("GetTodo", new { id = item.Id }, item);
  }
  [HttpPut("{id}")]
  public IActionResult Update(long id, [FromBody] TodoItem item)
  {
      if (item == null || item.Id != id)
      {
          return BadRequest();
      }
```

```
        var todo = _context.TodoItems.FirstOrDefault(t => t.Id ==
id);
        if (todo == null)
        {
            return NotFound();
        }
        todo.IsComplete = item.IsComplete;
        todo.Name = item.Name;

        _context.TodoItems.Update(todo);
        _context.SaveChanges();
        return new NoContentResult();
    }
```

11. Finally, add the `Delete` request underneath the `Post` requests:

```
[HttpDelete("{id}")]
    public IActionResult Delete(long id)
    {
        var todo = _context.TodoItems.FirstOrDefault(t => t.Id ==
id);
        if (todo == null)
        {
            return NotFound();
        }

        _context.TodoItems.Remove(todo);
        _context.SaveChanges();
        return new NoContentResult();
    }
```

12. You can now deploy this Web API to Azure using the **Publish** function in Visual Studio 2017. Right-click the **Solution Explorer** and click on **Publish**. The publishing wizard now opens. In there, select **Microsoft Azure App Service**, choose **Select Existing**, and click on **Publish**:

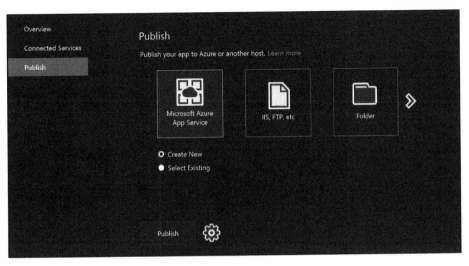

Publishing the Web API to Azure from Visual Studio 2017

13. In the next screen, select the Azure Web App that is already there from the previous sections in this chapter and click on the **OK** button:

Selecting the Azure Subscription from Visual Studio 2017

14. The Web API is now published to Azure.

 This sample application is based on a sample from the Microsoft site. When you need any further instructions or information about the sample app, please refer to the following Microsoft site: `https://docs.microsoft.com/en-us/aspnet/core/tutorials/first-web-api`.

Securing your Web API

To secure your Web API, you can use several options. You can use options provided by Azure or you can use your own authentication providers. A best practice is, however, to use the standard authentication options that are available for Azure App Services.

You can use the following services in Azure to secure your Web API:

- **Azure Active Directory (Azure AD)**: Azure AD offers traditional username and password identity management, roles, and permissions management from the cloud. In addition, it offers more enterprise solutions, such as multi-factor authentication, applications monitoring, solution monitoring, and alerting.
- **Azure Active Directory Business to Consumer**: Azure Active Directory Business to Consumer (B2C) is a cloud identity-management solution for mobile and web applications. It offers out-of-the-box authentication providers that can be leveraged from your apps and custom APIs. Examples of out-of-the-box authentication providers are Facebook, and Google.
- **Active Directory Federation Services**: You can use Active Directory Federation Services (ADFS) to secure your web API using the on-premises identities that are present in your organization. ADFS can be configured in conjunction with Azure AD in a hybrid mode. You can then use the same APIs, such as the Microsoft Graph, to connect to your on-premises identities when you are using only Azure AD.
- **API Management**: You can use API Management to secure your Web API as well. You can use advanced security policies, API keys, throttling for preventing DDOS attacks, and more, to add an additional layer of security on top of your Web API.

In the *Design, security, and identity* section of `Chapter 9`, *Securing Your Resources*, we will cover the available authentication providers in more detail. This section gives a quick overview of the providers that are leveraged inside your Web APIs.
API Management is covered in more detail in `Chapter 4`, *Implementing Serverless and Microservices*.

Summary

In this chapter, we have covered the design web applications objectives. We've covered Azure Web Apps, App Service plans, how to design Web Apps for Containers, how to design Web Apps for high availability, scalability, and performance, and how you can design and secure custom Web APIs.

In the next chapter, we will proceed with the serverless and microservice objectives.

Questions

Answer the following questions to test your knowledge of the information in this chapter. You can find the answers in the *Assessments* section at the end of this book:

1. Is Redis Cache a memory key value datastore?
    1. Yes
    2. No
2. Is the Basic tier of Redis Cache well suited for production environments?
    1. Yes
    2. No
3. Can you use Azure B2B as an authentication provider for your applications?
    1. Yes
    2. No

Further reading

You can check out the following links for more information on the topics that are covered in this chapter:

- **Web Apps Documentation**: https://docs.microsoft.com/en-us/azure/app-service/
- **Azure App Service plan overview**: https://docs.microsoft.com/en-us/azure/app-service/azure-web-sites-web-hosting-plans-in-depth-overview
- **Announcing App Service Isolated, more power, scale and ease of use**: https://azure.microsoft.com/nl-nl/blog/announcing-app-service-isolated-more-power-scale-and-ease-of-use/
- **App Service on Linux Documentation**: https://docs.microsoft.com/en-us/azure/app-service/containers/
- **CDN Documentation**: https://docs.microsoft.com/en-us/azure/cdn/
- **Redis Cache Documentation**: https://docs.microsoft.com/en-us/azure/redis-cache/
- **Integrating applications with Azure Active Directory**: https://docs.microsoft.com/en-us/azure/active-directory/develop/active-directory-integrating-applications
- **Active Directory B2C Documentation**: https://docs.microsoft.com/en-us/azure/active-directory-b2c/

Implementing Serverless and Microservices

4

In the previous chapter, we covered the objective of web applications. You read about web applications, App Service plans, containers, Web APIs, and more. You should now be aware of when to use these different features.

This chapter introduces serverless and microservices. It will cover serverless computing and what Azure has to offer regarding the creation of serverless applications, such as Azure Functions and Azure Logic Apps. You will read about how to design for serverless computing using Azure Containers and API Management. Finally, microservices-based solutions are covered. You will learn about containers for microservices and the different platforms that are available.

The following topics will be covered:

- Event-driven actions using Azure Functions
- Designing applications using Azure Functions and Logic Apps
- Designing for serverless computing using Azure Container Instances
- Container orchestrations and the different container orchestration platforms
- Azure Service Fabric
- API Management
- Cloud-native deployments versus migrating assets

Technical requirements

This chapter uses the following tools for the examples:

- Azure PowerShell: https://docs.microsoft.com/en-us/powershell/azure/install-azurerm-ps?view=azurermps-5.1.1

The source code for this chapter can be downloaded from here:

- https://github.com/SjoukjeZaal/AzureArchitectureBook/tree/master/Chapter%204

Event-driven actions using Azure Functions

Azure Functions is a serverless compute service that enables you to create event-driven actions and triggers without the need to provision or manage your own infrastructure. In Azure Functions, you can run a script or custom code that responds to events from Azure, third-party services, or on-premises systems. You can build HTTP-based API endpoints (called HTTP triggers) that can be accessed by a wide range of applications, as well as mobile and IoT devices. You can also create **timer triggers**, which can run based on a schedule. With Azure Functions, you pay only for the resources you consume.

Functions use an Azure storage account to store code and configuration bindings. It uses the standard Azure Storage, which provides blob, table, and queue storage for storing the files and triggers. You can use the same App Service plans for your functions as you use for web apps and APIs. Azure Functions can also be deployed in **App Service Environments (ASEs)**.

 For more information about Azure Functions and which events and triggers it supports, you can refer to the following site: https://docs.microsoft.com/en-us/azure/azure-functions/functions-overview. For more information about the different App Service plans and ASEs, you can refer to Chapter 3, *Designing Web Applications*.

Azure Functions can be created from the Azure Portal and from Visual Studio 2017 and can be created in a variety of programming languages, such as C#, F#, Node.js, Java, PHP, Batch, PowerShell, JavaScript, Python, and TypeScript. They can be created using ARM templates as well. They can be deployed on Windows or Linux and by using continuous deployment. At the time of writing this book, it supports Bitbucket, Dropbox, external repositories (Git or Mercurial), a Git local repository, GitHub, OneDrive, and Visual Studio Team Services as a deployment source. Continuous deployment can be configured from the Azure Portal.

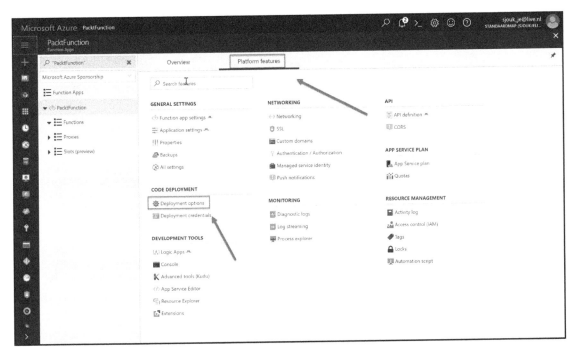

Continuous deployment for Azure Functions

 The Azure Functions tools in Visual Studio have been included since the 15.3 release. If you want to create them using Visual Studio 2017, update Visual Studio to at least version 15.3 or higher.

Consumption App Service plan

For Azure Functions, Microsoft introduced a new hosting plan where you share a pool of instances with functions from other customers. This plan is called the **Consumption plan**. This plan is more cost effective then the other available App Service plans because it automatically scales down and up, depending on the workload. When your function isn't running, you don't have to pay anything and when the function is running, instances are added dynamically and removed based on the number of incoming events. Functions hosted on the Consumption plan can run for a maximum of 10 minutes (the default timeout is 5 minutes, but this can be increased to 10 minutes). The Azure Function code and the binding configurations are stored on Azure File Storage on a separate storage account.

When you need your function to run continuously, or for it to run in the same App Service plan as other functions, or you need more CPU power, or you want to host your function on Linux, then it is best to use a dedicated App Service plan for your functions. All the other available App Service plans can be used for Azure Functions as well.

Designing application solutions using Azure Functions

In this demo, we are creating an Azure Function from the Azure Portal. This function is going to listen to an HTTP trigger and then add a message to a queue:

1. Navigate to the Azure Portal by opening `https://portal.azure.com/`.
2. Click on **New** and and type `Function App` in the search bar. Click the **Create** button.
3. A new blade opens up, where you can fill in the basic settings of the function. For the hosting plan, we are using a queue to store messages. When using the Consumption plan, queue storage is not part of your storage account, because it only uses Azure File Storage to store the function files. For the App Service plan, you can create a new App Service plan or pick an existing one. You can choose an ASE here as well. For the storage, by default, a new storage account is created. If you want to use an existing storage account, you can choose that as well. Add the following details and click on **Create**:

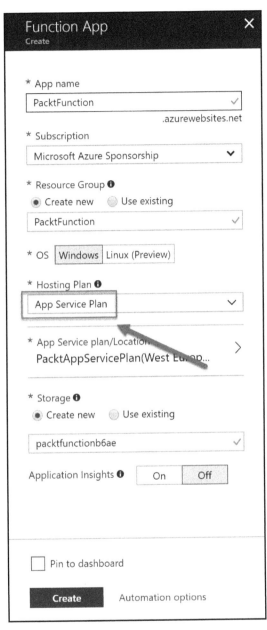

Creating an Azure Function from the Azure Portal

4. Once created, open the function from the Azure Portal and, in the left-hand menu, under **Function Apps**, select **Functions | New function**:

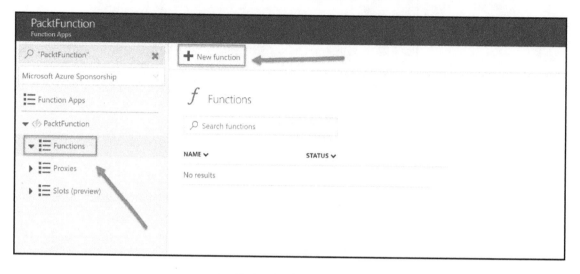

Azure Functions wizard from the Azure Portal

5. On the next screen, select **HTTP trigger**:

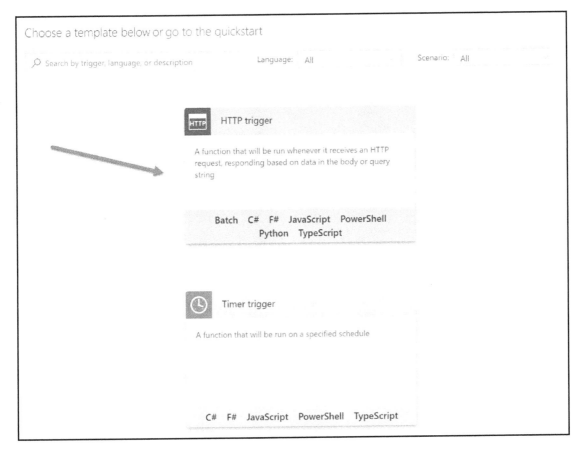

Selecting the HTTP trigger

6. The next step is the **HTTP trigger** settings. Fill in the following values. For the **Authorization level**, you can choose **Anonymous** right now. However, this is only for demo purposes; you should not choose that for your production functions. Click on **Create** and the trigger is created:

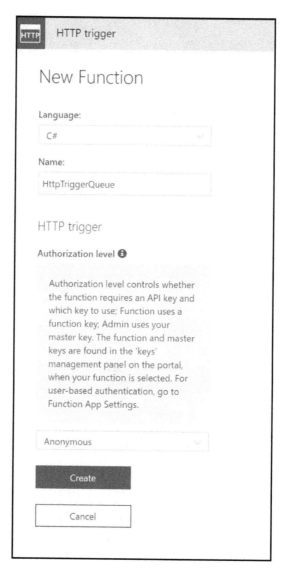

HTTP trigger settings

7. To configure the queue settings, click on **Integrate** | **New Output** and then select **Azure Queue Storage**. Click on **Select**:

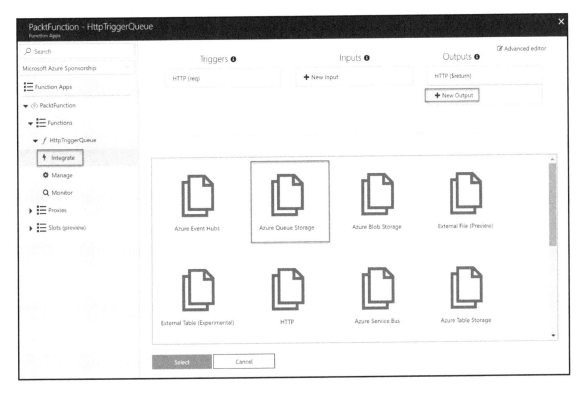

Configure queue

8. Under **Azure Queue Storage output**, keep the default settings and click on **Save**:

Configure queue

9. In the left-hand menu, select your function. The code editor will open. Replace the code with the following:

```
using System.Net;

public static async Task<HttpResponseMessage>
Run(HttpRequestMessage req, ICollector<string> outputQueueItem,
TraceWriter log)
{
    log.Info("C# HTTP trigger function processed a request.");
    // parse query parameter
    string name = req.GetQueryNameValuePairs()
        .FirstOrDefault(q => string.Compare(q.Key, "name", true) ==
0)
        .Value;

    // Get request body
```

```
dynamic data = await req.Content.ReadAsAsync<object>();

// Set name to query string or body data
name = name ?? data?.name;

outputQueueItem.Add("Name passed to the function: " + name);

return name == null
     ? req.CreateResponse(HttpStatusCode.BadRequest, "Please
pass a name on the query string or in the request body")
     : req.CreateResponse(HttpStatusCode.OK, "Hello " + name);
}
```

10. The preceding code adds a message inside the queue and then you need to click on **Save**:

11. To test the code, click the **Test** tab on the right-hand side of the screen. You can provide a message inside the JSON call and click on **Save and run**:

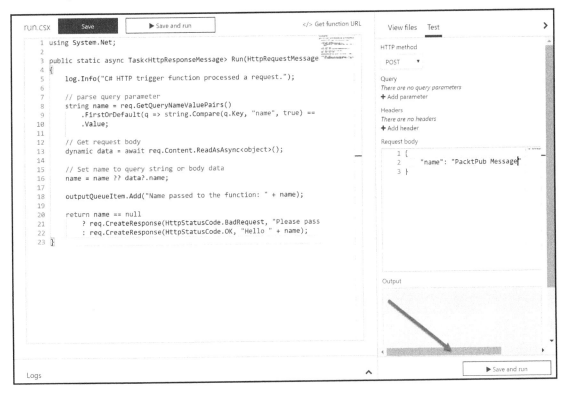

Testing the function

12. The default code generates an output message, which is displayed inside the output window. To see what is added to the queue, open the **Azure Storage Explorer** and connect to your Azure account using your credentials. In the left-hand tree view, navigate to the function storage account and click on **Queues**. The added message can be found there:

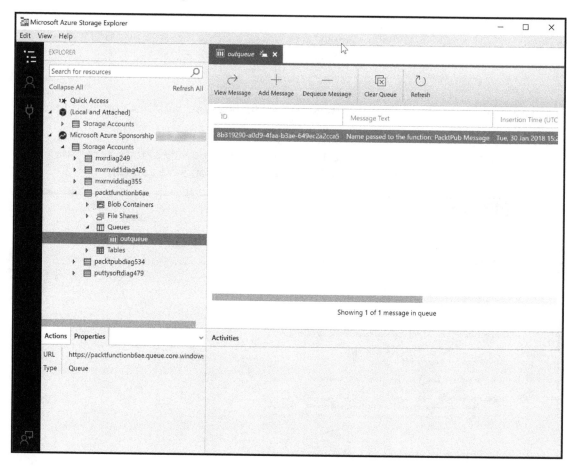

Queue message inside the Azure Storage Explorer

 The Azure Storage Explorer is part of the Azure Tools for Visual Studio. You can view blob, queue, and table data from your storage accounts in Azure. You can also download the Azure Storage Explorer from this direct link: `https://go.microsoft.com/fwlink/?LinkId=708343clcid=0x409`.

Durable Functions

At the time of writing this book, Durable Functions is still in preview. Durable Functions is an extension of Azure Functions and Azure WebJobs, and it provides the ability to create stateful functions with state management capabilities, checkpoints, and a restarting mechanism.

It introduces a new orchestrator function that has a couple of advantages. These are as follows:

- Workflows can be created in code; JSON schemas are not needed.
- It can call other functions synchronously and asynchronously. The output can be stored in local variables.
- It saves the state of the function when VMs are waiting and rebooting.

Workflow-driven applications using Logic Apps

Logic Apps, another service for the serverless offering from Azure, has a lot of overlap with Azure Functions. They can both be used to integrate apps or services. The main difference between the two is that Azure Functions are event-driven and Logic Apps are more workflow-driven. You can use Logic Apps to automate your business processes using a visual designer from the Azure Portal (developers can create them in Visual Studio as well), whereas Azure Functions are completely written in code. You can, however, call Azure Functions from within a Logic App.

With Logic Apps, you can build apps that integrate numerous cloud services and on-premises applications. These can be Azure services, third-party cloud services, different data stores and databases, and LOB applications. Azure Logic Apps provide a number of pre-built connectors that you leverage inside your workflow. Besides that, you can also create your own connectors using Visual Studio. Each connector provides an API, which can be called from inside the Logic App. Authentication is added to this connector as well.

 You can refer to the following article for an overview of all the available connectors for Azure Logic Apps: `https://docs.microsoft.com/en-us/azure/connectors/apis-list`.

Besides using the Visual Editor, you can create and make adjustments to the Workflow Definition Language schema manually as well. This schema is created using JSON and can be created from scratch using Visual Studio or can be adjusted inside the Azure Portal. They both use the Code View editor (Visual Studio uses the same editor as the Azure Portal). Some capabilities can only be added to the schema directly and cannot be made from the Visual Editor. Examples of this are date and time formatting and string concatenation. Logic App definition files can be added to ARM templates and deployed using PowerShell, CLI, or REST APIs.

Here is an example of the JSON code-behind file:

```
{
  "$schema":
"https://schema.management.azure.com/providers/Microsoft.Logic/schemas/2016
-06-01/workflowdefinition.json#",
  "contentVersion": "1.0.0.0",
  "parameters": {
    "order": {
      "defaultValue": {
        "quantity": 10,
        "id": "mycustomer-id"
      },
      "type": "Object"
    }
  },
  "triggers": {
    "Request": {
      "type": "request",
      "kind": "http"
    }
  },
  "actions": {
    "order": {
      "type": "Http",
      "inputs": {
        "method": "GET",
        "uri": "http://www.packt.com/?id=@{parameters('customer').id}"
      }
    },
    "ifTimingWarning": {
      "type": "If",
      "expression":
"@less(actions('customer').startTime,addseconds(utcNow(),-1))",
      "actions": {
        "timingWarning": {
          "type": "Http",
```

```
            "inputs": {
               "method": "GET",
               "uri":
  "http://www.packt.com/?recordLongOrderTime=@{parameters('customer').id}&cur
  rentTime=@{utcNow('r')}"
               }
            }
         },
         "runAfter": {
            "order": [
               "Succeeded"
            ]
         }
      }
   },
   "outputs": {}
}
```

Designing application solutions using Logic Apps

In this demo, we are creating the same functionality as we did in the previous Azure Function demo. We are adding a message to a queue. This way, you can see the difference between an event-driven approach and a workflow-driven approach. The steps are as follows:

1. Navigate to the Azure Portal by opening `https://portal.azure.com/`.
2. Click on **New** and and type `Logic App` in the search bar. Click on the **Create** button.

3. A new blade opens up where you can fill in the basic settings of the Logic App. Add the following and click on **Create**:

Azure Logic App settings

4. When you navigate to the Logic App in the Azure Portal, the designer is opened. Click on the HTTP request trigger:

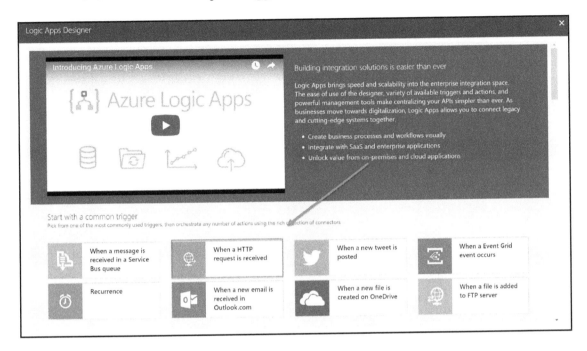

Azure Logic App designer

5. The workflow canvas will open. Click the top action, **When a HTTP request is received**, and add the following JSON schema to it:

```
{
    "type": "object",
    "properties": {
        "name": {
            "type": "string"
        }
    }
}
```

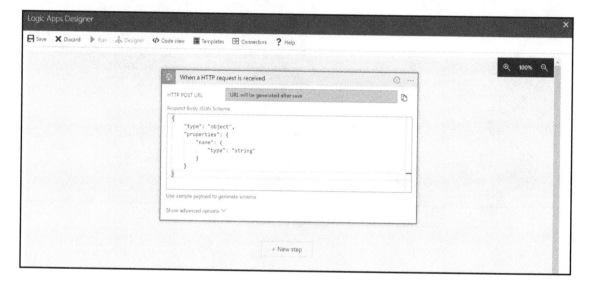

Azure Logic App designer

6. Click on **New step** to add an action. Click **Add an Action**, and inside the search box type `Azure Queue`. Select **Azure Queues - Put a message on a queue**:

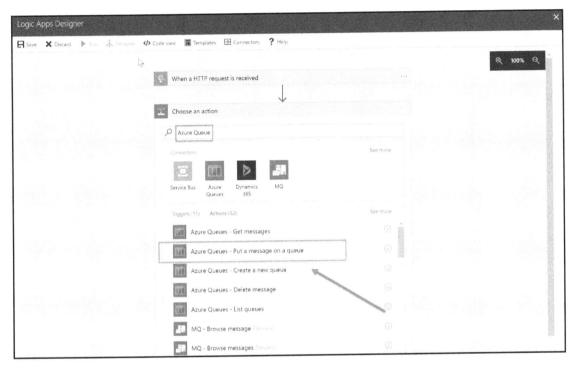

Add action in the Azure Logic App designer

7. Give your connection a name, such as `PacktQueueConnection`. You can then select a storage account from the different storage accounts that are available inside your Azure subscription. Pick the one that is used for the Azure Function as well. Click on **Create**.

8. Select the **outqueue** and add the following message: `Name passed to the Logic App:`. Then add the **name** parameter after the colon and click on **Save**:

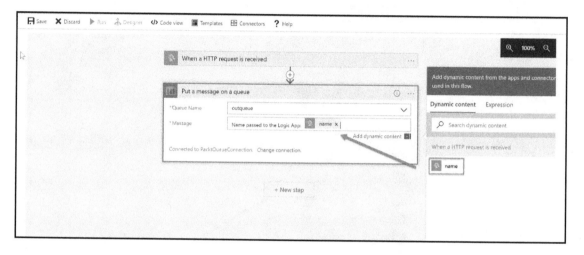

Configuring the message

9. Go to the **Overview** settings page of the Logic App and copy the **Callback url** to the clipboard:

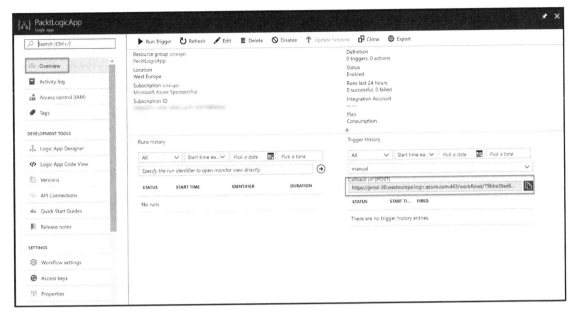

Retrieving the API request URL

10. Now open Postman, or some other tool for testing APIs, and paste the request URL. Add the same message to the **Body** as we used in the Azure Function example and click **Enter**:

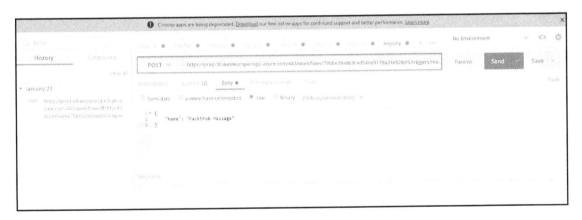

Creating a POST request in Postman

11. Open the **Azure Storage Explorer** tool again and you'll see the queue message created by the Logic App in there:

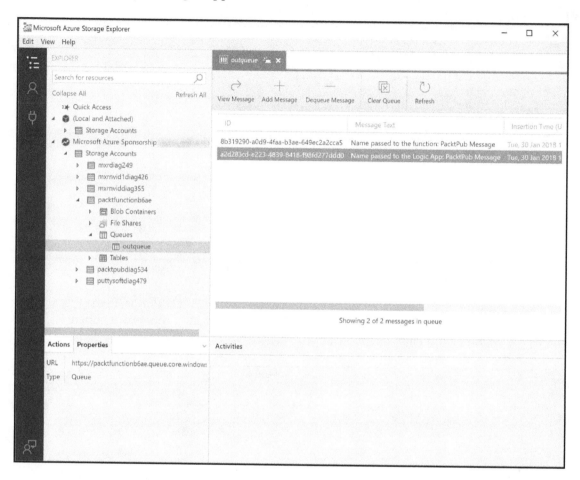

Queue message created by the Logic App

 Postman can be downloaded from the following URL: `https://www.getpostman.com/`.

Designing for serverless computing using Azure Container Instances

Containers are a broadly accepted open standard, and have significantly changed the way applications are developed and deployed. A container is an application packaging and deployment mechanism that simplifies the way we develop and deploy software. With the use of a container, we can add all the different artifacts that make the application run, such as configuration files, databases, and Web APIs, in an isolated package and deploy it everywhere. This eliminates unexpected failures that usually pop up when deploying software to different environments, such as development, test, or production environments. And any further knowledge of those different environments, such as which operating system it's using, is not needed anymore. If your application runs on your development environment, it will run on all environments. Because of the isolation, containers also solve the problem of running different versions of runtimes or applications that can interfere with each other.

Azure provides **Azure Container Instances** (**ACI**), which provide a hosted environment for running containers in Azure without managing the VMs and the underlying infrastructure. One ACI is a single Docker container, and you pay only for the resources you consume (per second for each running instance). It offers **Role-Based Access Control** (**RBAC**) on the instance, and you can track the usage at the individual container level. Containers can be deployed on Windows and Linux.

Containers can be created using PowerShell, CLI, and in the Azure Portal.

Creating containers

Containers can be easily created. In this example, the container is created from the CLI, with only a few parameters. To create a container, open the Azure Cloud Shell from the Azure Portal, select the `Bash` tab, and add the following code:

This step is optional. You can use this if you want to check and change the default selected Azure subscription:

```
az account show
az account set -s "Your-Subscription-Name"
```

Next, create the resource group and the container:

```
az group create --name packtcontainergroup --location "West Europe"
az container create -g packtcontainergroup --name packtcontainer --image
library/nginx --ip-address public
```

 You can also install CLI 2.0 on your Windows device using the following URL: https://azure.microsoft.com/nl-nl/blog/azure-cli-2-0-new-commands-features-available-now-in-azure-cloud-shell/.

Container orchestrations

A set of containers is managed by a container orchestration. An orchestration provides a single entity from where you manage scheduling, scaling, health monitoring, failover, networking, and application upgrades for your container instances. Also, continuous integration and continuous deployment are handled at the orchestration level.

ACI offers a layered approach for orchestrating your containers. ACI provides you with the features to manage one single container. It can manage simple applications, task automation, and build jobs for the isolated containers. For more advanced scenarios, where you need full container orchestration, including service discovery across multiple containers, automatic scaling, and coordinated application upgrades, you need to use orchestration platforms.

Orchestration platforms handle the tasks of managing a cluster of containers. The orchestration platform is only responsible for the multi-container architecture and doesn't have to worry about the underlying infrastructure because this is handled by Azure (using ACI).

Container orchestrations offer the following features and capabilities:

- **Scaling**: The orchestrator can add or remove container instances. This can be done manually or automatically.
- **Service discovery**: This allows containers to locate each other, even when the IP addresses are changed, and when the containers are moved between physical host machines.
- **Networking**: This provides a network that can be used by the underlying containers for communication across multiple host machines.
- **Scheduling**: The scheduler will use the container image and the resource request to locate a suitable VM to run the container on.
- **Health monitoring**: This monitors the health of the containers and can automatically provide rescheduling.
- **Application upgrades**: This provides coordinated container upgrades and rollbacks.
- **Failover**: This checks the current state of the machines and reschedules containers from unhealthy to healthy machines.
- **Affinity/anti-affinity**: This determines that a set of containers should run near each other to improve the performance of the application, or far away from each other to improve the availability of the application.

Azure offers support for different orchestration platforms. Platforms that are supported on Azure are Azure Container Service (AKS), Kubernetes, DC/OS (powered by Apache Mesos), Docker Swarm, and Azure Service Fabric.

Azure Service Fabric

Azure Service Fabric is an orchestration platform from Microsoft that can be used to deploy, manage, and package microservices and containers. It is similar to Docker Cloud and Kubernetes, where Service Fabric is fully bound to the Azure platform.

The difference between the three is that Service Fabric is the only one that is fully bound to the Azure Platform. Examples of this tight integration with the Azure platform includes the fact that Azure Service Fabric can use API Management, Event Hub, and IoT Hub out of the box as stateless gateways. When using other providers, stateless gateways are mostly built manually. You can import Docker images in Azure Fabric as well, but the orchestration of the Docker containers is then fully handled by Azure Service Fabric.

Azure Service Fabric offers a lightweight runtime for building distributed, scalable, stateless and stateful microservices that can run inside containers. Using Service Fabric, you can deploy the microservices and containers across a cluster of machines. On top of that, it offers comprehensive application management capabilities to deploy, provision, upgrade and patch, delete, and monitor applications and services on containers. Service Fabric is tailored to create full cloud-native applications that can start small and eventually scale up to thousands of machines over time.

Service Fabric can be deployed inside your own data center as well, on Windows Server machines. On Azure, Service Fabric can be deployed on Windows, Linux, and Azure Stack. There are a number of Azure PaaS solutions or resources that run on Service Fabric, such as Azure SQL Database, Cosmos DB, Intune, IoT Hub, Event Hubs, Skype, Cortana, Power BI, and Microsoft Dynamics.

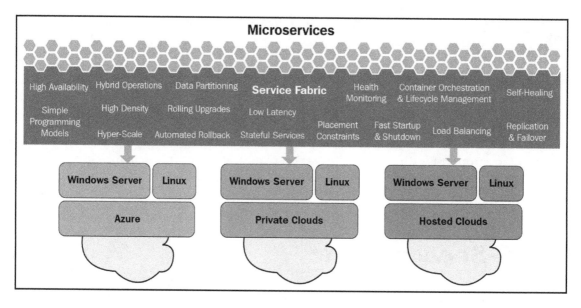

Azure Service Fabric overview

Applications use the Service Fabric programming models to create and manage your services. There are Service Fabric APIs that can be used in custom applications to take full advantage of the platform's features and application frameworks. You can deploy guest executables, which don't use the Service Fabric APIs, but can use the capabilities of the underlying platform. Guest executables are treated as stateless services and are deployed across different nodes inside a cluster. They can benefit from the affinity, anti-affinity and failover, application life cycle management, and discovery capabilities, for instance.

Service Fabric supports two different programming models that can be used to build scalable and stateful services in Visual Studio 2017. They are called the Reliable Services and the Reliable Actor programming model. By leveraging these models inside your code, Azure can guarantee that the services are consistent, scalable, reliable, and available inside Azure Service Fabric. Service Fabric integrates with ASP.NET Core as well, so you can write both stateless and stateful ASP.NET Core applications that take advantage of these reliable collections and the orchestration capabilities of Service Fabric.

 For more information on the available programming models for Azure Service Fabric, you can refer to the Microsoft documentation: `https://docs.microsoft.com/en-us/azure/service-fabric/service-fabric-reliable-services-introduction`. For more information on the Reliable Actor programming model, you can refer to: `https://docs.microsoft.com/en-us/azure/service-fabric/service-fabric-reliable-actors-introduction`.

Life cycle management

With Azure Service Fabric, you can manage the entire life cycles of your microservice applications. It supports all the different tasks, from developing the microservices to deployment, management, and maintenance. To accomplish this, Azure Service Fabric provides different roles that can operate independently. These different roles are as follows:

- **Service developer**: Develops generic microservices that can be leveraged in different applications. The developer uses the Reliable Services and Reliable Actor programming model to create the microservices.
- **Application developer**: Creates applications by using the various services developed by the service developer. The application developer creates the application manifest.
- **Application administrator**: Creates the application configuration files and creates the deployment packages. The administrator uses PowerShell to create the application packages.
- **Operator**: Deploys the application, monitors the application's health and performance after deployment, and maintains the physical infrastructure. The operator uses PowerShell, CLI, or the REST API to deploy the application.

For more information on the Service Fabric application life cycle features, you can refer to the following article: https://docs.microsoft.com/en-us/azure/service-fabric/service-fabric-application-lifecycle.

API Management

API Management is an Azure service that can be used to expose different types of apps to the outside world as APIs. You can import your custom APIs or serverless apps, such as Azure Functions, Web APIs, Logic Apps, or Service Fabric Apps.

You can also use API Management for your internal organization and use it as a service repository that all developers can use to compose their applications or services.

API Management offers an API Gateway, a Management portal, and a Developer portal, which are covered in more detail in the following sections.

API Gateway

The API Gateway acts as a bridge between your app and the outside world. This app can be a custom API, or any other backend application. The API Gateway accepts API calls and routes them to the backend. It provides extra features, such as enhanced security, by adding policies and authentication methods. It can verify API keys, JWT tokens, certificates, and more. You can create transformations without using code modifications, and enforce usage quotas and rate limits. It adds support for caching and throttling, and can log call metadata for analytics purposes.

API Management portal

The API Management portal is where you define and import your custom APIs. You can package your APIs into **products** in there as well. APIs inside API Management are exposed as products to developers and can be configured with a title, description, and terms of use. Products can even be **open** or **protected.** For protected APIs, developers need a subscription. Open APIs can be used without a subscription.

API Management uses **groups** to manage the visibility of products to developers. There are three different types of group:

- **Administrators**: Administrators can create APIs, operations, and products that are used by developers and manage API Management service instances.
- **Developers**: Developers are the customers that build applications using your APIs. Developer portal users are part of this group. They can be granted access to the Developer portal and leverage the APIs in their custom applications.
- **Guests**: Guest users are only granted read-only access to the developer portal. They may be future customers or developers, or users that only need to have view access on the different products.

Inside the API Management portal, you can set up policies, such as access restriction policies and transformation policies. You can get insights from analytics and create different versions of the APIs.

Developer portal

API Management also offers a developer portal, from where developers can access your APIs and read API documentation. It provides a console from where APIs can be tested. From there, developers can subscribe to different products. Future customers can visit the portal, view the products with their included operations, and sign up for a subscription. Developers can get insights about their usage from there as well.

The look and feel of the Developer portal can be customized. You can add custom content and add custom styles and your company branding to the portal as well.

Cloud-native deployments versus migrating assets

Most organizations are moving to the cloud for cost reduction and to speed up the development process of applications. To migrate an application to Azure, there are a couple of strategies you can use. Which one to use depends on the type of application and the priorities and needs of the organization.

Organizations are moving to the cloud to reduce costs and speed up the development process of applications. There are a couple of strategies you can use to migrate your applications to the cloud. Which strategy you use will depend on the type of application and the needs and priorities of the organization. Not all applications are worth the investment of moving to a PaaS model or developing a cloud-native app. For modern applications, you can choose to migrate to a cloud-optimized or cloud-native app, but with applications that are existing or legacy assets, the key is to spend minimal time and money (no re-architecting or code changes) while moving them to the cloud in order to realize the significant benefit therein.

There are three different migration levels from which you can choose:

- **Cloud infrastructure-ready**: In this approach, you simply move your current application and host it inside of Azure VMs. There are no code changes needed for this approach.
- **Cloud DevOps-ready**: By using this approach, you are using containers for developing and deploying your applications. This decouples your application from the infrastructure layer, which reduces the failures that are caused by the application dependencies. You can also leverage continuous development and integration on the orchestration level, which makes the deployment process a lot faster.
- **Cloud-optimized**: This migration approach targets the modernizing of your mission-critical applications. This type of modernization usually requires you to re-architect your application for the cloud. New code needs to be written, and you can create cloud-native applications and leverage microservices architectures.

Summary

In this chapter, we have covered serverless and microservices. We covered Azure Function, Azure Logic Apps, and the main differences between them. We also covered Azure containers services and container orchestrations. We explained what Azure Service Fabric is and what API Management is. Next, we talked about when to choose to migrate your assets to the cloud and when to choose a cloud-native deployment model.

This concludes the design compute infrastructure objective and, in the next chapter we will proceed with the design networking implementation objective, starting with robust networking implementations.

Questions

Answer the following questions to test your knowledge of the information in this chapter. You can find the answers in the *Assessments* section at the end of this book.

1. Can you use API Management as a stateless gateway for your microservices hosted in Azure Service Fabric?
    1. Yes
    2. No
2. Can you deploy Kubernetes containers to Azure Container Instances?
    1. Yes
    2. No
3. Is Azure Service Fabric suitable for DevOps environments?
    1. Yes
    2. No

Further reading

You can check the following links for more information about the topics that are covered in this chapter:

- **Introducing Azure Functions**: https://azure.microsoft.com/nl-nl/blog/introducing-azure-functions/
- **Azure Functions Documentation**: https://docs.microsoft.com/en-us/azure/azure-functions/
- **Durable Functions overview**: https://docs.microsoft.com/en-us/azure/azure-functions/durable-functions-overview
- **Azure Logic Apps Documentation**: https://docs.microsoft.com/en-us/azure/logic-apps/
- **API Management documentation**: https://docs.microsoft.com/en-us/azure/api-management/
- **Azure Container Instances Documentation**: https://docs.microsoft.com/en-us/azure/container-instances/
- **Azure Container Instances and container orchestrators**: https://docs.microsoft.com/en-us/azure/container-instances/container-instances-orchestrator-relationship
- **Azure Service Fabric Documentation**: https://docs.microsoft.com/en-us/azure/service-fabric/

5
Robust Networking Implementations

In the previous chapter, we covered the serverless and microservices objectives. We covered how to design serverless computing and which features Azure provides for creating them. We also covered microservices-based solutions, and the differences between all the different Azure features and when to use them.

This chapter introduces the networking objectives. It starts with how to design Azure Virtual Networks. This consists of designing solutions that use Azure networking services, such as designs for load balancing using Azure Load Balancer and Azure Traffic Manager, defining DNS, DHCP, and IP strategies, determining when to use Azure Application Gateway, and when to use multi-node application gateways, Traffic Manager, and Load Balancers.

After that, it covers designing external connectivity for Azure Virtual Networks. In this chapter, you will learn how to determine when to use Azure VPN, ExpressRoute, virtual network peering architecture, when to use **User Defined Routes** (**UDRs**), and when to use VPN gateway site-to-site failover for ExpressRoute.

Lastly, this chapter covers how to design security strategies by determining when to use network virtual appliances, how to design a perimeter network (DMZ), and determine when to use a **Web Application Firewall** (**WAF**), **Network Security Group** (**NSG**), and virtual network service tunneling.

The following topics will be covered in this chapter:

- Designing Azure Virtual Networks
- When to use Azure Application Gateway
- When to use multi-node application gateways, Azure Traffic Manager, and Load Balancers
- Designing external connectivity for Azure Virtual Networks
- Designing security strategies

Technical requirements

This chapter uses the following tools for the examples:

- Azure PowerShell: `https://docs.microsoft.com/en-us/powershell/azure/install-azurerm-ps?view=azurermps-5.1.1`

The source code for this chapter can be downloaded here:

- `https://github.com/SjoukjeZaal/AzureArchitectureBook/tree/master/Chapter%205`

Azure Virtual Network

An **Azure Virtual Network** (**VNet**) is a virtual representation of a traditional network, hosted in the cloud. It is totally software-based, where traditional networks use cables, routers, and more. VNets provide a secure and isolated environment and they connect Azure resources with each other. By default, the different resources are not reachable from outside of the virtual network. You can, however, connect multiple VNets to each other or connect a VNet to your on-premises network as well. All the Azure resources that are connected inside the same VNet must reside in the same region and subscription.

When you create a VNet, one subnet is automatically created as well. You can create multiple subnets inside the same VNet (there is a maximum of 1000 subnets allowed per VNet). Connecting multiple VNets to each other is called **virtual network peering**. There is a maximum of 10 peerings allowed per Azure subscription.

The smallest subnet that can be used in Azure is the /29 subnet, which consists of eight addresses and the largest is /8, which consists of 16 million addresses.

> For more information on subnetting, you can refer to the Subnet Mask Cheat Sheet: `https://www.aelius.com/njh/subnet_sheet.html`.

IP addresses

A virtual network in Azure can have private and public IP addresses. Private IP addresses are only accessible from within the virtual network and public IP addresses can be accessed from the internet as well. You can access private IP addresses from a VPN Gateway or an ExpressRoute connection. Both private and public IP addresses can be static or dynamic, but when you create a new VNet, the IP address is static by default. You can change the IP address to static from the Azure Portal, PowerShell, and CLI.

Dynamic and static IP address configuration in the Azure Portal

- **Dynamic**: Dynamic IP addresses are assigned by Azure automatically and are selected from the configured subnet's address range from the virtual network where the Azure resource resides. The IP address is assigned to the Azure resource upon creation or start. The IP address will then be released when the resource is stopped and deallocated (when you stop the VM from the Azure Portal, the VM is deallocated automatically as well) and added back to the pool of available addresses inside the subnet by Azure.
- **Static**: Static IP addresses (private and public) are pre-assigned and will remain the same until you delete the assignment. You can select a static private IP address manually. They can only be assigned to non-internet facing connections, such as an internal Load Balancer. You can assign a private IP address to a connection to your on-premises network or to an ExpressRoute circuit as well. Public static IP addresses are created by Azure automatically and they can be assigned to internet facing connections, such as an external Load Balancer.

Public IP address

Public IP addresses can be used for internal communication between Azure services and external communication over the internet. You can use IPv4 and IPv6 for public IP addresses, but the support for IPv6 is limited. At the time of writing, you can only assign IPv6 addresses to external Load Balancers.

Azure assigns the public IP address to the network interface when the Azure resource is started or created. When a outbound connection is initiated, Azure will map the private IP address to the public IP address (SNAT). Return traffic to the resource is allowed as well.

Public IP addresses are typically used for VMs, internet-facing Load Balancers, VPN gateways, and application gateways. There is a maximum of 60 dynamic public IP addresses and 20 static public IP addresses per subscription. The first five static IP address are free, the rest have a cost.

> The following document is beyond the scope of this book, but definitely interesting—*Understanding outbound connections in Azure*: `https://docs.microsoft.com/en-us/azure/load-balancer/load-balancer-outbound-connections?toc=%2fazure%2fvirtual-network%2ftoc.json`.

Private IP address

Private IP addresses support IPv4 and IPv6 as well, but support for IPv6 is also limited. They can only be assigned dynamically and IPv6 addresses cannot communicate with each other inside a VNet. The only way to use IPv6 addresses is by assigning them to an internet-facing Load Balancer, where the frontend IP address is an IPv4 address and the backend is an IPV6 address.

Private IP addresses are typically used for VMs, internal Load Balancers, and application gateways. A VPN cannot have a private IP address because it is always internet-facing. There is a maximum of 4096 private IP addresses per VNet. You can, however, create multiple VNets (50 per subscription).

These limits are based on the default limits from the following page: `https://docs.microsoft.com/en-us/azure/azure-subscription-service-limits?toc=%2fazure%2fvirtual-network%2ftoc.json#networking-limits`. You can open a support request to raise the limits. The limits can't be raised above the maximum limit, as described in the limit table.

Creating a public IP address

In the following example, we are going to create a static public IP address using PowerShell:

1. Navigate to the Azure Portal by opening `https://portal.azure.com/`.
2. Open the Azure Cloud Shell and make sure PowerShell is selected.
3. Add the following command:

   If necessary, select the right subscription:

   ```
   Select-AzureRmSubscription -SubscriptionId "********-****-****-****-***********"
   ```

   Create the IP address:

   ```
   New-AzureRmPublicIpAddress -Name PublicPacktIP -ResourceGroupName PacktPub -AllocationMethod Static -Location "West Europe"
   ```

4. This is the easiest way to create a static IP address. However, you still have to assign it to a Azure resource. It is only created now. I've used an existing resource group for this example. If you don't have one, you need to create it before creating the IP address.

DNS

Besides IP addresses, VMs can also be addressed by using hostnames or **fully qualified domain names (FQDN)**. You can configure a DNS label for this on a public IP address. For Azure services that are all hosted inside the same VNet, Azure internal DNS can be used for name resolving. If you want to use DNS for multiple VNets, you have to set up your own DNS server. For instance, if you add the DNS label `packtuniquedns`, the FQDN will become **packtuniquedns.westeurope.cloudapp.azure.com**. This FQDN will then map to the public IP address of the Azure resource.

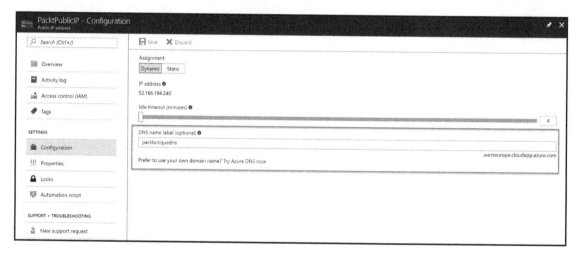

Built-in DNS name resolving

You can point your DNS to the Azure resource by adding a CNAME record as well. So instead of using the default DNS suffix, you can use Azure DNS to assign a custom hostname to the resource. If you want your Azure resource to be reached with a hostname without the www prefix, you need to add an A record. CNAME will only work with the www prefix.

For more information on this, you can refer to the following articles—*Create a fully qualified domain name in the Azure Portal for a Linux VM*: https://docs.microsoft.com/en-us/azure/virtual-machines/ linux/portal-create-fqdn and *Use Azure DNS to provide custom domain settings for an Azure service*: https://docs.microsoft.com/en-us/azure/ dns/dns-custom-domain?toc=%2fazure%2fvirtual-network%2ftoc. json#public-ip-address.

Creating a VNet with two subnets

In this example, we are going to create a VNet with two subnets from the Azure Portal. You can use PowerShell, CLI, and an ARM template as well. We are going to create a VNet and subnets according to the following diagram:

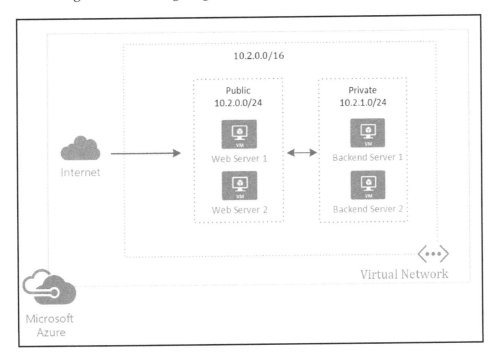

A VNet with two subnets

Take the following steps to create the VNet:

1. Navigate to the Azure Portal by opening `https://portal.azure.com/`.
2. Click on **New** and type `virtual network` in the search bar to create a new virtual network:

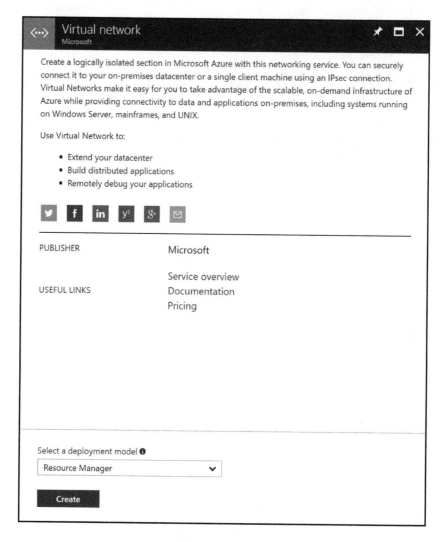

Creating a new virtual network

3. A new blade opens up, where you can fill in the settings. Add the following values:

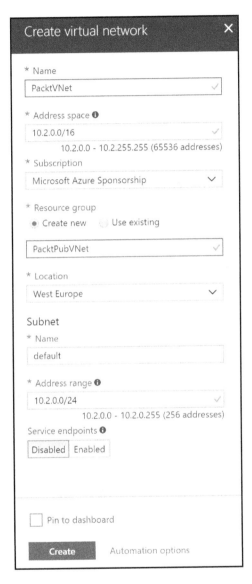

VNet and subnet settings

4. Click on **Create**. You can only create one subnet when creating a VNet from the Azure Portal. So, the second one needs to be added after creating the VNet.

5. Go to the VNet **Settings** and choose **Subnets** from the left-hand menu and click **+ Subnet** in the top menu, as shown in the following screenshot:

Adding a second subnet

6. A new blade will open up. Enter the following values and click on **OK**:

Second subnet settings

Azure Load Balancer

Azure Load Balancer is a Load Balancer which can be used for VMs, containers, and apps. It works at the transport layer (layer four in the OSI network reference stack) by distributing network traffic in the same Azure data center. It offers an external and an internal Load Balancer.

The external Load Balancer provides a single endpoint with a public IP address that is called by all client applications and services, and then distributes the incoming traffic over multiple healthy VMs, containers, or apps to provide scaling, high availability, and performance. The internal Load Balancer has the same features as the external, but it uses a private IP address.

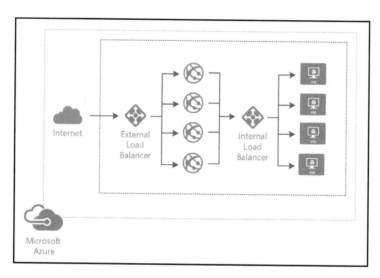

External and internal Load Balancer

There are two versions of Azure Load Balancer:

- **Basic**: The basic Load Balancer is free to use. It can be configured as an internet-facing Load Balancer, as an internal Load Balancer, and it can forward traffic to a specific VM. For the internet-facing Load Balancer, the public IP address is mapped to the private IP address by the Load Balancer. When traffic comes in, Azure distributes it to the Azure resource by using the internal IP address. It offers hashed-based distribution, port forwarding, automatic reconfiguration when you scale down or up, service monitoring, and source NAT.

- **Standard**: At the time of writing, the standard Load Balancer is still in preview. On top of all the features that the basic Load Balancer offers, the standard version offers enterprise scale. You can use standalone VMs or VMs up to 1000 instances using the standard Load Balancer. It also offers diagnostic insights for public and internal Load Balancer configurations, high reliability by using HA ports, and rules for individual ports. You can use NSGs (which we will discuss later in this chapter) and availability zones.

For more information on the standard Load Balancer, you can refer to the following article: `https://docs.microsoft.com/en-us/azure/load-balancer/load-balancer-standard-overview`.

Probes

The Azure Load Balancer uses probes to define the health of your servers and services that are leveraging the Load Balancer. There are two different types of probes: the HTTP and the TCP Probe.

For cloud services (such as VMs, web apps, APIs, and more), it uses a **guest agent probe**. In this scenario, there is a guest agent installed on your VM that responds with an HTTP 200 OK response. Every 15 seconds, the Load Balancer sends a message to the cloud service to which the agent responds. You can also create a custom HTTP Probe with your own logic that overrrides the logic of the default guest agent. The TCP Probe uses a three-way handshake to set up the connection.

When health logging is enabled, the data is stored in an Azure storage account. You can view this log data by using different Azure tools, such as PowerShell or CLI, the REST API, or the Azure Portal. You can also use Power BI to visualize and analyze the data using pre-defined dashboards provided by the *Azure Audit Logs content pack for Power BI.*

For more information and to download the Azure Audit Logs content pack for Power BI, you can refer to `https://docs.microsoft.com/en-us/power-bi/service-connect-to-azure-audit-logs`.

Azure Traffic Manager

Azure Traffic Manager spreads the workload over multiple regions and data centers in the world. It will handle the load and locate the closest geographical region or most suitable region at the DNS level. The client makes a DNS request and, based on the location of the DNS, Azure Traffic Manager will locate the nearest region in Azure and sends that location back to the client via a DNS response. The client then calls the location directly, without any further interference of Azure Traffic Manager. Traffic Manager also monitors the endpoints, so in case of a failure inside one region, the Traffic Manager will send back the endpoint of a different healthy region.

This differs from the Azure Load Balancer, where the client calls the IP address of the Load Balancer and the Load Balancer distributes the traffic over multiple cloud services, such as VMs, containers, or web apps. Also, the Azure Load Balancer spreads traffic over multiple instances in the same region and data center, whereas Traffic Manager can span over multiple regions and data centers.

You can use both the Azure Load Balancer and Azure Traffic Manager in a highly available and high-performing architecture, such as the one shown in the following diagram:

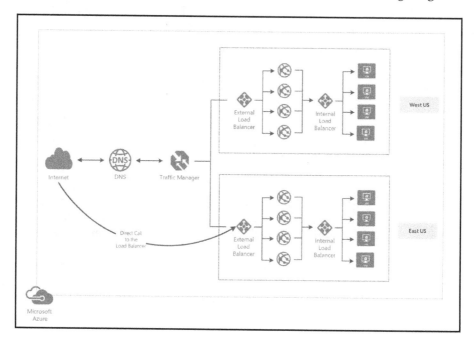

Azure Traffic Manager

 Azure Traffic Manager was also discussed in `Chapter 3`, *Designing Web Applications*, in the section about high availability and performance for your web apps. The different routing methods that are available for Azure Traffic Manager are also described there.

Azure Application Gateway

The Azure Application Gateway offers an **Application Delivery Controller** (**ADC**), which operates on the application layer (layer seven in the OSI network reference stack).

It provides web load balancing, so it provides load balancing on layer seven, which is for HTTP(S) only. It also provides a web application firewall, which can be leveraged to protect your apps from common web-based attacks, such as cross-site scripting, SQL injection, and session-hijacking (this is described in more detail in the *Network Security Strategies* section in this chapter). It can decrypt HTTPS traffic, so you can install your SSL certificates on the application gateway instead of onto the different web servers. This way, the web servers don't have to take care of this and management will be easier because it is all in one place. Application Gateway will then encrypt the response before it is sent back to the client. It can also provide URL-based content routing, so traffic can be routed to specific backends. For example, a call to a CDN that is hosted on a dedicated backend can be called directly, which reduces unnecessary routing. It also provides health monitoring and advanced diagnostics.

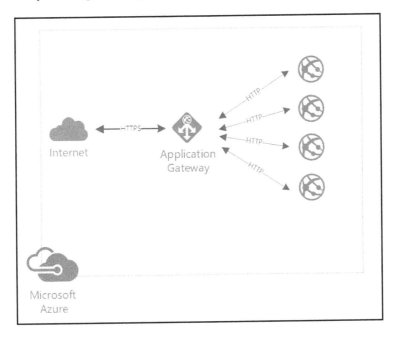

Azure Application Gateway

For more information on Azure Application Gateway and the different features, you can refer to `https://docs.microsoft.com/en-us/azure/traffic-manager/traffic-manager-overview`. This page also gives an overview of all the differences between the Azure Load Balancer, Azure Traffic Manager, and the Azure Application Gateway.

External connectivity for Azure Virtual Networks

The cloud is becoming more popular everyday, but for the next few years, most organizations will still have an on-premises infrastructure that will be used and maintained. In fact, some organizations will never move to the cloud completely because of business requirements or some sort of legacy system that is still in use and cannot be moved for some reason or other. Also, security requirements could be a reason for keeping a part of your data on-premises. So, there will always be a need for hybrid environments. From a networking perspective, Azure offers various features to set up seamless connections from your on-premises infrastructure to Azure and vice versa.

Azure VPN

Azure VPN provides a secure gateway that can be used to connect your on-premises infrastructure with Azure and to connect multiple VNets with each other by sending an encrypted message from one location to the other. Most organizations use VPN connections to let remote workers connect to their private network.

Azure VPN offers multiple ways to set up a secure connection, such as site-to-site VPN, point-to-site VPN, and ExpressRoute. They are described in the following sections. When setting up an Azure network gateway for one of these connection types, you have to choose between the different SKUs that Azure offers. Azure VPN offers the following SKUs:

- **Basic**: Provides a maximum of 10 site-to-site/VNet-to-VNet tunnels and a maximum of 128 point-to-site connections. The average bandwidth is 100 Mbps.
- **VpnGw1**: Provides a maximum of 30 site-to-site/VNet-to-VNet tunnels and a maximum of 128 point-to-site connections. The average bandwidth is 650 Mbps.
- **VpnGw2**: Provides a maximum of 30 site-to-site/VNet-to-VNet tunnels and a maximum of 128 point-to-site connections. The average bandwidth is 1 Gbps.
- **VpnGw3**: Provides a maximum of 30 site-to-site/VNet-to-VNet tunnels and a maximum of 128 point-to-site connections. The average bandwidth is 1.25 Gbps.

You can set up route-based or policy-based VPN types. Which one to use depends on the compatibility of your VPN device and the VPN connection type you want to use.

Policy-based means that you have to write your own routing-table entries. This can be suitable for small organizations, but most will rather do this dynamically. Policy-based routing also has some restrictions; you can only set up one site-to-site VPN tunnel using IKEv1 and no point-to-site tunnel.

Route-based means that the routing-table entries are added dynamically and that you can use all the VPN connection types and IKEv2.

Site-to-site VPN

A **site-to-site** (**S2S**) VPN is designed to create secure connections between a location, such as an office for instance, and Azure over the internet. You can then connect from every server or computer from that location using the same VPN connection. It requires a compatible VPN device or **Routing and Remote Access Service** (**RRAS**) and a public IP address for your VPN device. The RRAS can be deployed on a Windows server by activating the remote access server role.

The S2S VPN gateway creates a connection over a IPsec/IKE (IKEv1 or IKEv2) VPN tunnel. **Internet Protocol Security** (**IPSec**) is an open standard for securing connections over the internet and **Internet Key Exchange** (**IKE**) is a key management protocol standard used in conjunction with IPSec. It is a method for exchanging keys for encryption and authentication.

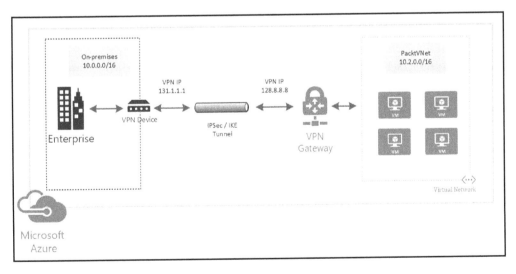

Site-to-site VPN connection

For a list of compatible VPN devices and the supported VPN types, you can refer to the following overview: https://docs.microsoft.com/en-us/ azure/vpn-gateway/vpn-gateway-about-vpn-devices.

VNet-to-VNet VPN

VNet-to-VNet is a connection type that can be set up as well. In this case, you are creating a connection between multiple Azure VNets. A typical reason for setting up this type of connection, could be for geo-redundancy. This connection type is the same as the S2S connection type.

Point-to-site VPN

A **point-to-site** (P2S) VPN is designed to create secure connections between an individual client computer over IKEv2 or SSTP. The connection is established by starting it from the client computer using a script. These connections are used for remote workers that log on to the private network from a different location or they can be used when you have a few clients that need to connect to the VPN.

Secure Socket Tunneling Protocol (SSTP) is a VPN tunnel that creates a connection through an SSL/TLS channel. By using SSL/TLS over port 443, the connection can pass through all firewalls and proxy servers.

P2S connections don't require a VPN device or a public IP address for the client computer. They can be used in conjunction with the S2S connection as well as through the same VPN gateway, as long as the requirements for both the connections are the same.

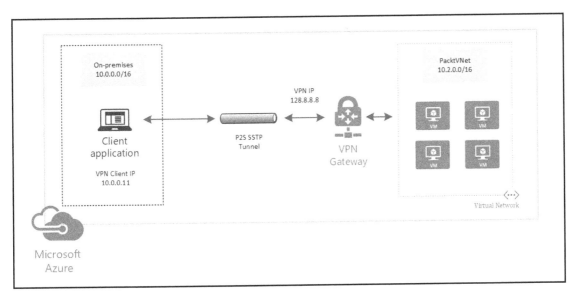

Point-to-site VPN connection

ExpressRoute

ExpressRoute is the most advanced type of VPN connection. It offers a fast connection from your on-premises infrastructure to the Azure via your internal WAN, unlike S2S connections, which go over the internet. By using your WAN, ExpressRoute can provide faster speeds, lower latency, and higher security than an S2S connection. The maximum bandwidth that can be provided per ExpressRoute circuit is 10 GBps. With ExpressRoute, you can also set up hybrid connections with Office 365 and Dynamics 365. ExpressRoute also guarantees a connection uptime SLA, whereas S2S doesn't.

ExpressRoute offers the following connection models:

- **Any-to-any (IPVPN)**: With this type of connection, you integrate your WAN with Azure using an IPVPN provider. The provider is then responsible for setting up the secure connection between your on-premises network and Azure. WAN providers typically offer a layer three connection.
- **Point-to-point Ethernet**: With this type of connection, you connect through point-to-point Ethernet links. Point-to-point providers typically provide a layer two connection.

- **Co-located at a Cloud Exchange**: With this type of connection, you can order connections through the provider's Ethernet exchange. These providers typically offer layer two cross-connections and managed layer three cross-connections.

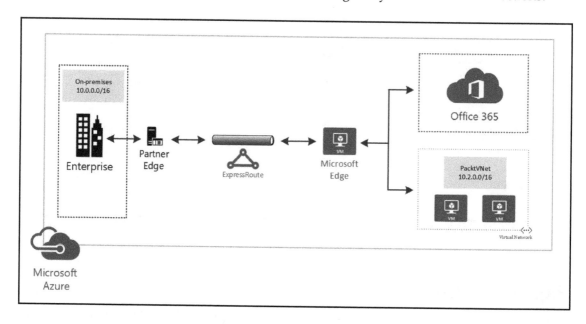

ExpressRoute VPN connection

Network security strategies

With all the hacking incidents nowadays, a strong network security strategy is key. It is not secure to just create a public IP address and expose your Azure resource to the internet. This will make you vulnerable for attacks. Design your networks with security in mind and reduce what is exposed to the internet. You can use the features that Azure provides for securing your networks. Azure offers support for different security strategies, which are described in the following section.

DMZ

A **demilitarized zone** (**DMZ**) or perimeter network is a physical or logical boundary between the internal and the external network of an organization. The external network can be the internet. The purpose is to add an additional security layer to the internal network. You don't open any ports from the internal network to the internet, but only to the DMZ. Azure offers multiple features that you can use to create a DMZ, such as **Network Security Groups** (**NSGs**), firewalls, and **User Defined Routes** (**UDRs**).

The following diagram shows an example of a physical DMZ created using a frontend VNet with two VMs in it. Only this VNet is connected to the internet.

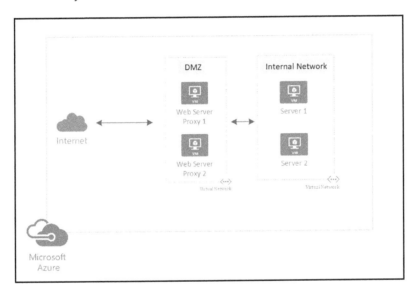

Simple DMZ example

Network Security Groups

A NSG is an access control list inside Azure where you can add inbound and outbound rules. When a connection is established between VMS, VNets, or other cloud services, this list is checked to see whether the connection is allowed or denied.

NSGs can be applied to one or more subnets or individual **network interfaces** (**NIC**). This means that all resources that are associated with this subnet or NIC will automatically have all the rules applied.

NSG rules are processed in priority order, with lower numbers before higher numbers, and they can be applied to inbound or outbound traffic.

Creating a NSG

Follow these steps to create a NSG:

1. Navigate to the Azure Portal by opening `https://portal.azure.com/`.
2. Click **New**, type `Network Security Group` in the search bar, and create a new one:

New NSG

3. A new blade opens up. Add the following settings and click on **Create**:

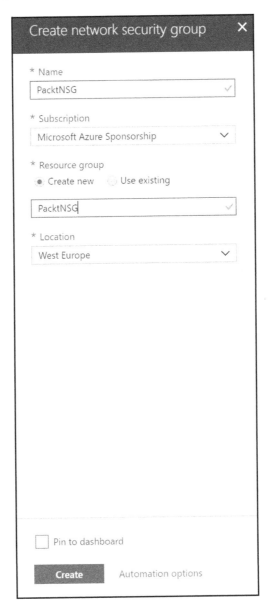

New NSG settings

4. A NSG is created with some default inbound and outbound security rules. They are low-priority rules, as they have a high number, so there is a lot of room to add custom rules. To add a custom rule, click on **Inbound security rules** in the left-hand menu:

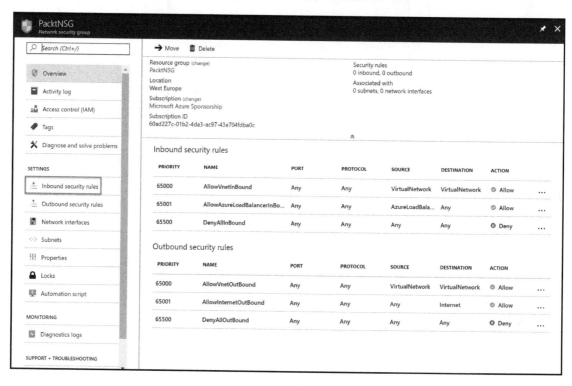

NSG default Inbound and Outbound rules

5. Click the **Add** button and add the following values to create rules that allow traffic from port 80:

New rule

6. You can now associate this NSG with an NIC or a subnet by clicking on **Network Interfaces** or **Subnets** from the left-hand menu:

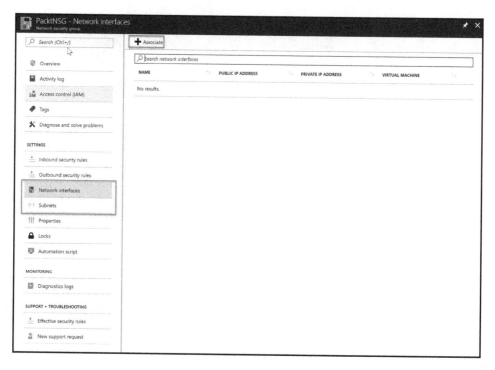

Associate the NSG with a NIC or subnet

User Defined Routes

When you create subnets, Azure creates system routes that enable all resources in a subnet to communicate with each other. You can override the system routes by creating UDRs. This way, you can force traffic to follow a particular route.

For instance, you have a network that consists of two subnets and you want to add a VM that is used as a DMZ and has a firewall installed on it. You want traffic only to go through the firewall and not between the two subnets.

To create UDRs and enable IP forwarding, you have to create a routing table in Azure. When this table is created and there are custom routes in there, Azure prefers the custom routes over the default system routes.

Creating User Defined Routes

To create UDRs, follow these steps:

1. Navigate to the Azure Portal by opening `https://portal.azure.com/`.
2. Click on **New**, type `Routing Table` in the search bar, and create a new one.

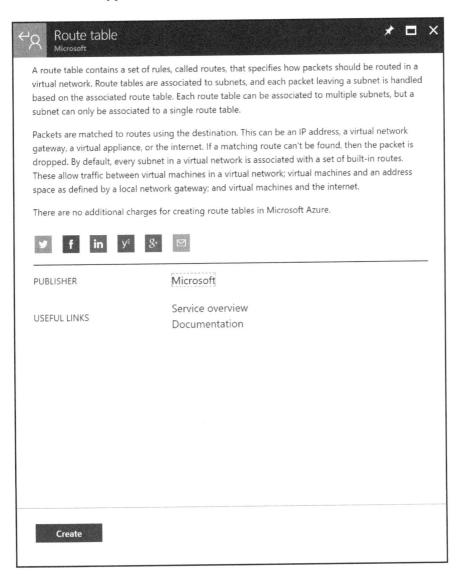

A route table contains a set of rules, called routes, that specifies how packets should be routed in a virtual network. Route tables are associated to subnets, and each packet leaving a subnet is handled based on the associated route table. Each route table can be associated to multiple subnets, but a subnet can only be associated to a single route table.

Packets are matched to routes using the destination. This can be an IP address, a virtual network gateway, a virtual appliance, or the internet. If a matching route can't be found, then the packet is dropped. By default, every subnet in a virtual network is associated with a set of built-in routes. These allow traffic between virtual machines in a virtual network; virtual machines and an address space as defined by a local network gateway; and virtual machines and the internet.

There are no additional charges for creating route tables in Microsoft Azure.

PUBLISHER — Microsoft

USEFUL LINKS — Service overview / Documentation

Create

Create a new routing table

3. Add the following values:

Route table settings

4. A new and empty route table is created. To add custom routes, click on **Routes** in the left-hand menu:

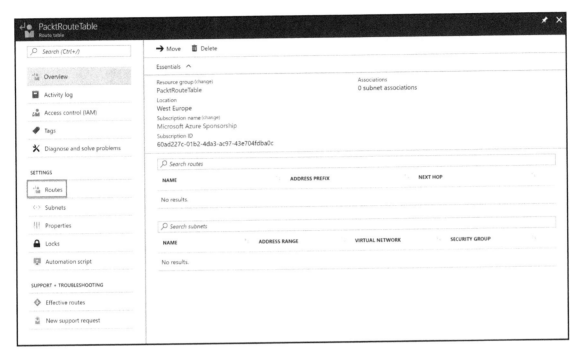

Empty route table

5. Click the **Add** button in the top menu and add the following values to create a custom route. In this example, we want all internet traffic to go through the firewall. So, add a `0.0.0.0/0` as the **Address prefix**. The **Next hop type** is a `Virtual appliance`; this is the firewall. And last, the **Next hop address**; this will be the internal IP address of the firewall:

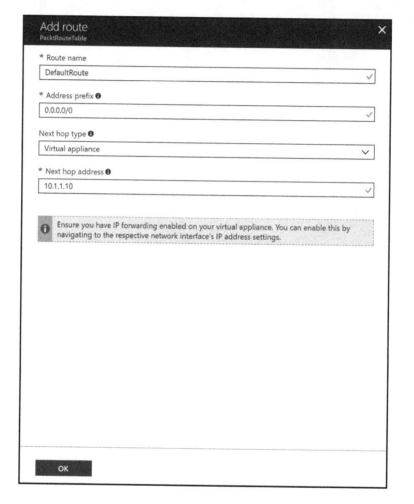

Add custom route

 For more detailed instructions on how to create UDPs and a virtual appliance, you can refer to the following tutorial: `https://docs.microsoft.com/en-us/azure/virtual-network/create-user-defined-route-portal`.

Virtual network service tunneling

With **virtual network service tunneling,** all your external traffic is forced to go through a site-to-site VPN tunnel. Without this, external traffic will always go directly from Azure to the internet. This gives you the opportunity to audit the traffic.

Forced tunneling uses the UDRs to define the routing. Instead of choosing the virtual appliance, you now choose the virtual network gateway:

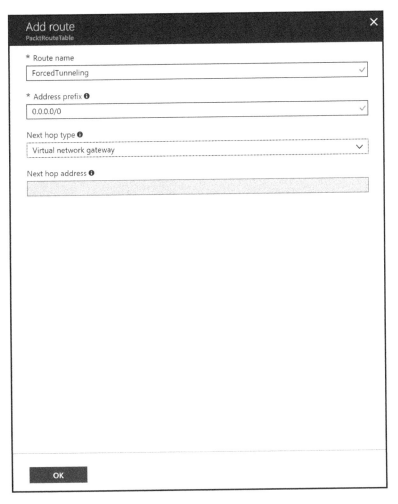

Virtual network service tunneling

For more information about virtual network service tunneling and an example on how to create it using PowerShell, you can refer to the following tutorial: https://docs.microsoft.com/en-us/azure/vpn-gateway/vpn-gateway-forced-tunneling-rm.

Web Application Firewall

The WAF is part of the application gateway and it provides a firewall to protect your web apps from hacking attacks. It is based on rules from the OWASP core rule set 3.0. It can protect a maximum of 20 applications behind an application gateway and it provides monitoring for your applications using Azure Monitor (in the future, monitoring will be added to the Azure Security Center as well).

OWASP is an open standard for application security. For more information on the rule set, you can refer to the OWASP website: https://www.owasp.org/index.php/Category:OWASP_ModSecurity_Core_Rule_Set_Project.

By default, it protects your application from the following:

- From SQL injection attacks
- From cross-site scripting attacks
- From command injection, HTTP request smuggling, HTTP response splitting, and remote file inclusion attacks
- Against HTTP protocol violations and anomalies
- Against bots, crawlers, and scanners
- It detects common application misconfigurations

You can also add or customize the rules and rule group to suit the needs of your application. You can refer to the following tutorial to customize rules: https://docs.microsoft.com/en-us/azure/application-gateway/application-gateway-customize-waf-rules-portal.

Summary

In this chapter, we have covered the networking objectives. We've covered how to design Azure Virtual Networks. We've discussed IP addresses and Azure DNS. We also covered when to use the Azure Application Gateway, Azure Traffic Manager, and Azure Load Balancer. We then looked at designing external connectivity for Azure VNets using different VPN connections, and finally, we talked about designing different security strategies.

In the next chapter, we will cover hybrid applications.

Questions

Answer the following questions to test your knowledge of the information in this chapter. You can find the answers in the *Assessments* section at the end of this book:

1. When you create a new routing table in Azure, is the system routing table deleted?
    1. Yes
    2. No

2. Are NSG rules processed by priority number from high to low?
    1. Yes
    2. No

3. Does DMZ consist of a firewall?
    1. Yes
    2. No

Further reading

You can check out the following links for more information on the topics that are covered in this chapter:

- **Azure Virtual Network**: https://docs.microsoft.com/en-us/azure/virtual-network/virtual-networks-overview
- **Virtual Network Peering**: https://docs.microsoft.com/en-us/azure/virtual-network/virtual-network-peering-overview
- **Azure Load Balancer overview**: https://docs.microsoft.com/en-us/azure/load-balancer/load-balancer-overview
- **Overview of Traffic Manager**: https://docs.microsoft.com/en-us/azure/traffic-manager/traffic-manager-overview
- **Overview of Application Gateway**: https://docs.microsoft.com/en-us/azure/application-gateway/application-gateway-introduction
- **About VPN Gateway**: https://docs.microsoft.com/en-us/azure/vpn-gateway/vpn-gateway-about-vpngateways
- **ExpressRoute overview**: https://docs.microsoft.com/en-us/azure/expressroute/expressroute-introduction
- **Filter network traffic with network security groups**: https://docs.microsoft.com/en-us/azure/virtual-network/virtual-networks-nsg
- **User Defined Routes**: https://docs.microsoft.com/en-us/azure/virtual-network/virtual-networks-udr-overview#custom-routes
- **Web Application Firewall**: https://docs.microsoft.com/en-us/azure/application-gateway/application-gateway-web-application-firewall-overview

6
Connecting Hybrid Applications

In the previous chapter, we covered the networking objective. We covered how to design virtual networks in Azure and how to design solutions that use virtual networks. We also covered external connectivity for Azure VNets and how to design security strategies for networking solutions.

This chapter introduces the designing connectivity for the hybrid applications objective. It starts with how to design connectivity to on-premises data from Azure applications using the different services that Azure provides.

The following topics will be covered:

- Azure Relay service
- Azure Data Management Gateway for Data Factory
- Azure On-premises Data Gateway
- Azure App Service Hybrid Connections
- Azure App Service Virtual Network Integration
- Azure AD Application Proxy
- Joining VMs to domains

Azure Relay service

With Azure Relay services you can connect your on-premises application with a gateway in Azure, without having to open a firewall connection or make any other big adjustments to your on-premises network.

You can create an Azure Relay service in the Azure Portal. Inside the Azure Relay service, a secure connection is created by using an outbound port and a bi-directional connection to your on-premises application. This connection is dedicated to one client and encrypted using **Transport Layer Security (TLS)**. The on-premises application imports the Azure Relay namespace and makes a call to the Azure Relay service in the Azure Portal using access keys for authentication:

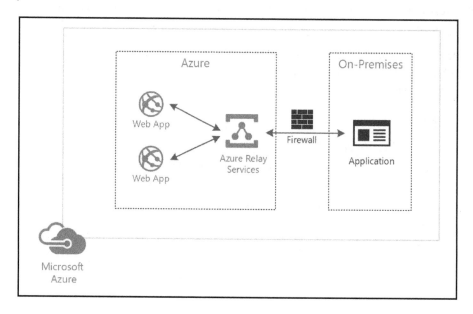

Azure Relay services

Azure Relay services support peer-to-peer traffic, one-way, request/response traffic, publish/subscribe scenarios, and bi-directional socket communication for increased point-to-point efficiency.

The difference of using Azure Relay services instead of using a VPN to create a hybrid connection, is that the Azure Relay service can be scoped to one application on a single machine instead of using one connection for all sorts of connection types.

Azure Relay services offer two features, hybrid connection and WCF Relays which are different implementations, but both share the same gateway.

Hybrid connections

With hybrid connections a rendezvous point is established in the cloud. An application can then connect to this using HTTP and web sockets. You can use all programming languages that support web sockets, such as .NET Core, JavaScript, and NodeJS and multiple remote procedure models.

 For more information about the Azure Relay hybrid connections protocol you can refer to the following website: `https://docs.microsoft.com/en-us/azure/service-bus-relay/relay-hybrid-connections-protocol`. For more information on how to get started with relay hybrid connections, you can refer to the following tutorial: `https://docs.microsoft.com/en-us/azure/service-bus-relay/relay-hybrid-connections-dotnet-get-started`.

WCF Relays

WCF Relays (formerly Service Bus Relays) uses the .NET Framework and WCF to establish a connection and sending a message. The on-premises application uses WCF Relay bindings which creates WCF channels that integrate with the Azure Service Bus.

 For more information on **How to use Azure Relay WCF Relays with .NET,** you can refer to the following article: `https://docs.microsoft.com/en-us/azure/service-bus-relay/relay-wcf-dotnet-get-started`.

Azure Data Management Gateway for Data Factory

Azure Data Factory offers a data-integration service which you can use to create workflows that automate movement and transformation of data. With Data Factory, you can create data workflows that can aggregate data from different data stores and transform and process data using Azure services, such as Azure Machine Learning, Azure HDInsight Hadoop, and Azure Data Lake Analytics and Output data to different data stores.

Azure Data Management Gateway for Data Factory acts as a bridge to connect your on-premises to the cloud. It consists of a client agent which is installed on the on-premises system and which then connects to Azure Data Factory. This agent copies your data to the cloud. The gateway can be scaled out by installing the agent on multiple on-premises environments and increasing the data movement jobs that can run simultaneously on a node. Data is processed in parallel using the jobs.

You don't have to open firewall ports to copy the data. It sends data securely over HTTP using certificates. It also offers a monitoring and management feature from Azure Data Factory in the Azure Portal.

 Azure Data Management Gateway for Data Factory supports a variety of data sources which are listed here: `https://docs.microsoft.com/en-us/azure/data-factory/v1/data-factory-data-movement-activities#supported-data-stores-and-formats`.

Azure On-premises Data Gateway

The Azure On-premises Data Gateway acts as a bridge between your on-premises data sources and Azure. It can connect to a number of Azure services, such as Azure Analysis Services, Azure Logic Apps, Microsoft Flow, Power Apps, and Power BI. For the on-premises side, there are a number of products which can be connected to the gateway, such as SQL Server, SQL Analysis Services, SharePoint, and more.

 For an overview of the on-premises data sources that are supported for the Azure On-premises Data Gateway, you can refer to the following website: `https://docs.microsoft.com/en-us/azure/analysis-services/analysis-services-datasource`.

To use the Azure On-premises Data Gateway, a client needs to be installed on the on-premises environment. This client consists of a Windows service which is responsible for setting up the connection with Azure. In Azure, a Gateway Cloud Service needs to be created. The client then communicates with the Gateway Cloud Service using the Azure Service Bus.

When a request for data is created by one of the Azure services, The cloud gateway service creates a query and encrypts the on-premises credentials. This query and the credentials are then sent to a queue inside the gateway. The gateway then sends the query to the Azure Service Bus.

The on-premises client polls the Azure Service Bus regularly and when a message is waiting inside the Service Bus, it decrypts the credentials from the on-premises data source and then runs the query on it to retrieve the data.

The data is returned to the Gateway Cloud Service by using the Azure Service Bus again. The Gateway Cloud Service is responsible for routing the data between the different Azure services.

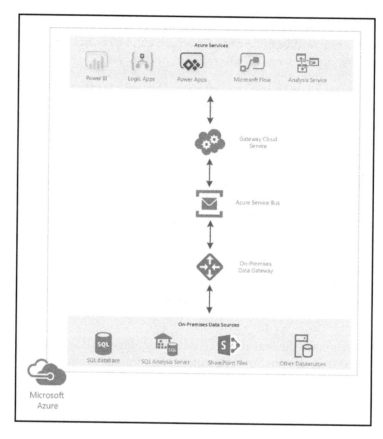

Azure On-premises Data Gateway architecture

Azure App Service Hybrid Connections

Azure App Service Hybrid Connections is both part of the Azure App Service and is a separate feature in Azure. It uses the Azure Relay service to establish a connection between applications that are hosted in Azure and applications that are hosted in your on-premises environment. It creates an application endpoint in the cloud which your app can connect to. It uses the Azure Relay services to establish the connection.

The hybrid connection manager connects to the Azure Relay service, and the application itself connects to the Azure Relay services as well. Azure Relay services is then responsible for setting up a TCP tunnel over which they both can safely communicate. By using the TCP connection, you don't have to open a firewall port on the on-premises server.

Inside Azure App Service, a hybrid connection is created to access application resources on the on-premises environment. You can create a hybrid connection from the Azure Relay service but it is best to create the connection from within the app settings in Azure:

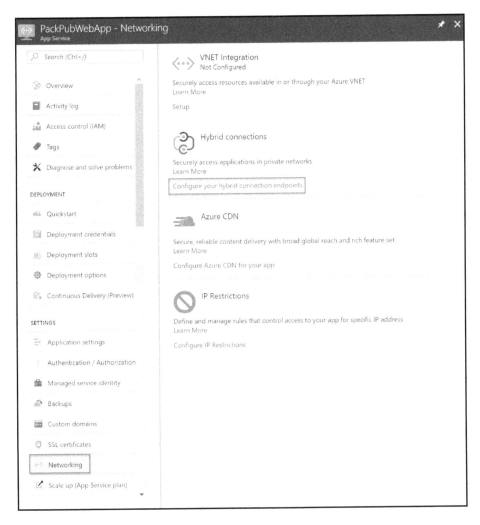

Azure App Service Hybrid Connections settings

Azure App Service Virtual Network Integration

You can use the Azure App Service Virtual Network Integration to deploy your application inside a VNet. This enables access from your application to other services, VMs, or databases that are deployed inside the same VNet as well.

To establish the connection from your application to the VNet, Azure App Service VNet integration uses a point-to-site VPN with a dynamic routing gateway. By using the point-to-site type of VPN connection, there is only one connection created for the VM on which your app is hosted. Other resources that are deployed inside the same App Service plan, are not connected. When you want to set up a connection for that resources as well, you have to set up a separate point-to-site VPN connection for each resource that resides in the App Service plan.

This point-to-site VPN connects to an Azure VPN Gateway, which is connected to the VNet. When a VNet is connected to your on-premises network using the Azure VPN Gateway and a site-to-site VPN, you can use the connection to connect the resource with the resources which reside in the on-premises network as well.

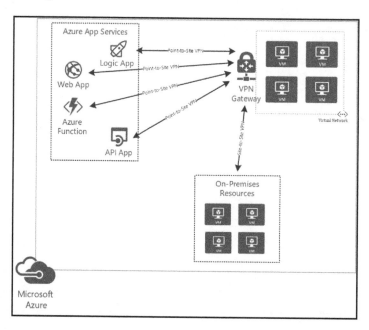

Azure App Service VNet Integration.

App VNet Integration supports communication over UDP and TCP. You can connect to the App by using it's private IP address. Public IP addresses don't have to be created for your App. They can be accessed by their private IP address by all the services that are deployed inside the same VNet.

The VNet Integration can be used for apps that use the Basic, Standard, or Isolated App Service plans. Inside the App Service plan, you can create up to five VNets. However, you can only assign your application to one VNet at a time.

VNet Integration can be set up from the App Settings in the Azure Portal under **Networking**:

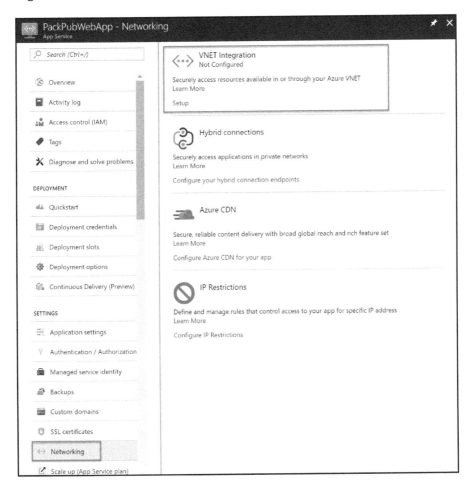

Azure App Service VNet integration from the Azure Portal

Another way for VNet Integration for your App is by using an **Application Service Environment** (**ASE**), which is described in Chapter 3, *Designing Web Applications*. An ASE is deployed inside a VNet as well.

There are some constraints when using VNet Integration for your apps. VNet Integration cannot enable private site access for your app. Private site access makes your app only accessible from resources inside the same virtual network. Private site access can only be accomplished using an Application Service Environment configured with an **Internal Load Balancer** (**ILB**).

For more information on how to create an ASE with an ILB, you can refer to the following article: https://docs.microsoft.com/en-us/azure/app-service/environment/create-ilb-ase.

Azure AD Application Proxy

With the Azure Active Directory Application Proxy, you can access on-premises web applications from the cloud. It provides **Single Sign On** (**SSO**) and secure remote access for your web applications. Applications are integrated with Azure Active Directory and published through the Azure Portal. You don't have to make any adjustments to your on-premises network or use a VPN connection to use the Azure AD Application Proxy for your applications.

The type of applications that can work with Azure AD Application Proxy, are web APIs, web applications that use integrated Windows Authentication for authentication, use form-based or header-based access, applications integrated with the **Active Directory Authentication Library** (**ADAL**), and applications hosted behind a remote desktop gateway.

Azure AD Application Proxy uses two components that need to be configured:

- **Connector**: The connector is a lightweight agent that needs to be installed inside the on-premises network on a Windows Server. It facilitates the network connection between your on-premises application and the Application Proxy service in Azure. It only uses outbound connections, so you don't have to install it in a DMZ or open any inbound ports.

- **External endpoint**: The external endpoint is how your users access the web application. This can be an direct URL or this can be accessed from the MyApps portal. Users authenticate with Azure AD and then they are routed to the on-premises application, through the connector.

 The MyApps portal can be accessed using the following URL: `https://myapps.microsoft.com`. It offers a web portal where all users who have a Azure AD account, can view and launch the applications to which they have been granted access.

Joining VMs to domains

The last way for creating hybrid applications is by joining an Azure VM to an on-premises domain. You can connect an Azure Virtual Machine, which has your application deployed in it for instance, with an on-premises domain using Azure AD Domain Services. To set up this connection, you don't have to install and manage a domain controller in Azure.

Azure AD Domain Services is a feature which can be enabled inside your Azure subscription. It creates a managed domain which is fully integrated with the Azure AD tenant and available inside Azure VNets. On-premises VMs and Azure VMs can then join this managed domain and use the usernames, passwords, and group memberships from Azure AD to log in or authenticate. Applications that are deployed inside these VMs can benefit from this as well.

Azure AD Domain Services provides group policies, LDAP and Kerberos/NTLM authentication' which is compatible with Windows Server Active Directory. You can use this feature for cloud-only Azure AD tenants and for hybrid Azure AD tenants, where the on-premises identities are synced with Azure using Azure AD Connect.

Enabling Azure AD Domain Services

To enable Azure AD Domain Services inside your Azure tenant, you can take the following steps:

1. Navigate to the Azure Portal by opening `https://portal.azure.com/`.
2. Click on **New** and type `Azure AD Domain Services` in the search bar.

3. Azure AD Domain Services is automatically mapped to your Azure AD tenant, so the only thing you have to specify in the next blade is the resource group and the location and click **OK**:

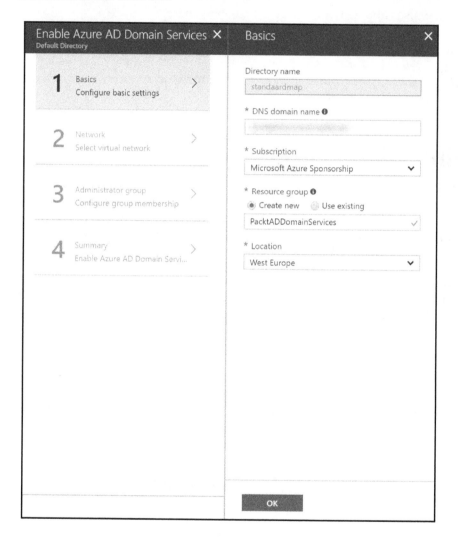

Enable Azure AD Domain Services

4. In the next blade, you can create a new VNet or associate Azure AD Domain Services with a VNet. Note that it is recommended to create a separate subnet for it and click **OK**:

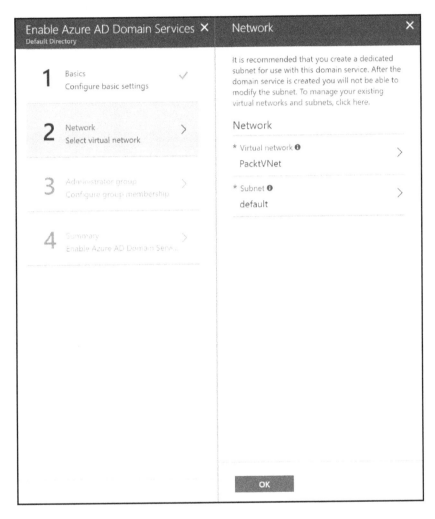

Set VNet

5. There is automatically a group created called **AAD DC Administrators**. You can add users to this group in here:

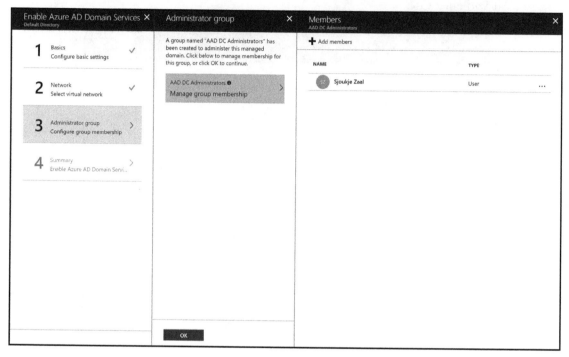

Add administrators

6. The last blade provides a summary of the settings. Click on **OK** to create the service:

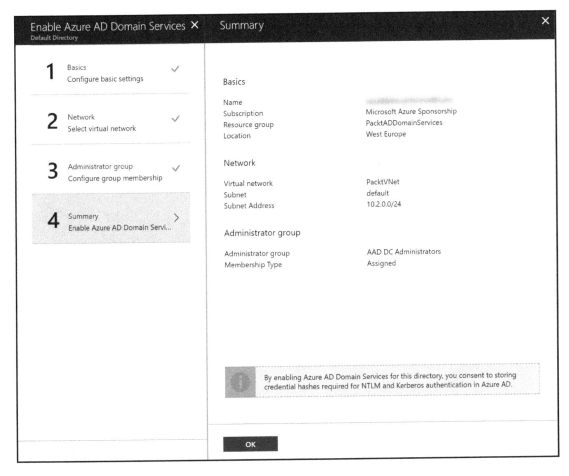

Summary

Adding the VM to the managed domain

Next is to add a VM to the managed domain which is created in the previous step:

1. Open a VM, which was created earlier, from the Azure Portal or create a new VM. Make sure the VM is deployed in the same VNet as the Azure AD Domain Service (but in a separate subnet).

2. Start the VM, connect to it and log in using the credential you provided when the VM was created.

3. Open **Server Manager** | **Local Server** and click on **WORKGROUP**, as shown in the following screenshot:

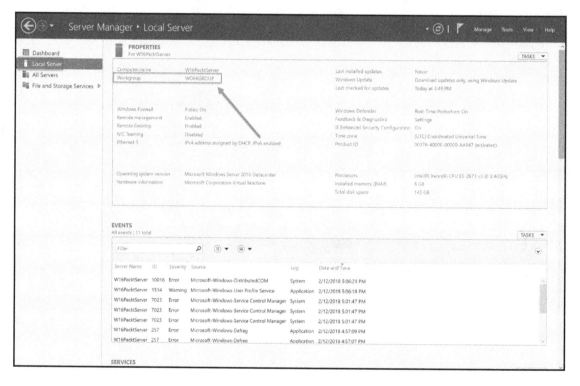

Local Server settings

4. Add the name of the managed domain of Azure AD Domain Services and add the VM to it.

Summary

In this chapter, we covered the designing connectivity for hybrid applications objective. We covered the different services that Azure offers for connecting on-premises applications, data, and services with Azure. You should now know, when to use the different features inside your own solutions and architectures.

The next chapter will focus on the different storage solutions that Azure offers.

Questions

Answer the following questions to test your knowledge of the information in this chapter. You can find the answers in the *Assessments* section at the end of this book.

1. You want to use Azure App VNet Integration to secure your application from outside access. Will this work?
   1. Yes
   2. No

2. You want to connect your on-premises domain with Azure Active Directory as easy as possible. Can we use Azure Active Directory Domain Services for this without using Azure AD Connect?
   1. Yes
   2. No

3. Can we add applications deployed in Azure App Services to a VNet?
   1. Yes
   2. No

Further reading

You can check the following links for more information about the topics that are covered in this chapter:

- **What is Azure Relay?**: https://docs.microsoft.com/en-us/azure/service-bus-relay/relay-what-is-it
- **Service Bus Relay Documentation**: https://docs.microsoft.com/en-us/azure/service-bus-relay/
- **Data Management Gateway**: https://docs.microsoft.com/en-us/azure/data-factory/v1/data-factory-data-management-gateway
- **Connecting to on-premises data sources with Azure On-premises Data Gateway**: https://docs.microsoft.com/en-us/azure/analysis-services/analysis-services-gateway
- **Azure App Service Hybrid Connections**: https://docs.microsoft.com/en-us/azure/app-service/app-service-hybrid-connections.
- **How to provide secure remote access to on-premises applications**: https://docs.microsoft.com/en-us/azure/active-directory/active-directory-application-proxy-get-started
- **Join a Windows Server virtual machine to a managed domain**: https://docs.microsoft.com/en-us/azure/active-directory-domain-services/active-directory-ds-admin-guide-join-windows-vm-portal

7
Using Storage Solutions

In the previous chapter, we covered the designing connectivity for hybrid applications objective. We covered how to design hybrid applications. We also covered external connectivity for Azure VNets and how to design security strategies for networking solutions.

This chapter introduces the designing data implementations objective by starting with storage solutions. This chapter covers the different storage solutions that are available in Azure, such as Azure Blob Storage and Azure Files. It will also help you determine when to use one of these storage solutions. It will also cover designing for NoSQL storage and when to use the different NoSQL services inside Azure, such as Azure Table Storage and Cosmos DB. And finally, it covers searching your data with Azure Search.

By the end of reading this chapter, you should know when to use which storage option for your solutions.

The following topics will be covered:

- Azure Storage types and replication types
- Azure Blob Storage
- Azure Table Storage
- Azure Queue Storage
- Azure File Storage
- Azure Disk Storage
- StorSimple
- Cosmos DB Storage
- Azure Search

Technical requirements

This chapter uses the following tools for the examples:

- Azure PowerShell: `https://docs.microsoft.com/en-us/powershell/azure/install-azurerm-ps?view=azurermps-5.1.1`
- Visual Studio 2017: `https://www.visualstudio.com/downloads/`

The source code for this chapter can be downloaded from the following link:

- `https://github.com/SjoukjeZaal/AzureArchitectureBook/tree/master/Chapter%207`

Azure Storage and replication types

Every application needs some sort of storage solution. Azure offers several different types of storage, from storing files and documents to storing datasets. The first step to take is creating a storage account. When you create a storage account, you have to determine whether you want your data to be accessible locally or globally. Another thing to take into consideration is which account type to choose.

Storage account types

Azure Blob Storage offers three different account types which can be used for Blob, Table, File, and Queue storage. Azure offers the following storage types.

General-purpose v1 (GPv1)

The General-purpose Storage (V1) account is the oldest type of storage account. It offers storage for page blobs, block blobs, files, queues, and tables, but it is not the most cost-effective storage account type. It is the only storage account type that can be used for the classic deployment model. It doesn't support the latest features such as access tiers.

Blob storage

The Blob storage account offers all the features of StorageV2 accounts except that it supports only block blobs (and append blobs). Page blobs are not supported. It offers access tiers, which consists of hot, cool, and archive storage and which is covered later in this chapter.

General-purpose v2 (GPv2)

StorageV2 is the newest type of storage account and it combines the V1 storage with Blob storage. It offers all the latest features such as access tiers for Blob storage with a reduction in costs. Microsoft recommends using this account type over the V1 and Blob storage account type.

V1 storage accounts can be upgraded to V2.

 For more information on pricing and billing for these different account types, you can refer to the following pricing page: `https://azure.microsoft.com/en-us/pricing/details/storage/`.

Storage replication types

Data that is stored in Azure is always replicated to ensure durability and high availability. This way, it is protected from unplanned and planned events, such as network or power outages, natural disasters, and terrorism. It also ensures that during these types of events, your storage account still meets SLA.

Data can be replicated within the same data center, across zonal data centers within the same region and across different regions. These replication types are named **Locally Redundant Storage (LRS)**, **Zone Redundant Storage (ZRS)**, and **Geo-redundant Storage (GRS)**, and they are covered in more detail in the upcoming sections.

 You choose a replication type when you create a new storage account. Storage accounts can be created inside the Azure Portal as well as from PowerShell or CLI.

Locally Redundant Storage

LRS is the cheapest option, which replicates the data three times within the same data center. When you make a write request to your storage account, it will synchronously be written during this request to all three replicas. The request is committed when the data is completely replicated. With LRS, the data will be replicated across multiple update domains and fault domains within one storage scale unit.

Zone Redundant Storage

ZRS is currently in preview and only available in US East 2 and US Central. It replicates three copies, across two or three data centers. The data is written synchronously to all three replicas in one or two regions. It also replicates the data three times inside the same data center where the data resided, just like LRS.

Geo-redundant Storage

GRS replicates the data three times within the same region such as ZRS, as well as three copies to other regions asynchronously.

Azure Blob Storage

Azure Blob Storage offers unstructured data storage in the cloud. It can store all kinds of data, such as documents, VHDs, images, and audio files.

There are two types of blobs that you can create. There are **page blobs**, which are used for the storage of disks. So, when you have VHD which need to be stored and attached to your VM, you will create a page blob. The maximum size of a page blob is 1 TB. The other one is **block blobs**, which are basically all the other types of data that you can store in Azure, such as files and documents. The maximum size of a block blob is 200 GB. However, there is a third blob type named append blob, but this one is used internally by Azure and can't be used in order to store actual files.

There are a couple of ways that you can copy blobs to your blob storage account. You can use the Azure Portal (only one at a time) or Azure Storage Explorer, or you can copy your files programmatically using .NET, PowerShell, or CLI or by calling the REST API.

Access tiers

Blob storage accounts use access tiers to determine how frequently the data is accessed. Based on this access tier, you will get billed. Azure offers three storage access tiers, hot, cool, and archive.

Hot

The Hot access tier is most suitable for storing data accessed frequently and data that is in active use. For instance, you would store images and style sheets for a website inside the Hot access tier. The storage costs for this tier are higher than compared to the other access tiers, but you pay less for accessing the files.

The Hot access tier is optimized for storing data that is accessed frequently. It has higher storage costs than Cool and Archive storage, but you pay less for accessing the files. This access tier is most suitable for data that is in active use.

Cool

The Cool access tier is most suitable for storing data that is not accessed frequently (less then once in 30 days). Compared with the Hot access tier, the Cool tier has lower storage costs, but you pay more for accessing the files. This tier is most suitable for storing backups and older content that is not viewed often.

Archive

The Archive storage tier is set on the blob level and not on the storage level. It has the lowest costs for storing data and the highest cost for accessing data compared with the Hot and Cool access tiers. This tier is for data that will remain in the archive for at least 180 days, and it will take a couple of hours of latency before it can be accessed. This tier is most suitable for long-term backups or compliance and archive data.

A blob in the Archive tier is offline and cannot be read (except for the metadata), copied, overwritten, or modified.

Azure Table Storage

Azure Table Storage is a NoSQL data store, which can be used for a big amount of semi-structured, non-relational data. It is more cost-effective than relational databases because it stores the data on cheaper servers that provide horizontal scale and high performance. NoSQL uses schemaless design, and data is stored based on key/attribute values. You can store flexible datasets in it, and it can store any number of entities in a table, up to the maximum capacity of the storage account (which is 500 TB).

Azure Table Storage is most suitable for datasets that don't require complex joins, stored procedures, and foreign keys. You can access the data using the OData protocol and LINQ Queries.

Creating a storage account

Before you can upload any data or files to Azure Storage, a storage account needs to be created. This can be done using the Azure Portal, PowerShell, CLI, or Visual Studio.

In this demo, we are going to create a storage account with PowerShell:

```
Login-AzureRmAccount
```

If necessary, select the right subscription:

```
Select-AzureRmSubscription -SubscriptionId "********-****-****-****-
***********"
```

Create a resource group:

```
New-AzureRmResourceGroup -Name PacktPubStorage -Location WestEurope
```

Create the storage account:

```
New-AzureRmStorageAccount -ResourceGroupName PacktPubStorage -AccountName
packtpubstorage -Location WestEurope -SkuName "Standard_GRS"
```

Uploading data to Azure Table Storage

In this demo, we are going to use Visual Studio 2017 to upload data to a Azure Table inside the storage account, which was created in the previous step.

1. Click on **File | New | Project**, and in the **New Project** window, select **Windows Classic Desktop | Console App**. Name the project and click on **OK**:

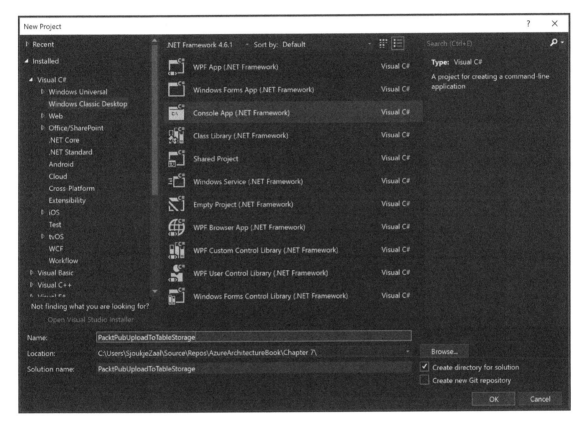

Create a new project

2. Next is to import the NuGet packages. There are two packages that need to be installed:

    - **Windows Azure Storage**: This library provides access to the Azure Storage account and the data. It can be used for blobs, files, tables, and queues.
    - **Microsoft Windows Azure Configuration Manager**: This library provides a unified API to load configuration settings regardless of where the application is hosted.

3. Add the following piece of XML to the `App.config`. The actual `ConnectionString` value can be obtained from the **Access Key** settings in the Azure Portal:

```xml
<configuration>
  <startup>
    <supportedRuntime version="v4.0"
sku=".NETFramework,Version=v4.5.2" />
  </startup>
  <appSettings>
    <add key="StorageConnectionString"
value="DefaultEndpointsProtocol=https;AccountName=packtpubstorage;A
ccountKey=account-key" />
  </appSettings>
</configuration>
```

4. Add a new class to the project and name it `Contact.cs`. Replace it with the following code:

```csharp
using Microsoft.WindowsAzure.Storage.Table;

namespace PacktPubUploadToTableStorage
{
    class Contact : TableEntity
    {
        public Contact(string lastName, string firstName)
        {
            this.PartitionKey = lastName;
            this.RowKey = firstName;
        }

        public Contact() { }

        public string Email { get; set; }
    }
}
```

5. Add the following code to the `Main()` method of the `Program.cs`:

```
using Microsoft.Azure;
using Microsoft.WindowsAzure.Storage;
using Microsoft.WindowsAzure.Storage.Table;

namespace PacktPubUploadToTableStorage
{
    class Program
    {
        static void Main(string[] args)
        {
            CloudStorageAccount storageAccount =
CloudStorageAccount.Parse(CloudConfigurationManager.GetSetting("Sto
rageConnectionString"));
            // Create the table client.

            // Create the table client.
            CloudTableClient tableClient =
storageAccount.CreateCloudTableClient();

            // Retrieve a reference to the table.
            CloudTable table =
tableClient.GetTableReference("packtpubContact");

            // Create the table if it doesn't exist.
            table.CreateIfNotExists();

            // Create a new contact entity.
            Contact contact1 = new Contact("Zaal", "Sjoukje");
            contact1.Email = "sjoukje@packtpub.com";

            // Create the TableOperation object that inserts the
contact.
            TableOperation insertOperation =
TableOperation.Insert(contact1);

            // Execute the insert operation.
            table.Execute(insertOperation);
        }
    }
}
```

6. Run the project. You can then open up the Azure Storage Explorer and navigate to the storage account and the container. You can see the data row that has been added:

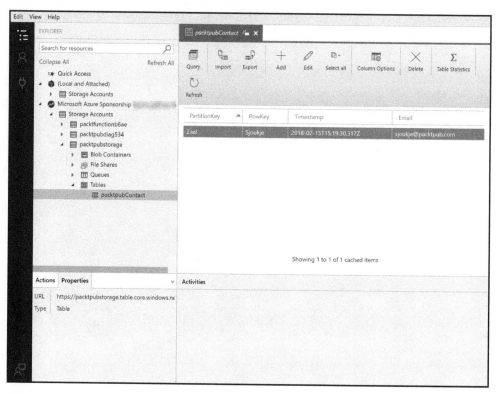

Added data row

 For more information on working with Azure Table Storage from .NET, you can refer to the following tutorial: https://docs.microsoft.com/en-us/azure/cosmos-db/table-storage-how-to-use-dotnet.

Azure Queue Storage

Azure Queue Storage offers a message queue that can be used by applications. Message queues offer an asynchronous communication mechanism where a sender adds an message to the queue, which can be received by the receiver at a later time. Applications can benefit of this because they can decouple components, which can scale independently from each other.

You can send and receive messages from Queue Storage using the Azure Storage Client Libraries and the REST API.

Azure queue storage is covered in more detail in `Chapter 13`, *Implementing Messaging Solutions*.

Azure File Storage

With Azure File Storage, you can create file shares in the cloud. You can access your files using the Server Message Block (SMB) protocol, which is an industry standard and can be used on Linux, Windows, and macOS devices. Azure Files can also be mounted as if it is a local drive on these same devices as well, and they can be cached for fast access on Windows Server using Azure File Sync (preview).

File shares can be used across multiple machines, which makes them suitable for storing files or data that are accessed from multiple machines, such as tools for development machines, or configuration files or log data. Azure File share is part of the Azure Storage Client Libraries and offers an Azure Storage REST API which can be leveraged by developers in their solutions.

Azure Disk Storage

The disks that are used for virtual machines are stored in Azure Blob Storage as page blobs. Azure stores two disks for each virtual machine, the actual operating system (VHD) of the VM and a temporary disk that is used for short-term storage. This data is erased when the VM is turned of or rebooted.

There are two different performance tiers that Azure offers, Standard Disk Storage and Premium Disk Storage.

Standard Disk Storage

Standard Disk Storage offers HDD drives to store the data on and is the most cost-effective storage tier from which you can choose. It can only use LRS or GRS for supporting high availability for your data and applications.

Standard Disk Storage offers HDDs and is more cost-effective. Standard Disk Storage can only use LRS or GRS.

Premium Disk Storage

With Premium Disk Storage, your data is stored on SSDs. Not all Azure Virtual Machine series can use this type of storage. It can only be used with DS, DSv2, GS, LS, or FS series Azure Virtual Machines. It offers high-performance and low-latency disk support.

Unmanaged versus Managed Disks

Managed Disks were covered in `Chapter 1`, *Working with Azure Virtual Machines*, and they handle the storage account creation for you. With Unmanaged Disks, which are the traditional disks used for VMs, you needed to create a storage account manually and then select that storage account when you created the VM. With Managed Disks, this burden is handled for you by Azure. You select the disk type and the performance tier (Standard or Premium), and the managed disk is created. It also handles scaling automatically for you.

Managed Disks are recommended by Microsoft over Unmanaged Disks.

StorSimple

StorSimple is an integrated storage solution that spans across on-premises environments and cloud storage. It answers a lot of storage problems, such as data growth, capacity management, backup, archiving, and disaster recovery, by offering a hybrid solution, which consists of a cloud integrated storage system and Azure Cloud Storage.

With StorSimple, you can store your active data on the on-premises storage system, which offers lower latency and high throughput. Database files are a part of active data for instance. Data that is less active such as documents, SharePoint files, archive data, and VM storage are more suitable for cloud storage. Using StorSimple, you can put that data in Azure Cloud Storage.

StorSimple supports iSCSI and SMB to connect to your data, and compared to more affordable Cloud Storage, it eliminates redundant data and compresses it to reduce costs. You can use Azure Premium storage in conjunction with StorSimple for higher performance and reduced latency.

To accomplish this, StorSimple offers the following storage area network (SAN) solutions, StorSimple Virtual Array and StorSimple 8000 Series.

StorSimple Virtual Array

The StorSimple Virtual Array runs on your existing hypervisor infrastructure on your on-premises environment. It manages the storage across the on-premises environment and Azure Cloud Storage. It also provides cloud backup, fast restore, disaster recovery features, and item-level recovery. It supports Hyper-V 2008 R2 and higher and VMWare 5.5 and higher.

The StorSimple Virtual Array is the most cost-effective StorSimple solution because it offers a download that can be installed on a virtual machine on Hyper-V or VMWare inside your data center or office. It can then be configured as an iSCSI server (SAN) or a file server (NAS). It can be managed from the StorSimple Manager service inside the Azure Portal:

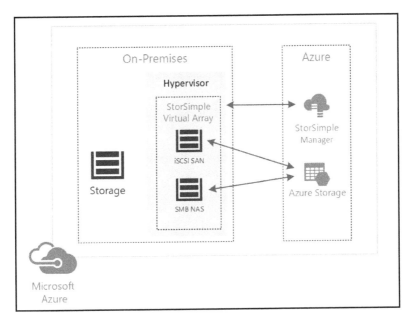

StorSimple Virtual Array

 For more information about the StorSimple Virtual Array, you can refer to https://docs.microsoft.com/en-us/azure/storsimple/storsimple-ova-overview.

StorSimple 8000 Series

With the StorSimple 8000 Series, Microsoft offers a physical device that can be leased and installed inside your on-premises environment. It uses SSD drives for the most active data, HDD drives for data that is used less frequently, and it stores archival data inside Azure Cloud Storage. It also offers redundant controllers to manage the storage tiering and automatic failover.

The StorSimple storage array is installed inside the on-premises environment and offers iSCSI access. It can connect with other SAN storage devices inside the network (up to six network ports). It uses the Virtual Appliance Manager to replicate data to Azure Cloud Storage. The Virtual Appliance Manager is installed inside an Azure VM. It can provide an iSCSI interface to virtual machines in Azure as well. The StorSimple Manager helps you manage the data from the Azure Portal. It can also manage your snapshots, which are stored on-premises. The Snapshot Manager is a **Microsoft Management Console** (**MMC**) snap-in which runs on a Windows-Server based host:

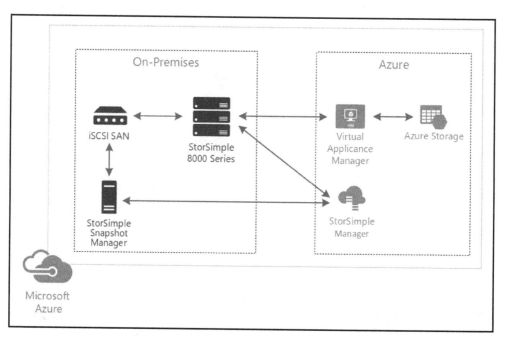

StorSimple 8000 Series

The StorSimple 8000 Series offers Windows PowerShell for StorSimple and a StorSimple adapter for SharePoint.

For more information about the StorSimple 8000 Series, you can refer
to `https://docs.microsoft.com/en-us/azure/storsimple/storsimple-`
`overview`.

Cosmos DB Storage

Cosmos DB (former DocumentDB) storage is the premium offering for Azure Table Storage.
It's a multimodel and globally distributed database service which is designed to
horizontally scale and replicate your data to any number of Azure regions. By replicating
and scaling the data, Cosmos DB can guarantee low latency, high availability, and high
performance anywhere in the world. You can replicate or scale data easily inside the Azure
Portal by selecting the available regions on the map.

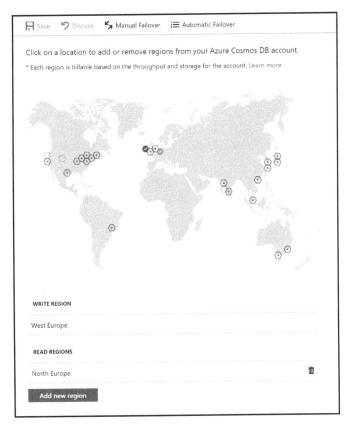

Scaling and replicating data inside the Azure Portal

This high availability and low latency makes Cosmos DB most suitable for mobile applications, games, and applications that need to be globally distributed. The Azure Portal also uses Cosmos DB for data storage.

Cosmos DB is completely schema-less, and you can use a number of existing APIs with available SDKs to communicate with it. So, if you are using a specific API for your data and you want to move your data to Cosmos DB, all you need to do is change the connection string inside your application and the data is stored in Cosmos DB automatically. Cosmos DB supports the following APIs for storing and interacting with your data:

- **SQL API**: With the SQL API, you can use SQL queries as a JSON query language against the dataset inside Cosmos DB. Because Cosmos DB is schema-less, it provides autoindexing of the JSON documents. Data is stored on SSD drives for low latency, and it is lock-free, so you can create real-time queries for your data. Cosmos DB also supports writing stored procedures, triggers, and user-defined functions (UDFs) in JavaScript and it supports ACID transactions inside a collection.
- **MongoDB API**: MongoDB is an open source document database that provides high performance, high availability, and automatic scaling by default. Using it inside Cosmos DB provides automatic sharding, indexing, replication, and encryption of your data on top of this. MongoDB also provides an aggregation pipeline which can be used to filter and transform the data in multiple stages. It also supports creating a full-text index, and you can integrate it easily with Azure Search and other Azure services as well.
- **Gremlin (Graph) API**: The Gremlin API is part of the Apache TinkerPop project, which is an open source Graph computing framework. A Graph is a way of storing objects (nodes) based on relationships. Each object can have multiple relations with other objects. You can interact with the data using JavaScript.
- **Table API**: The Azure Table API can be used for applications that are written for using Azure Table Storage, but need the premium features, such as global distribution, automatic indexing, low latency, and high throughput.
- **Cassandra API**: The Cassandra API can be used for applications that are written for Apache Cassandra. Apache Cassandra is an open source distributed NoSQL database that offers scalability and high availability. Cosmos DB offers no operations management, SLA, and automatic indexing on top of this.

In the future, new APIs will be added to Cosmos DB as well.

Multi-model APIs available for Cosmos DB

If you want to get started with developing applications using one of these multimodel APIs, you can refer to `https://docs.microsoft.com/en-us/azure/cosmos-db/`. There are a lot of examples for multiple programming languages available there.

Azure Search

Azure Search is an Azure service that provides a rich search experience over content stored in Azure SQL Database, Azure Cosmos DB, and Azure Blob Storage. For Azure Blob Storage, it supports indexing for multiple file formats, such as CSV, JSON, plain text files, RTF, EML, ZIP, XML, HTML, various Microsoft Office formats, and PDF.

It offers full text search and text analysis, linguistic analysis with analyzers in 56 languages, geo-search, user experience features, such as search suggestions, paging, sorting, and hit highlighting, and monitoring and reporting features.

Azure Search uses partitions for storing search indexes and for providing I/O for read/write operations. Azure Search offers different service tiers which can be combined inside a tenant. The different tiers offer different amounts of storage capacity and scalability. For the more expensive service tiers, multiple instances of the search service can be created, which are named replicas.

Azure Search offers the following service tiers:

- **Free**: This offers a shared service with other tenants in Azure. It offers 50 MB of storage, a maximum of 3 indexes per service up to 10,000 documents each, and it cannot scale out.
- **Basic**: This offers a dedicated service with 2 GB of storage and a maximum of 5 indexes per service. You can scale up to 3 search units per service (1 partition and 3 replicas).
- **Standard S1**: This offers a dedicated service with 25 GB of storage and a maximum of 50 indexes per service. You can scale up to 36 search units per service (12 partitions and 12 replicas).
- **Standard S2**: This offers the Standard S1 features but with 100 GB of storage and a maximum of 200 indexes per service on top of it.
- **Standard S3**: This offers 200 GB of storage and all the Standard S2 features.
- **Standard HD**: This is an option that can be enabled for Standard S3 pricing tiers. On top of all the features that Standard S3 provides, you can have a maximum of 1,000 indexes per service.

It is recommended that you always provision a free search service tier per subscription, so it can be used for testing or for lightweight searches. You can then create other Search Services next to it for production workloads. For more information about the available SKUs for Azure Search, you can refer to https://docs.microsoft.com/en-us/azure/search/search-sku-tier.

Summary

In this chapter, we covered the designing data implementations objective. We covered the different storage solutions that are available in Azure and when to use them. We also covered designing for NoSQL Storage and when to use the different Azure services such as Azure Table Storage and Cosmos DB. Finally, we briefly covered Azure Search.

The next chapter will cover scalable data implementations.

Questions

Answer the following questions to test your knowledge of the information in this chapter. You can find the answers in the *Assessments* section at the end of this book.

1. Is Cosmos DB more suitable for gaming applications than Azure Table Storage?
    1. Yes
    2. No
2. Can you use Azure Search with Azure Data Factory to search for data?
    1. Yes
    2. No
3. You want to create a Graph database in Cosmos DB. Is the MongoDB API the appropriate API for this to leverage in your custom applications?
    1. Yes
    2. No

Further reading

You can check the following links for more information about the topics that are covered in this chapter:

- **Azure Storage Account Options**: https://docs.microsoft.com/en-us/azure/storage/common/storage-account-options
- **Azure Storage replication**: https://docs.microsoft.com/en-us/azure/storage/common/storage-redundancy
- **Azure Table Storage overview**: https://docs.microsoft.com/en-us/azure/cosmos-db/table-storage-overview
- **Introduction to Azure Files**: https://docs.microsoft.com/en-us/azure/storage/files/storage-files-introduction
- **About disks storage for Azure Windows VMs**: https://docs.microsoft.com/en-us/azure/virtual-machines/windows/about-disks-and-vhds
- **StorSimple Documentation**: https://docs.microsoft.com/en-us/azure/storsimple/
- **Welcome to Azure Cosmos DB**: https://docs.microsoft.com/en-us/azure/cosmos-db/introduction
- **Azure Search Documentation**: https://docs.microsoft.com/en-us/azure/search/

8
Scalable Data Implementations

In the previous chapter, we covered the storage solutions objective. We covered some of the different storage features that Azure offers, as well as when and how to use them. We also covered designing for NoSQL storage, and when to use the available solutions.

This is the second chapter of the Domain Design Data Implementation objective. It covers designing for Azure data services, including a high-level overview of the services and solutions that Azure provides. It also covers relational databases in Azure. This consists of the Azure SQL Database and how to design for performance, availability, and two open source relational databases, such as MySQL and PostgreSQL on Azure.

By the end of this chapter, you should know which data service or relational database to use for your solutions and when.

The following topics will be covered:

- Azure Data Catalog
- Azure Data Factory
- Azure SQL Data Warehouse
- Azure Data Lake
- Azure Analysis Services
- Azure SQL Database
- Azure Database for MySQL
- Azure Database for PostgreSQL

Technical requirements

The source code for this chapter can be downloaded from `https://github.com/ SjoukjeZaal/AzureArchitectureBook/tree/master/Chapter%208`.

Azure Data Catalog

Azure Data Catalog provides a central repository where you can find all of the data sources that are used inside your organization. Most employees inside an organization are not aware of where enterprise data is located or who is responsible for that data. With Azure Data Catalog, any user (such as a developer or analyst, for instance) can discover and consume the data source from a central place.

Azure Data Catalog provides one data catalog per Azure AD Tenant, even if you have multiple subscriptions associated with the tenant. A copy of the data source metadata and the location of the data source is added to the catalog. The data itself remains at the original location. Azure Data Catalog offers search functionality to easily discover the data, as well.

You can import a data source in the Azure Data Catalog using the tooling that Microsoft provides. Azure Data Catalog supports a variety of data sources that can be published using the import tool, such as Azure Blob Storage, Azure Data Lake, SQL Server, and third-party data sources such as Oracle, MySQL, and more. When a data source is added to the catalog, the metadata can be enriched to provide extra information to the users.

There are two different versions of the Azure Data Catalog—**Free** and **Standard:**

- **Free**: Offers unlimited users and 5,000 registered data assets; the data assets are discoverable by all users
- **Standard**: Offers unlimited users, 100,000 registered data assets, and asset-level authorization, restricting visibility

The Azure Data Catalog can also be used programmatically by calling the Data Catalog REST API. It provides calls for registering and deleting data, and for working with annotations.

For a complete overview of the data sources that Azure Data Catalog supports, you can refer to the article at `https://docs.microsoft.com/en-us/azure/data-catalog/data-catalog-dsr`. For more information about the Data Catalog REST API, you can refer to the article at `https://docs.microsoft.com/en-us/rest/api/datacatalog/#search-syntax-reference`.

Azure Data Factory

Azure Data Factory is a cloud service for big data processing and analytics. It uses raw data from various data sources to create valuable insights for business decision makers, analysts, and data scientists. The following features are used to process and compose the data into data-driven workflows:

- **Data pipelines**: Represent a group of activities that perform a unit of work.
- **Activities**: One activity represents a step in a pipeline. For instance, you can create a Copy Activity to copy data from an Azure Blob Storage account to an HDInsight cluster. Azure Data Factory supports three types of activities: data movement activities, data transformation activities, and data control activities.
- **Datasets**: These represent the data from the data stores which are used for input and output.
- **Linked services**: Azure Data Factory uses linked services to connect to the data sources. You can relate this to connection strings. There are two types of linked services—one for connecting to a data store and one for connecting to compute resources.
- **Triggers**: A trigger starts the execution of the data pipeline. Data Factory supports schedule triggers and tumbling window triggers, which run on a periodic interval. There is no trigger to start the pipeline from custom code. If you want to start it from inside an application, the best method is to change the start time of the schedule trigger to the time you want to start the operation, from inside your code.
- **Pipeline run**: This is an instance of data pipeline execution.
- **Parameters**: You can pass arguments to parameters inside the pipeline. They are key-value pairs.
- **Control flow**: This represents an orchestration of activities. You can process activities in sequence, create for-each iterators, and more.

You can create a Data Factory service and data pipelines from the Azure Portal using the Azure Data Lake UI (only from Edge or Chrome), .NET, Python, PowerShell, ARM, or by calling the REST API.

 At the time of writing this book, Azure offers two versions of Azure Data Factory: V1 and V2. V2 is currently in preview. For a detailed overview of the differences between the versions, you can refer to `https://docs.` `microsoft.com/en-us/azure/data-factory/compare-versions`. Azure Data Factories can only be created in the East US, East US2, and West Europe regions. However, they can access data stores and compute services in other Azure regions to move data between data stores or process data using compute services.

Azure SQL Data Warehouse

Azure SQL Data Warehouse offers an Enterprise Data Warehouse in the cloud. It uses **Massively Parallel Processing** (**MPP**) combined with Azure Storage, to provide high performance and scalability. To create valuable insights into the data stored inside the Data Warehouse, Azure uses Hadoop/Spark and machine learning.

Data is stored in relational tables with columnar storage. When using columnar storage, the data is written and read in columns, instead of the rows used in traditional row-oriented databases. So, when you query the data, columnar storage skips all of the irrelevant data by immediately jumping to the appropriate column. This will make your queries run a lot faster. For instance, when you want to look up the average age of all of your customers, columnar storage will jump to the age column immediately, instead of looking at each row for the age column. This also provides better compression of the data, which results in lower storage costs.

By using MPP, Azure SQL Data Warehouse decouples the storage layer from the compute layer, which makes it easy to scale out. MPP uses multiple compute nodes to process the data. A client application or storage solution uses PolyBase T-SQL commands to add data to the control node. The control node runs the MPP engine, which uses the **Data Movement Service** (**DMS**) for moving the data between the nodes. It is also responsible for optimizing the queries for parallel processing. When optimized, the MPP engine will pass the queries on to the available compute nodes to execute them in parallel. The compute nodes will then be responsible of storing the data inside Azure Storage:

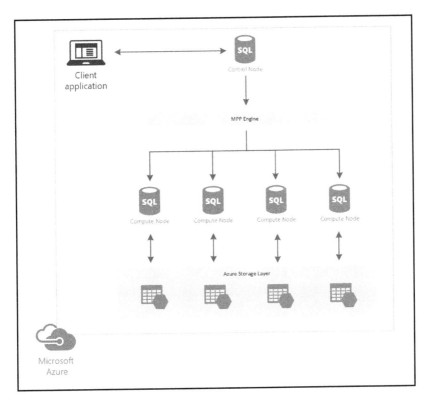

MPP architecture

Decoupling the storage layer from the compute layer is also more cost-effective. You can independently scale out the compute nodes of the storage layer, or pause the compute capacity so that you only have to pay for the storage.

Azure Data Lake

Azure Data Lake is a big data storage and analytics service that can store an unlimited amount of structured, semi-structured, or unstructured data. It is based on the Hadoop Yes Another Resource Negotiator (YARN) cluster management platform, which can scale dynamically across Azure SQL Server instances or instances of Azure SQL Data Warehouse.

For more information about Hadoop YARN, you can refer to the Hadoop website at `https://hadoop.apache.org/docs/current/hadoop-yarn/ hadoop-yarn-site/YARN.html`.

Hadoop YARN offers three types of solutions:

- Azure Data Lake Store
- Azure Data Lake Analytics
- Azure HDInsight

Azure Data Lake Store

Azure Data Lake Store is a storage repository for big data workloads, where you can store raw data. A data lake is a container where you can store all kinds of data, such as structured, semi-structured, and unstructured data. Data is still unprocessed when it is added to the data lake. This is different from a data warehouse, where you store structured and processed data.

Azure Data Lake Store is built for Hadoop, which is available from the HDInsight cluster in Azure. It uses the Hadoop filesystem to store the data. Applications call the WebHDFS-compatible REST APIs to add data to the filesystem. It offers unlimited storage, and data can be analyzed using Hadoop analytic frameworks such as MapReduce or Hive. Azure HDInsight clusters can also be configured by using an out-of-the-box connection to directly access data stored in the Azure Data Lake Store. You can use Azure Data Lake Store data inside machine learning models, and you can create batch queries or store data inside a data warehouse:

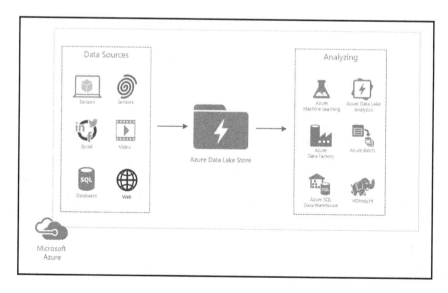

Azure Data Lake Store

Azure Data Lake Analytics

Azure Data Lake Analytics is a feature of Azure Data Lake that can be used to analyze your data. Your data can come from various data sources, and after the data is analyzed, it can be written to various data sources as well. It works with Azure Data Lake Store, Azure Blob Storage, and Azure SQL Database.

Azure Data Lake Analytics uses a serverless approach; you don't have to manage a cluster, and you only pay for the actual analysis of your data. It can scale dynamically, and it is integrated with Azure AD for authentication.

It comes with two price packages:

- **Pay-as-you-go**: Here, you pay only for your use, per minute. There is no further commitment
- **Monthly commitment**: This price package comes with a couple of different possibilities, where you pay upfront for a certain amount of hours—100, 500, or 1,000 hours, and so on

 For more information on the different price packages, you can refer to `https://azure.microsoft.com/en-us/pricing/details/data-lake-analytics/`.

Azure Data Analytics uses U-SQL to analyze the data. U-SQL is the big data query language, and it can be used in combination with C#, R, Python, and Cognitive Services. You can create scripts from the Azure Portal and create jobs to execute them on the data. You can use Visual Studio, Visual Studio Code, PowerShell, and CLI for submitting U-SQL scripts, as well.

Analyzing your data using Data Lake Analytics

In this demo, we are going to create a Data Lake Analytics account and analyze some data, storing it in Azure Data Lake Store afterwards. An Azure Data Lake Store account is mandatory for Data Lake Analytics, so we will create that as well:

1. Navigate to the Azure Portal by opening `https://portal.azure.com/`.

2. Click on **New** and type **Data Lake Analytics** in the search bar.
3. A new blade opens up. At the time of writing this book, Data Lake Analytics can only be created in the regions Central US, East US 2, and North Europe. Add the following settings:

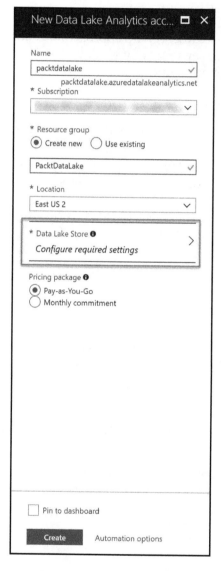

Create an Azure Data Lake Analytics account

4. Click **Data Lake Store** to create the account for storing your data:

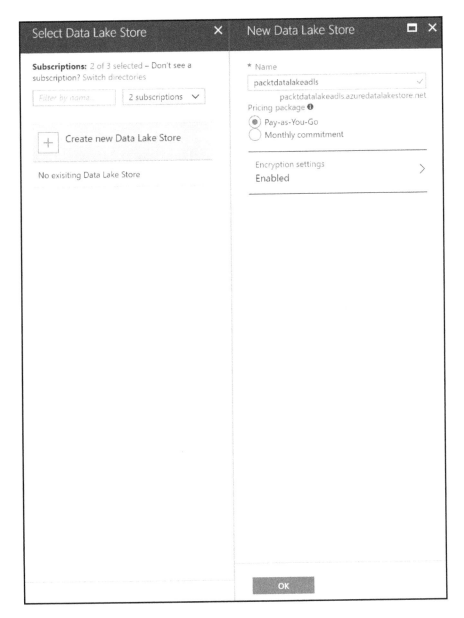

Create an Azure Data Lake Store

5. Click **OK** twice to create both the Data Lake Store and the Data Lake Analytics account.

6. You can now navigate to the Data Lake Analytics account. Next, upload the sample file `SearchLogs.tsv` to Azure Data Lake Store. Click on **Data explorer** in the left-hand menu:

Data Explorer

7. Create a new folder and name it `input`. Upload `SearchLogs.tsv` to the folder:

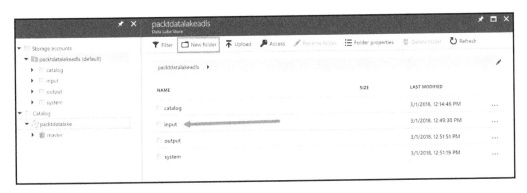

Create a new input folder

8. Next, click on **New job**:

Azure Data Lake overview

9. Name the job, and add the following code to it. This extracts the raw data from the `SearchLog` file and creates a new file with headers, and then stores it in a folder called `output` in the Azure Data Lake Store:

```
@searchlog =
    EXTRACT UserId int,
            Start DateTime,
            Region string,
            Query string,
            Duration int?,
            Urls string,
            ClickedUrls string
    FROM "/input/SearchLog.tsv"
    USING Extractors.Tsv();

OUTPUT @searchlog
    TO "/output/SearchLog-first-u-sql.csv"
    USING Outputters.Csv();
```

10. Run the job. The following output will be displayed:

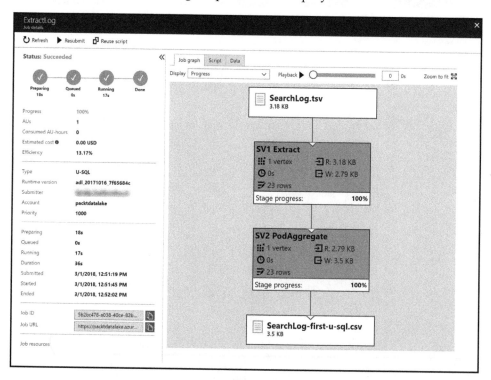

Azure Data Lake output

11. You can now see the result in the Data Explorer. There is a new folder called `output` added, where the output file is stored.

Azure HDInsight

Azure HDInsight is a service which deploys Hadoop components in the form of clusters in the cloud. Apache Hadoop is a very popular open source framework for processing and analyzing big data. The Hadoop components on Azure make it very easy to process data because Azure handles the creation of the clusters.

HDInsight offers the following cluster types:

- **Apache Hadoop**: Hadoop can process data in parallel using MapReduce, a programming language that can process data efficiently.
- **Apache Spark**: Spark can process data in parallel as well by using in-memory processing for better performance. You can use it with SQL, streaming data, and machine learning solutions.
- **Apache HBase**: This offers a NoSQL database on Hadoop which can be used as input or output for MapReduce jobs.
- **Microsoft R Server**: Offers a server for hosting and managing R scripts. R is mostly used by data scientists, and provides scalable methods for analyzing data.
- **Apache Storm**: Offers processing for large streams of data in a very fast way. You can use this to analyze real-time sensor data, for instance.
- **Apache Interactive Query (Preview)**: Hive queries can now run faster using the in-memory caching mechanism.
- **Apache Kafka**: Offers streaming for data pipelines, message queuing, and applications.

Azure HDInsight uses Azure Blob Storage and Azure Data Lake Store as storage solutions. You can build applications on Azure HDInsight using Java, Python, and .NET by using the HDInsight .NET SDK and more.

Azure Analysis Services

Azure Analysis Services use the same architecture that SQL Server Analysis uses, and provides enterprise-grade data modeling in the cloud.

You can easily create a hybrid environment by connecting Azure Analysis Services with your on-premises SQL Analysis Servers. Data from various sources, such as SQL Server Analysis, SQL Server, Azure SQL Server, and more, can then easily be combined. Inside Azure Analysis Services, the models can be processed much faster when compared to on-premises environments. This way, client applications such as Power BI, Excel, Reporting Services, and other third-party applications, can query the data and deliver dashboards much faster:

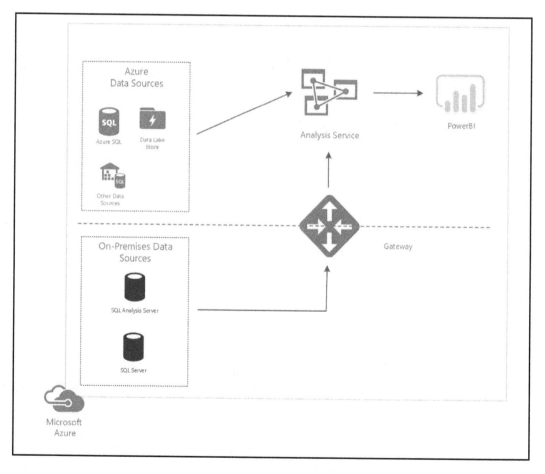

Azure Analysis Services

Azure SQL Database

Azure SQL Database offers a relational database in the cloud. It uses the SQL Server on-premises code base, but by using Azure SQL Database over SQL Server on-premises, you don't have to manage the underlying platform, the operating system, or buy any licenses. Besides that, Microsoft releases updates for Azure SQL Database first, and then for SQL Server.

Azure SQL Database offers scalability without causing any downtime for your databases. It offers column base indexes, which make your queries perform much faster. There is built-in monitoring for your databases and built-in intelligence for increasing the performance of your database automatically, and it provides high availability by providing automatic backups and Point-in-time restores. You can also use active geo-replication, for global applications.

Azure SQL Database offers the following tiers for your databases:

- **Elastic Database Pools**: Elastic pools is a feature that helps in managing and scaling databases that have unpredictable usage demands. All databases in an Elastic Pool are deployed on the same database server and share the same resources. By managing the pool of databases and not the individual databases, they can share performance and scaling. The performance of this tier is expressed in **elastic Database Transaction Units (eDTUs)**.
- **Individual databases**: This is a good fit if you have a database with predictable performance. Scaling is done for each database separately. The performance of this tier is expressed in **Database Transaction Units (DTUs)**.

For more information about **Database Transaction Units (DTUs) and elastic Database Transaction Units (eDTUs)**, you can refer to the article at `https://docs.microsoft.com/en-us/azure/sql-database/sql-database-what-is-a-dtu`.
There are a number of different service plans and pricing tiers available for Azure SQL Database. As they change often, you can refer to the pricing page for an overview at `https://azure.microsoft.com/en-us/pricing/details/sql-database/`. However, it is strongly advised to look at the different plans for the 70-535 exam.

SQL Server Stretch Database

SQL Service Stretch Database was introduced in SQL Server 2016, and is a feature that can move or archive your cold data from your on-premises SQL Server to the Azure SQL Database. This results in better performance for your on-premises server, and the stretched data resides in the cloud, where it is easily accessible for other applications.

Inside SQL Server, you can mark a table as a stretch candidate, and SQL Server will move the data to Azure SQL Database transparently. Large transactional tables with lots of historical data can benefit from enabling for stretch. These are mostly massive tables with hundreds or millions of rows in them, which don't have to be queried frequently.

High availability

Even when your databases are hosted in Azure, there is still a chance that failures and outages will occur. In the case of an outage (such as a total regional failure, which can be caused by a natural disaster, an act of terrorism, war, a government action, or a network or device failure external to the data centers of Microsoft), your data still needs to be accessible.

To create highly available SQL Server databases on Azure, you can use failover groups and active geo-replication, which are covered in more detail in the following sections.

Active geo-replication

Geo-replication is a business continuity feature that allows you to replicate the primary database, up to four read-only secondary databases, in the same or different Azure regions. You can use the secondary databases to query data, or for failover scenarios when there is a data center outage. Active geo-replication has to be set up by the user or the application manually.

Failover groups

Failover groups is a feature that automatically manages the failovers. It automatically manages the geo-replication relationship between the databases, the failover at scale, and the connectivity. To use failover groups, the primary and the secondary databases need to be created inside of the same Azure subscription.

Automatic failover supports replication of all of the databases that are created in the same failover group to only one secondary database server, in a different region. This is different when using active geo-replication, which can replicate up to four secondary databases.

You can set and manage geo-replication from the Azure Portal, PowerShell, Transact SQL, and the REST API.

Configuring active geo-replication and failover groups

In this example, we are going to set up active geo-replication and failover groups for a single database. Note that this can be done for an Elastic Pool, as well:

1. Navigate to the Azure Portal by opening `https://portal.azure.com/`.
2. First, create the SQL Database. Click on **New** and type `SQL Database` in the search bar.
3. On the next screen, add the following settings in the creation blade and click on **Create**, as shown in the following screenshot:

Create SQL Database

4. Click on **Create a new server**, add the following settings, and click on **Select**:

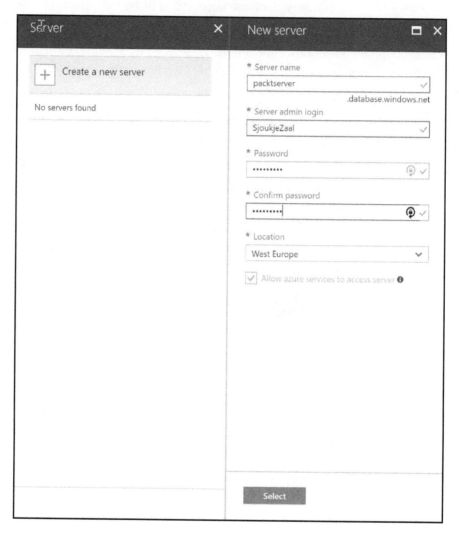

Create SQL Server

5. Click the pricing tier; in this blade, you can select the pricing tier and the DTUs and eDTUs that you want to configure for the database. For now, you can keep the default settings and click **Apply**:

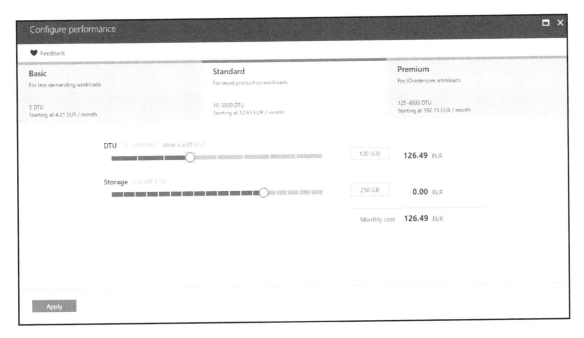

Select pricing tier

6. Click on **Create** to create the database.

7. Navigate to the database and, in the left-hand menu, click **Geo-Replication**. There, you can configure to which regions you want your database to be replicated. You can select every region, but the paired region is recommended. You can also click the top banner to create a failover group for your database:

Geo-replication settings

8. Select the region, and a new blade will pop up. In there, you have to create the second database in a new server. The steps for creating the new server are identical to the steps that were taken for the first server. Add the following settings, and click **OK**:

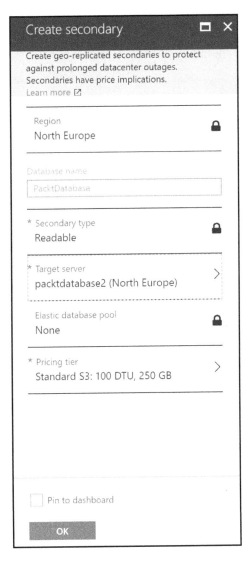

Create secondary server

9. To automatically replicate the database, you need to add it to a failover group. Click the banner and add the following settings. Pick the secondary database created in the previous step as a secondary server and click on **Create**:

Automatic Failover

Backup and recovery

Azure creates geo-redundant backups for each service tier automatically. These backups are then copied to **read-access geo-redundant storage** (**RA-GRS**). Azure SQL Database creates a full database backup every week, and a differential backup every hour. A differential backup creates a backup from the data that has changed since the last full backup. Azure SQL Database also creates a transaction log backup every 5 to 10 minutes.

The retention period of these backups varies for each service tier:

- **Basic**: Has a retention of 7 days
- **Standard**: Has a retention of 35 days
- **Premium**: Has a retention of 35 days

These retention periods can be extended by creating a **long-term backup retention policy**. By using the LTR policy, the retention period can be extended up to 10 years. The backups are copied to the Azure Recovery Services Vault, and data is encrypted at rest. The Azure Recovery Services Vault manages all of the backups and automatically removes backups that have expired. The LTR policy can be created from the Azure Portal or from PowerShell.

You can use the backups for the following restoring scenarios:

- **Point-in-time restore**: A database can be restored to any Point-in-time within the retention policy on the same logical server. A new database, which is fully accessible, is created. You can use Point-in-time restore for every service tier, and for single databases and databases deployed into elastic pools. A Point-in-time restore can be restored from the Azure Portal, PowerShell, or the REST API.
- **Deleted database restore**: A deleted database can be restored up to the time of deletion on the same logical server. You can restore a deleted database to an earlier Point-in-time as well. A deleted database restore can be executed from the Azure Portal, PowerShell, and the REST API.
- **Geo-restore**: Using geo-restore, you can restore a database backup to any server in any region. You can only use geo-restore for geo-redundant backups. Backups that are created manually are not supported. For this type of restore, you can use the Azure Portal, PowerShell, and the REST API.
- **Azure Recovery Services Vault restore**: You can use this type of restore for restoring a database to a certain Point-in-time in the available retention policy. This way, you can restore an old version of a database for an application, for instance. For this type of restore, you can use the Azure Portal, PowerShell, and the REST API, as well.

Azure Database for MySQL

Azure Database for MySQL is an implementation of the open source relational database MySQL in the cloud. The Azure offering offers the same functionality and capabilities as the MySQL Community Edition.

The MySQL Database is widely used by PHP developers, and for a lot of PHP applications, like the open source CMS WordPress, for instance. MySQL offers the following features and capabilities:

- **Open source**: MySQL is open source but owned by Oracle. It offers commercial versions as well.
- **ACID compliancy**: It offers Atomicity, Consistency, Isolation, Durability (ACID) transactions. This ensures that there is no data loss in the case of failure. MySQL offers ACID compliancy when using InnoDB and NDB Cluster Storage engines. InnoDB has been the default MySQL storage engine since version 5.6.
- **Replication**: MySQL offers master-standby replication, which includes single master to one standby and multiple standbys, circular replication (A to B to C, and back to A), and master to master.
- **Performance**: MySQL can under-perform at a heavy load and when it needs to execute complex queries. It is most suitable for web-based projects that need simple, straightforward data transactions.
- **Security**: MySQL offers security based on **Access Control Lists** (**ACLs**) for all connections, queries, and other operations. It offers support for SSL-encrypted connections between MySQL clients and servers.
- **NoSQL features**: MySQL only offers JSON data type support, and not support for indexing JSON.
- **Extensibility**: MySQL has no support for extensibility.
- **Concurrency**: MySQL only has multiversion concurrency control (MVCC) support in InnoDB.
- **Programming languages**: You can only use the MySQL programming language to communicate with the data in the database.

By running your MySQL Database on Azure, on top of all the features and capabilities that MySQL offers, Microsoft offers automatic scaling, high availability, encryption for data at rest, automatic backup and Point-in-time restore for up to 35 days, enterprise security and compliance, and more.

MySQL on Azure offers the following pricing tiers:

- **Basic**: Offers a maximum of 1 TB of storage, four logical CPUs, and locally redundant backups
- **General purpose**: Offers a maximum of 1 TB of storage, four logical CPUs, scalable I/O throughput, and locally redundant and geographically redundant backups
- **Memory optimized:** Offers a maximum of 1 TB of storage, five logical CPUs, scalable I/O throughput, and locally redundant and geographically redundant backups

 For more information about the features and capabilities that the MySQL Community Edition offers, you can refer to `https://www.mysql.com/products/community/`.

Azure Database for PostgreSQL

Azure Database for PostgreSQL is an implementation of the open source relational database PostgreSQL in the cloud. It is also based on the community version of the open source PostgreSQL database engine. PostgreSQL offers capabilities similar to MySQL, but there are differences as well.

It offers the following features and capabilities:

- **Open source**: PostgreSQL is completely open source.
- **ACID compliancy**: Offers ACID transactions.
- **Replication**: PostgreSQL provides master-standby replication, including single master to one standby and multiple standbys, hot standby/streaming replication, bi-directional replication, logical log streaming replication, and cascading replication.
- **Performance**: It supports a variety of performance optimizations, and is most suitable for systems that require the execution of complex queries and where read and write speeds are crucial. PostgreSQL performs well in OLTP/OLAP systems and with business intelligence applications.
- **Security**: PostgreSQL offers role-based and inherited role-based security. It offers native SSL support for client/server communications, and it offers row level security.

- **Concurrency**: PostgreSQL has full multiversion concurrency control (MVCC) support and is extremely responsive in high volume environments.
- **NoSQL features**: PostgreSQL supports JSON and other NoSQL features, such as native XML support, JSON indexing, and key-value pairs with HSTORE.
- **Extensibility**: PostgreSQL offers support for extensibility, such as adding new functions, types, new index types, and more.
- **Programming languages**: Offers programming language extensions for JavaScript, .Net, R, C/C++, Java, Perl, Python, Ruby, Tcl, and more.

On top of all of the features that PostgreSQL provides, Azure Database for PostgreSQL offers automatic scaling, high availability, encryption for data at rest, automatic backup and Point-in-time restore, and more.

PostgreSQL on Azure offers identical pricing tiers as MySQL on Azure:

- **Basic**: Offers a maximum of 1 TB of storage, four logical CPUs, and locally redundant backups
- **General purpose**: Offers a maximum of 1 TB of storage, four logical CPUs, scalable I/O throughput, and locally redundant and geographically redundant backups
- **Memory optimized**: Offers a maximum of 1 TB of storage, five logical CPUs, scalable I/O throughput, and locally redundant and geographically redundant backups

 For more information about the features and capabilities that the PostgreSQL database offers, you can refer to `https://www.postgresql.org/`.

Summary

In this chapter, we have completed the designing data implementations objective. We've covered the various data implementation solutions that Azure provides, such as the various Azure Data Services and the various relational databases that Azure offers. You should now know which database you should use in different scenarios, how to manage your backup and restore, and how to design for high availability and performance.

Next, we will kick off designing security and identity solutions with securing Azure resources.

Questions

Answer the following questions to test your knowledge of the information in this chapter. You can find the answers in the *Assessments* section at the end of this book:

1. Can you restore deleted databases in Azure?
    1. Yes
    2. No

2. Can you use SQL Server Stretch Database to extend your on-premises data storage to Azure?
    1. Yes
    2. No

3. Can you use T-SQL for analyzing data in Azure Data Analytics?
    1. Yes
    2. No

Further reading

You can check the following links for more information about the topics that are covered in this chapter:

- **Azure Data Catalog documentation**: https://docs.microsoft.com/en-us/azure/data-catalog/.
- **Get started with Azure Data Catalog**: https://docs.microsoft.com/en-us/azure/data-catalog/data-catalog-get-started.
- **What is Azure SQL Data Warehouse?**: https://docs.microsoft.com/en-us/azure/sql-data-warehouse/sql-data-warehouse-overview-what-is.
- **Overview of Azure Data Lake Store**: https://docs.microsoft.com/en-us/azure/data-lake-store/data-lake-store-overview.
- **Overview of Microsoft Azure Data Lake Analytics**: https://docs.microsoft.com/en-us/azure/data-lake-analytics/data-lake-analytics-overview
- **Introduction to Azure HDInsight and the Hadoop and Spark technology stack**: https://docs.microsoft.com/en-us/azure/hdinsight/hadoop/apache-hadoop-introduction.
- **Azure SQL Database documentation**: https://docs.microsoft.com/en-us/azure/sql-database/

- **Scaling out with Azure SQL Database**: `https://docs.microsoft.com/en-us/azure/sql-database/sql-database-elastic-scale-introduction`
- **Stretch Database**: `https://docs.microsoft.com/en-us/sql/sql-server/stretch-database/stretch-database`
- **Designing highly available services using Azure SQL Database**: `https://docs.microsoft.com/en-us/azure/sql-database/sql-database-designing-cloud-solutions-for-disaster-recovery`
- **Learning about automatic SQL Database backups**: `https://docs.microsoft.com/en-us/azure/sql-database/sql-database-automated-backups`
- **Recovering an Azure SQL Database using automated database backups**: `https://docs.microsoft.com/en-us/azure/sql-database/sql-database-recovery-using-backups`
- **What is Azure Database for MySQL?**: `https://docs.microsoft.com/en-us/azure/mysql/overview.`
- **What is Azure Database for PostgreSQL?**: `https://docs.microsoft.com/en-us/azure/postgresql/overview`

Securing Your Resources

9

In the previous chapter, we covered designing for the Azure Data Services objective. We've covered some of the different Azure Data Services as well as relational databases in Azure. We also covered backup and security strategies and designing for high availability and performance.

In this chapter, you will learn about the objective of the Design Security and Identity Solutions domains, by covering how to secure your resources, such as using Azure AD Connect, Multi-Factor Authentication (MFA), and more. It also covers how to use the different Identity Providers for your Azure Solutions.

The following topics will be covered:

- Azure Active Directory (Azure AD)
- Azure AD Connect
- Active Directory Federation Services (ADFS)
- Multi-Factor Authentication
- Azure Active Directory Business to Business (Azure AD B2B)
- Azure Active Directory Business to Consumer (Azure AD B2C)

Technical requirements

This chapter uses the following tools for the examples:

- Visual Studio 2017: `https://www.visualstudio.com/downloads/`

The source code for this chapter can be downloaded from the following link:

- `https://github.com/SjoukjeZaal/AzureArchitectureBook/tree/master/Chapter%209/`

Azure Active Directory

Azure Active Directory (Azure AD) offers directory and identity management from the cloud. It offers traditional username and password identity management and roles and permissions management. On top of that, it offers more enterprise solutions, such as MFA and applications monitoring, solution monitoring, and alerting. Azure AD can easily be integrated with your on-premises Active Directory to create a hybrid infrastructure.

Azure AD offers the following pricing plans:

- **Free**: This offers the most basic features, such as support for up to 500,000 objects, SSO, support for Azure AD Connect synchronization, and standard security reports
- **Basic**: This offers no object limit, SLA of 99.9%, Groups, self-service password reset, and support for the Application Proxy
- **Premium P1**: This offers Advanced Reporting, MFA, MDM auto-enrollment, Cloud app discovery, and Azure AD Connect Health
- **Premium P2**: Identity protection and Privileged Identity Management

> For a detailed overview of the different pricing plans and all the features that are offered for each plan, you can refer to the following pricing page: https://azure.microsoft.com/en-us/pricing/details/active-directory/.
> Note that Azure AD Premium is part of the Enterprise Mobility + Security Suite.

Azure AD can be leveraged in your custom apps and APIs as well for authorizing your users and securing your resources. It offers support for industry standard protocols such as OAuth2.0 and OpenID Connect and supports authentication for single and multitenant applications, as well as line of business (LOB) applications.

It offers two different endpoints that can be leveraged in your custom applications:

- **V1 endpoint**: This endpoint offers support for Microsoft work or school accounts only, and it uses the Azure Portal to register the apps in Azure AD. It uses the **Azure Active Directory Library** (**ADAL**) SDK to authenticate users within the application.
- **V2 endpoint**: This offers support for both Microsoft work or school accounts and personal accounts such as Outlook.com. It also offers a new registration portal located at apps.dev.microsoft.com, and that makes it much easier to register your application in Azure AD. It uses the **Microsoft**

Authentication Library (**MSAL**) in order to authenticate your users within the application. Using this endpoint, you can create one single App ID for multiplatform apps. If your applications consist of a separate web, Android, and IoS app, they can all use the same App ID. You can use dynamic consent, where you grant permissions only at the time you need them in the application itself and not up front when registering the app in Azure AD.

Microsoft Graph

Microsoft Graph is a set of APIs that connects multiple Azure services together and provides a single endpoint for developers to use in their custom applications.

Microsoft Graph is made up of relationships between the various Azure services. By calling the endpoint for a particular user, that is added to Azure AD, you can retrieve the documents where the user is working on, find his/her manager, retrieve the users meetings, get a list of devices, and much more.

Azure AD is integrated in Microsoft Graph as well, but it can be leveraged for more than Azure AD features only. In fact, nearly all SaaS products of Azure use Azure AD, such as Office 365, Intune, Dynamic 365, and Azure SQL. All of those Azure services are integrated in Microsoft Graph and can be leveraged inside your apps and APIs.

Microsoft Graph offers two different endpoints, the V1.0 endpoint, which consists of all the APIs that are general available and the beta endpoint, with the latter providing APIs that can still change over time.

To get started with the Graph API and to register your App in Azure AD, you can refer to: `https://developer.microsoft.com/en-us/graph`. This is a great starting point, where you can also download secure sample applications for multiple programming languages.
For an overview of all the Azure services that are integrated in Microsoft Graph, you can refer to this website as well.

Azure AD Connect

Azure AD Connect is a service that you can use to synchronize your on-premises Active Directory identities with Azure. This way, you can use the same identities for authentication on your on-premises environment as well as in the cloud and other SaaS applications.

The Azure AD Connect sync service consists of two parts, the Azure AD Connect sync component, which is a tool that is installed on a separate server inside your on-premises environment, and the Azure AD Connect sync service, which is part of Azure AD. The sync component can sync data from Active Directory and SQL Server to Azure. There is also a third component named the Active Directory Federation Services component, which can be used in a scenario where ADFS is involved. To monitor the on-premises identity infrastructure and the different Azure AD components, you can use a tool named Azure AD Connect Health.

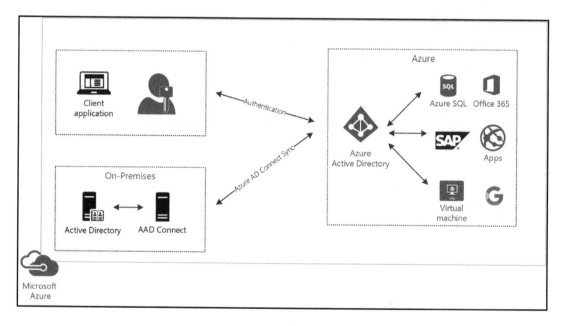

Azure AD Connect architecture

 For more information about how to install Azure AD Connect and syncing the user accounts and passwords, you can refer to https://docs. microsoft.com/en-us/azure/active-directory/connect/active-directory-aadconnect-select-installation. For more information about monitoring the Health, you can refer to: https://docs. microsoft.com/en-us/azure/active-directory/connect-health/ active-directory-aadconnect-health.

Azure AD Connect offers support for your users to sign in with the same passwords to both on-premises as cloud resources. It provides three different authentication methods for this, the password hash synchronization method, the pass-through authentication method, and the Federated SSO method (in conjunction with Active Directory Federation Services).

These three different authentication methods are covered in more detail in the upcoming sections.

Azure Active Directory password hash synchronization

Most organizations only have a requirement to enable user sign-in to Office 365, SaaS applications, and other Azure AD-based resources. The password hash synchronization method is well suitable for those scenario's.

Using this method, hashes of the user's password are synced between the on-premises Active Directory and Azure Active Directory. When there are any changes to the user's password, the password is synced immediately, so users can always log in with the same credentials on-premises as well as in Azure.

This authentication method also provides Azure AD Seamless Single Sign-On (SSO). This way, users are automatically signed in when they are using a domain-joined device on the corporate network. Users only have to enter their username when using Seamless SSO. To use Seamless SSO, you don't have to install additional software or components on the on-premises network. You can push this capability to your users using group policies.

Azure Active Directory pass-through authentication

Azure Active Directory pass-through authentication offers the same capability, such as Azure AD password hash synchronization. Users can log in to their Azure resources as well as on-premises resources using the same credentials. The difference is that passwords aren't synced with Azure AD using pass-through authentication. The passwords are validated using the on-premises Active Directory and are not stored in the Azure Active Directory at all.

This method is suitable for organizations that have security and compliance restrictions and aren't allowed to send usernames and passwords outside the on-premises network.

Pass-through authentication requires an agent to be installed on a domain-joined Windows Server that resides inside the on-premises environment. This agent then listens for password validation requests and only makes an outbound connection from within your network. It also offers support for MFA and Azure AD Conditional Access policies.

Azure AD pass-through authentication offers Azure AD Seamless SSO as well.

Active Directory Federation Services

Active Directory Federation Services (ADFS) is a standards-based service and a feature of Windows Server that you can enable on a Windows Server machine. It provides an authentication provider for external users to log in to an on-premises environment over the internet.

ADFS offers the following features:

- **Web SSO**: This provides SSO for federated users when they access applications that are installed in the on-premises data center.
- **Web Services (WS) - interoperability**: Applications or users that don't use the Windows identity model but are compatible with the WS-Federation specification can still authenticate to the ADFS server and your on-premises applications.
- **No external user account management**: External users can authenticate using their own organization or personal credentials. Inside ADFS, a trust is established using the external authentication provider and ADFS. The user can then federate using Security Assertion Markup Language (SAML) claims.

The Federated SSO Authentication method uses Azure AD Connect in conjunction with ADFS to offer federated Single Sign On to your users. You can deploy ADFS inside your on-premises data center or using Azure VMs. You can use the same Azure AD APIs, such as Microsoft Graph, to connect to your on-premises identities. Azure Active Directory is responsible for connecting to your on-premises environment via ADFS and takes care of the authentication process.

You can also expand the functionality of Azure AD using ADFS. You can implement custom claims or conditional policies that don't exist in Azure AD, or use you organization login screen with additional notifications or information or use a custom MFA provider. You can also create a trust between different environments using ADFS.

Multi-Factor Authentication

In today's world, securing your data and systems is key. MFA adds a second layer of security to user sign-ins and is now a best practice to secure data. It enables two-step verification, where you first sign in with what you know and then with something you have.

Azure MFA uses the following verification methods:

- **Something you know**: This is like a traditional password.
- **Something you have**: This is like a phone, by sending a text message, using a verification app, or receiving a phone call. Azure MFA also supports third-party OAUTH tokens.
- **Something you are**: This is like biometrics, using fingerprints or facial recognition.

Azure MFA is part of Office 365 and Azure services. It is easy to set up, and you can select which verification methods you want to use for your users. When you have requirements to add MFA to on-premises applications that are not published to the cloud using the Azure Application Proxy, you can choose to deploy a on-premises MFA server as well.

 If you want more information about the on-premises MFA Server and which features it offers, you can refer to: `https://docs.microsoft.com/en-us/azure/multi-factor-authentication/multi-factor-authentication-get-started-server`.

Azure MFA is included in the Azure Active Directory Premium Plans and the Enterprise Mobility + Security Suite. You can buy it as a standalone product as well.

You can leverage MFA in your custom applications using the MFA SDK as well. Users can sign in to the app using their existing credentials. The app sends a request to the Azure MFA service, and the Azure MFA service will send a request to a phone or other device. Once the user is authenticated, the Azure MFA service will send the response back to the application so that the user can be signed in. The MFA SDK can be used for multiple programming languages, such as C#, PHP, Ruby, and Java.

Enabling MFA in the Azure Portal

To enable MFA in the Azure Portal, take the following steps:

1. Navigate to the Azure Portal by opening `https://portal.azure.com/`.
2. Click on **Azure Active Directory** in the left menu.

3. In the next blade, click on **Users**. Click on **Multi-Factor Authentication** in the top menu:

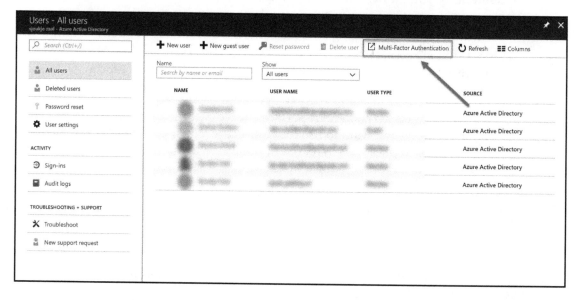

Enabling MFA - Azure Portal

4. The MFA portal is opened where you can enable MFA for each user.

Enabling MFA in Office 365

To enable MFA in the Office 365 admin center, take the following steps:

1. Navigate to the Office 365 admin center by opening `https://portal.office.com/adminportal/home`.
2. Go to **Users | Active Users**. Click **More | Setup Azure mult....** as shown in the following screenshot:

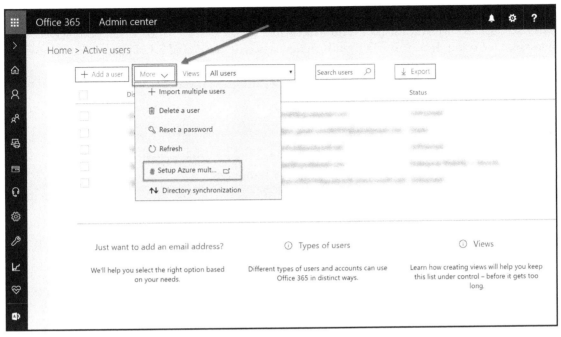

Enabling MFA - Office 365 Admin Center

3. The MFA portal of Office 365 is opened, which looks basically the same as the Azure MFA portal.

Azure Active Directory Business to Business

Azure Active Directory Business to Business (B2B) is a feature on top of Azure Active Directory, which enables organizations to work safely with external users. To be added to Azure B2B, external users don't need to have an Microsoft work or personal account that is added to an existing Azure AD tenant. All sorts of accounts can be added to Azure B2B. You don't have to configure anything in the Azure Portal to use B2B; this feature is enabled by default for all Azure AD tenants.

Azure B2B is integrated with Office 365 for external sharing. It also provides APIs that can be leveraged inside custom applications to let both internal and external users authenticate.

Azure AD Free features are available for external users at no cost. However, if you want external users to use Azure AD Premium features, such as MFA and conditional access, you need to have enough Azure AD Premium licenses with a ratio of 5:1. This means, for every Azure AD Premium license, you can add five external users. So for instance, if your organization wants to add 50 external users to Azure B2B, there should be 10 Azure AD Premium licensed being purchased.

Azure AD B2B offers the following features:

- **Management portal**: Separate portal for the external organization, where administrators can add, manage, and remove users.
- **Groups**: You can create groups for external users. You can use dynamic groups as well. Administrators can set up rules to populate groups based on user attributes.
- **Conditional access**: With conditional access, you can set certain conditions for your users. You can enforce external users to use MFA, or give them access to certain applications or only access from certain locations.
- **Sharing policies**: Not only administrators can invite external users. You can use policies to delegate these permissions to other external users. You can add the Guest Invitor role to the user, which is then allowed to send invites.
- **Auditing and reporting**: Just like normal users, there are auditing and reporting capabilities as well. You can look into the invitation history and acceptance details.

Azure Active Directory Business to Consumer

Azure Active Directory Business to Consumer (B2C) is a cloud identity-management solution for mobile and web applications. It offers out-of-the-box authentication providers that can be leveraged from within your apps and custom APIs using MSAL, which is used in other Azure AD applications as well (using the V2 endpoint).

This means that developers don't have to add additional SDKs manually; that is all handled by Microsoft. Next, to the authentication providers that are offered by Microsoft, it also provides the ability to add your own authentication providers.

Azure AD B2C offers the following authentication providers:

- **Social accounts**: They are Facebook, Google, LinkedIn, and more
- **Enterprise accounts**: They use open standards protocols, such as OpenID Connect or SAML
- **Local accounts**: They are accounts using email address/username and password

Your application needs to be registered inside the Azure B2C tenant. After registration, built-in policies can be configured for the app where you can enable different authentication methods, set claims, enable MFA, or create a password reset policy, that the App can use.

You then add the required configuration settings for the application that is registered in the Azure B2C tenant to your code, and all the earlier-mentioned settings can be used without any further configuration.

 You can refer to the following site for more information about Azure AD B2C: `https://docs.microsoft.com/en-us/azure/active-directory-b2c/active-directory-b2c-overview`.

Leveraging Azure AD B2C in your application

In this demo, we are creating an application that leverages the Azure AD B2C features for authentication. This consists of two steps, first is creating an Azure AD B2C tenant in the Azure Portal, and the second is creating the application.

To create the Azure AD B2C tenant in the Azure Portal, follow these steps:

1. Navigate to the Azure Portal by opening `https://portal.azure.com/`.
2. Click on **New** and type `Azure Active Directory B2C` in the search bar. Create a new tenant:

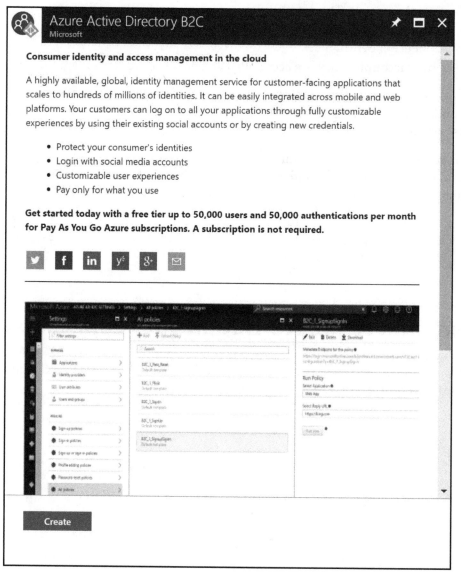

Creating Azure B2C tenant

3. Select **Create a new Azure AD B2C Tenant**, add the following settings, and click on **Create**:

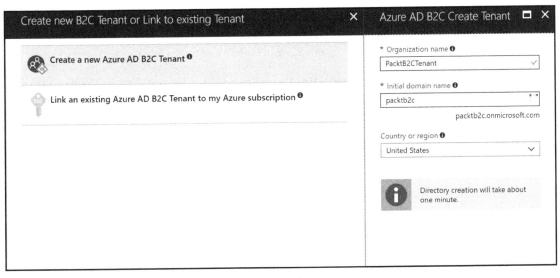

Adding the settings

4. You can select the tenant by opening the menu in the top-right corner of the Azure Portal:

Selecting Azure B2C tenant

5. After creation, you can navigate to the Azure B2C page in the portal.

 You can now set up different authentication providers inside the B2C tenant. For this demo, I've added a Google Identity provider. To add this, you can refer to the tutorial at: `https://docs.microsoft.com/en-us/azure/active-directory-b2c/active-directory-b2c-setup-goog-app`.

6. The next thing to do is to register the application. Click on **Applications** in the left menu and click on the **Add** button:

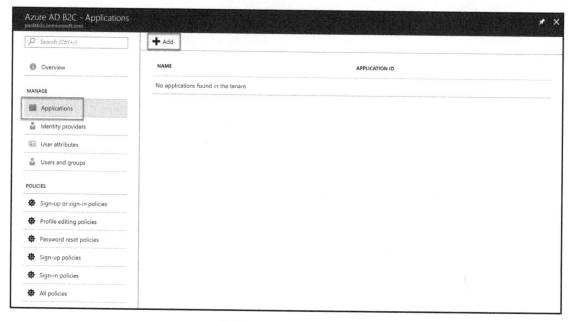

Registering the application in Azure B2C

7. We are going to create a Web App that authenticates to Azure B2C. We are using OpenID Connect sign in, so you have to enable **Allow implicit flow**. You need to add a **Reply URL** as well. Add the following settings and click on **Create**:

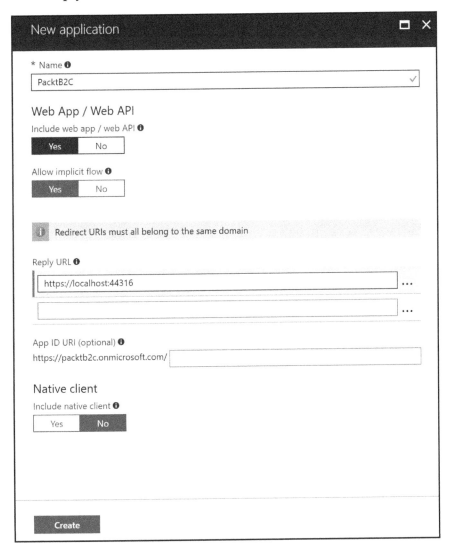

Adding App settings

8. When your app is created, click on the **App**. Copy the **Application ID** to your Notepad. The **Application Key** needs to be copied as well. Click on **Keys** in the left menu and click on **Generate key**:

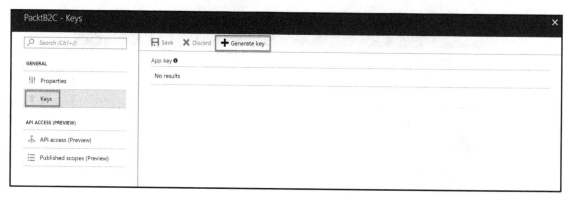

Generating the key

9. Immediately, click on **Save** and copy the key to the Notepad.

10. The next thing to do is to create a Google Identity Provider. Open **Identity providers** in the left menu and click on the **Add** button:

Adding Google Identity Provider

11. In the next blade, select the following settings:

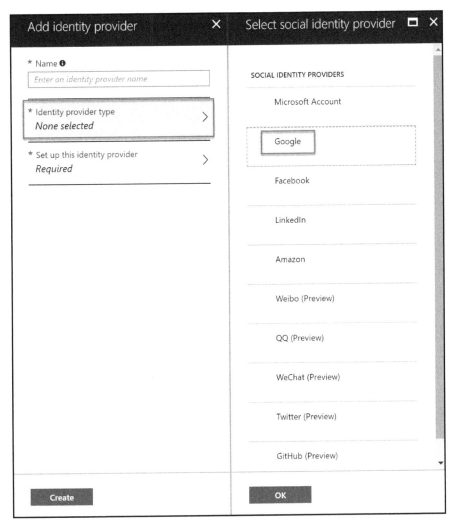

Selecting Google

12. Open a new browser tab and navigate to: `https://console.developers.google.com`. Create a new project and add call it `PacktB2C`. Go back to the API home page and click on **Credentials** in the left menu:

Retrieving App Credentials

13. Click on the **OAuth consent screen** settings in the top menu, add the following, and click on **Save**:

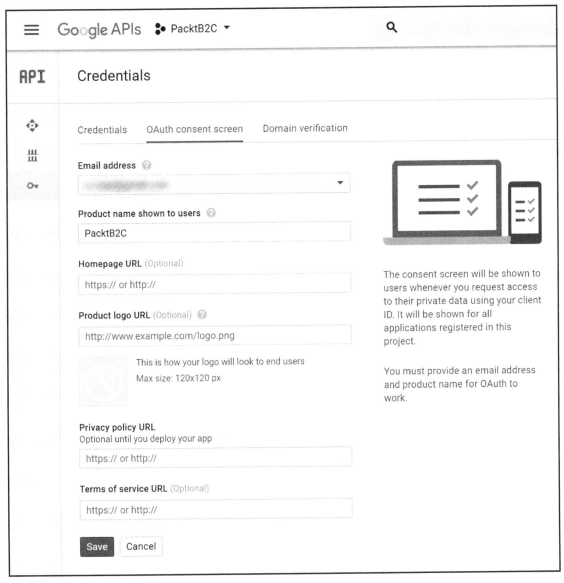

OAuth consent settings

14. Click on the **Credentials** consent settings in the top menu and add the following settings:

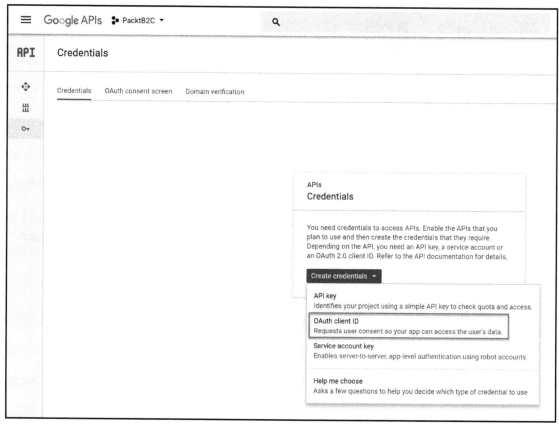

Creating OAuth credentials

15. Add the following settings to create the app:

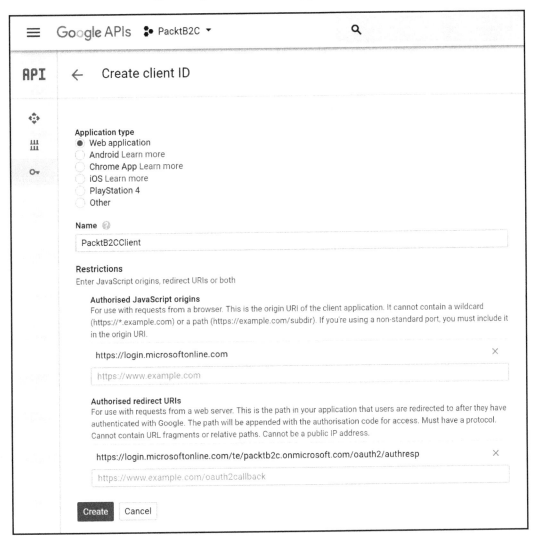

Registering the app

16. A popup appears with the **Client ID** and the **Client secret**. Copy it to the Notepad.

17. Go back to the Azure Portal and add the **Client ID** and the **Client secret** to the blade where we were registering the Identity Provider and click on **OK**:

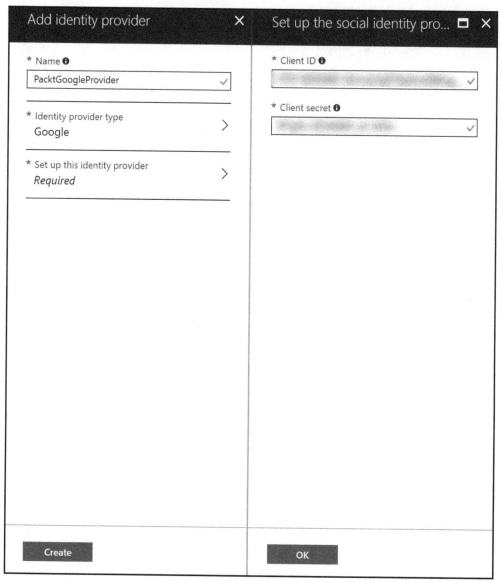

Adding Client ID and Client Secret

18. Next, you have to add **Sign-in Policy**. Click this in the left menu and click on **Add**. Add the following settings:

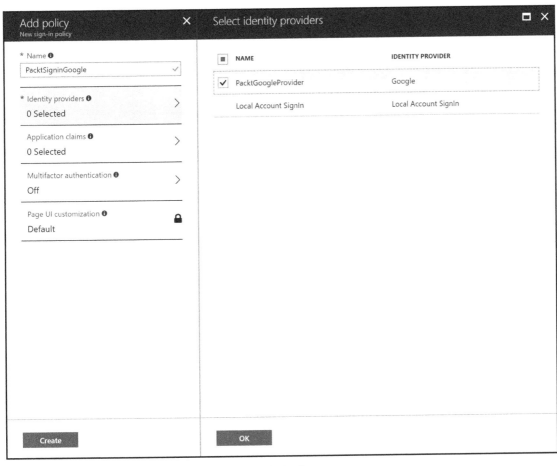

Adding the policy

19. Select the following application claims and click on **OK**, and then click on **Create**:

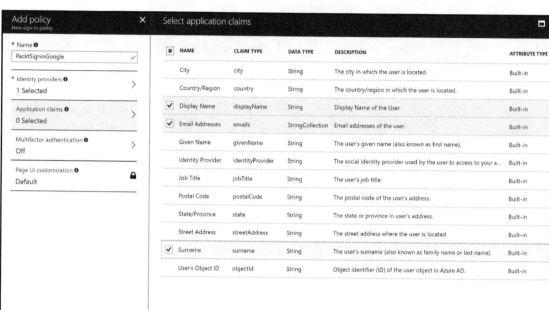

Selecting Google Claims

20. The sample application can be downloaded from GitHub. Open the `Web.config` of the application and update the settings with the values that were copied to the Notepad earlier. It will look as follows:

```
<appSettings>
    <add key="webpages:Version" value="3.0.0.0" />
    <add key="webpages:Enabled" value="false" />
    <add key="ClientValidationEnabled" value="true" />
    <add key="UnobtrusiveJavaScriptEnabled" value="true" />
    <add key="ida:Tenant" value="packtb2c.onmicrosoft.com" />
    <add key="ida:ClientId"
value="0c321f85-2f11-402a-84d7-0e3823947038" />
    <add key="ida:ClientSecret" value="3Tc\(J3.A7w1emrm.v4r|Dxj" />
    <!--<add key="ida:AadInstance"
value="https://login.microsoftonline.com/tfp/{0}/{1}/v2.0/.well-kno
wn/openid-configuration" />-->
    <add key="ida:AadInstance"
value="https://login.microsoftonline.com/{0}/v2.0/.well-known/openi
```

```
d-configuration?p={1}" />
    <add key="ida:RedirectUri" value="https://localhost:44316/" />
    <add key="ida:SignInPolicyId" value="B2C_1_PacktSigninGoogle"
/>
  </appSettings>
```

21. Run the application and click on the **Sign in** button. Make sure that the application runs on the IP address that you've configured in the Azure Portal as the **Reply URL**:

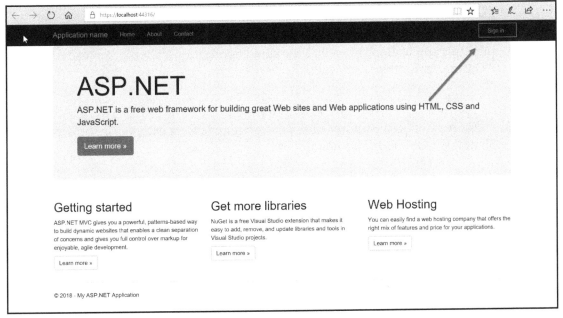

Signing into the application

22. You can now sign in using your Google account.

Summary

In this chapter, we covered how to secure your resources using the different capabilities that Azure provides. We covered Azure Active Directory and how to design a hybrid environment using Azure AD Connect. We covered ADFS, Azure B2B, and Azure B2C.

The next chapter will be about securing your data.

Questions

Answer the following questions to test your knowledge of the information in this chapter. You can find the answers in the *Assessments* section at the end of this book:

1. You are creating a meeting application that leverages data from Office 365. Users should be able to log in using their Azure Active Directory credentials. Can you use Microsoft Graph for this?
    1. Yes
    2. No

2. You want to create a hybrid environment and use single sign-on for both the on-premises applications as well as the cloud applications. Should you use Azure AD Connect for this?
    1. Yes
    2. No

3. Is Azure AD B2B the appropriate solution for enabling external sharing in your SharePoint Online environment?
    1. Yes
    2. No

Further reading

You can check the following links for more information about the topics that have been covered in this chapter:

- **Azure Active Directory Documentation**: https://docs.microsoft.com/en-us/azure/active-directory/
- **Azure AD Connect sync**: Understand and customize synchronization: https://docs.microsoft.com/en-us/azure/active-directory/connect/active-directory-aadconnectsync-whatis
- **Azure AD Connect user sign-in options**: https://docs.microsoft.com/en-us/azure/active-directory/connect/active-directory-aadconnect-user-signin
- **Active Directory Federation Services**: https://msdn.microsoft.com/en-us/library/bb897402.aspx
- **Deploying Active Directory Federation Services in Azure**: https://docs.microsoft.com/en-us/azure/active-directory/connect/active-directory-aadconnect-azure-adfs

- **Multi-factor Authentication Documentation**: `https://docs.microsoft.com/en-us/azure/multi-factor-authentication/`
- **What is Azure AD B2B collaboration?**: `https://docs.microsoft.com/en-us/azure/active-directory/active-directory-b2b-what-is-azure-ad-b2b`
- **Azure Active Directory B2C: Provide sign-up and sign-in to consumers with Microsoft accounts**: `https://docs.microsoft.com/en-us/azure/active-directory-b2c/active-directory-b2c-setup-msa-app`
- **Azure Active Directory B2C: Provide sign-up and sign-in to consumers with Facebook accounts**: `https://docs.microsoft.com/en-us/azure/active-directory-b2c/active-directory-b2c-setup-fb-app`
- **Azure Active Directory B2C: Provide sign-up and sign-in to consumers with Google+ accounts**: `https://docs.microsoft.com/en-us/azure/active-directory-b2c/active-directory-b2c-setup-goog-app`
- **Azure Active Directory B2C: Register your application**: `https://docs.microsoft.com/en-us/azure/active-directory-b2c/active-directory-b2c-app-registration`
- **Azure Active Directory B2C: Enable Multi-Factor Authentication in your consumer-facing applications**: `https://docs.microsoft.com/en-us/azure/active-directory-b2c/active-directory-b2c-reference-mfa`

10
Securing Your Data

In the previous chapter, we covered the securing your resources objective. We covered how to design solutions using Azure Active Directory, Azure B2B, and more. We also covered when to use these different Azure services.

In this chapter, we will cover how to design data security solutions for Azure services, such as using Azure Storage Encryption, Azure Disk Encryption, and Azure Key Vault.

By the end of this chapter, you will know how to secure your data using the different security features in Azure.

The following topics will be covered:

- Azure Key Vault
- Azure Storage Encryption
- Azure Disk Encryption
- Azure SQL Database Security
- Azure AD Managed Service Identity

Technical requirements

This chapter uses the following tools for the examples:

- Azure PowerShell: https://docs.microsoft.com/en-us/powershell/azure/install-azurerm-ps?view=azurermps-5.1.1

The source code for this chapter can be downloaded from the following link:

- `https://github.com/SjoukjeZaal/AzureArchitectureBook/tree/master/Chapter%2010`

Azure Key Vault

You can store cryptographic keys and secrets in Azure Key Vault, which can be used by various Azure services and custom applications. Azure uses it for storing keys for Azure Storage Service Encryptions and Azure Disk Encryption, which are covered later in this chapter. However, for instance, you can store your App client ID and secret in there as well and retrieve this inside your custom application. This way, you don't have to store these IDs and secrets in your web.config anymore, and they can be managed from one place, where it is secured and protected, inside the Azure Portal. You can store certificates and other authentication keys in there as well, and it offers a monitoring solution for key usage. Azure Key Vault is integrated with Azure AD, so you can set access policies on different users and groups to access the keys that are stored in there.

Azure Key Vault comes in two service tiers:

- **Standard**: This offers Geographic scaling and available.
- **Premium**: This offers Geo-availability and support for Hardware Security Modules (HSMs), by providing backups for HSM keys. HSMs are special computers that are only used for cryptographic operations. Handling this on the hardware itself offers better performance and security. The keys and secrets are encrypted in Azure Key Vault with adding some extra properties, which makes sure that it can only be used by that particular HSM.

Creating an Azure Key Vault in the Azure Portal

To create an Azure Key Vault Service in the Azure Portal and add a key, secret, and certificate to it, take the following steps:

1. Navigate to the Azure Portal by opening `https://portal.azure.com/`.
2. Click on **New** and type `Key Vault` in the search bar. Create a new Key Vault:

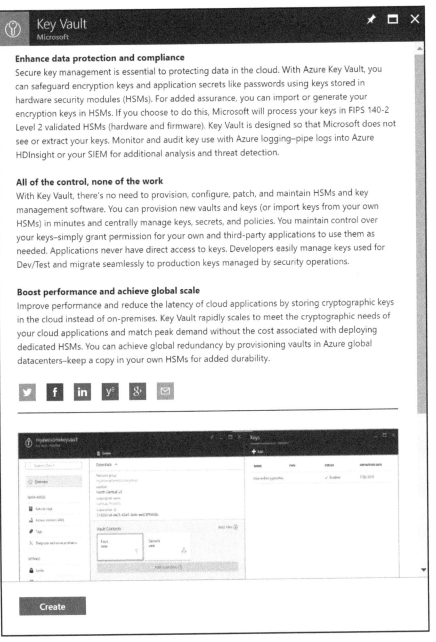

Enhance data protection and compliance

Secure key management is essential to protecting data in the cloud. With Azure Key Vault, you can safeguard encryption keys and application secrets like passwords using keys stored in hardware security modules (HSMs). For added assurance, you can import or generate your encryption keys in HSMs. If you choose to do this, Microsoft will process your keys in FIPS 140-2 Level 2 validated HSMs (hardware and firmware). Key Vault is designed so that Microsoft does not see or extract your keys. Monitor and audit key use with Azure logging–pipe logs into Azure HDInsight or your SIEM for additional analysis and threat detection.

All of the control, none of the work

With Key Vault, there's no need to provision, configure, patch, and maintain HSMs and key management software. You can provision new vaults and keys (or import keys from your own HSMs) in minutes and centrally manage keys, secrets, and policies. You maintain control over your keys–simply grant permission for your own and third-party applications to use them as needed. Applications never have direct access to keys. Developers easily manage keys used for Dev/Test and migrate seamlessly to production keys managed by security operations.

Boost performance and achieve global scale

Improve performance and reduce the latency of cloud applications by storing cryptographic keys in the cloud instead of on-premises. Key Vault rapidly scales to meet the cryptographic needs of your cloud applications and match peak demand without the cost associated with deploying dedicated HSMs. You can achieve global redundancy by provisioning vaults in Azure global datacenters–keep a copy in your own HSMs for added durability.

Creating a new Azure Key Vault

3. Add the following settings and click on **Create**:

Adding Azure Key Vault settings

4. Once the Key Vault is created, you can add a key and secret from the left menu:

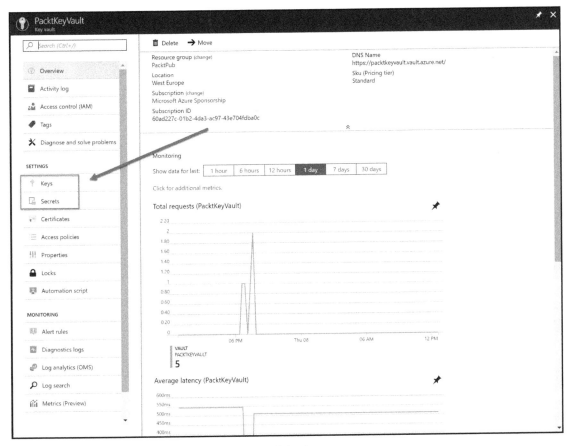

Key Vault settings

5. Click on **Keys** and then on **Generate/Import**. Here, you can set a number of settings, such as the key type and key size. Add the following settings and click on **Create**:

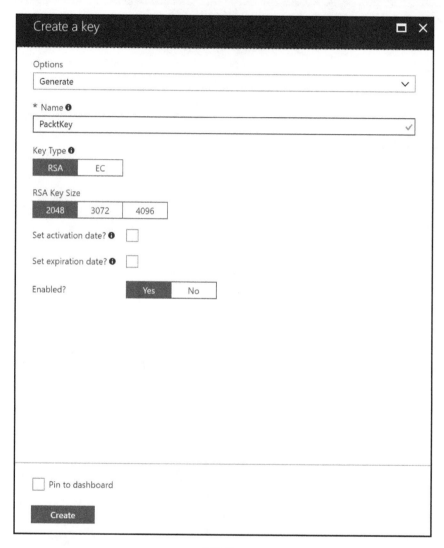

Adding Key

6. If you click on the **Key** and go to the properties of it, you can see that you can use this key for a number of operations; you can **Encrypt**, **Decrypt**, **Sign**, and **Verify** data, or you can protect another key using the **Wrap Key** and **Unwrap Key** operations:

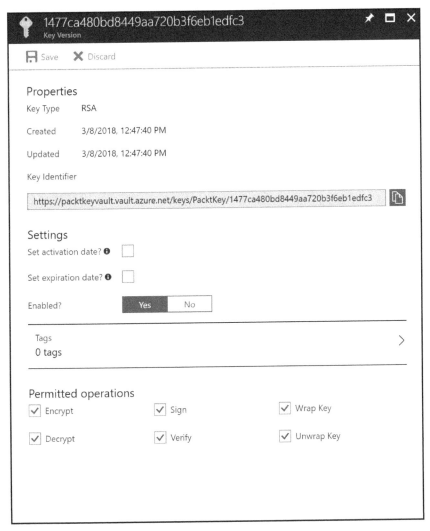

Key properties

7. To create a secret, click on **Secret** in the left menu and click
    on **Generate/Import**. For instance, you can add an App key and an App secret to
    this. Add the following settings and click on **Create**:

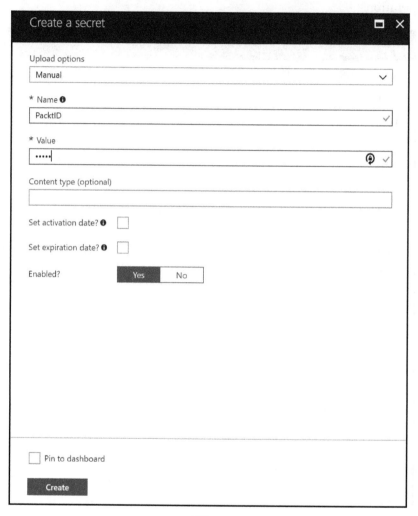

Add Secret

8. To create or upload a certificate, click on **Certificate** in the left menu and click on **Generate/Import**. You can add Certificate Authorities in here as well and let them issue the certificate. We are now creating a Self-Signed certificate for this example:

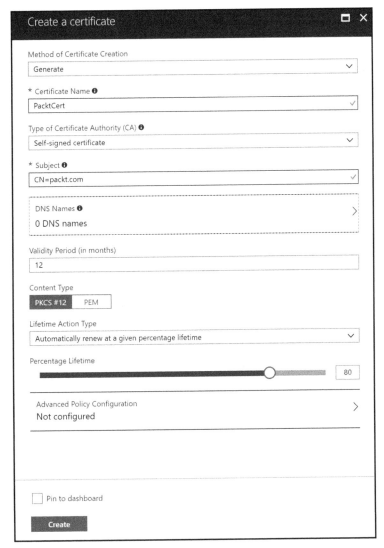

Creating Certificate

9. Click on **Create**. It may take some time before the certificate is created.

Azure Key Vault secrets in ARM templates

Besides leveraging the Azure Key Vault in your custom applications, you can also use secrets in ARM templates. You can add the secrets to the parameters JSON file. See the following example to see what your parameter will look like:

```
"packtPassword": {
"reference": {
"keyVault": {
    "id": "/subscriptions/<subscription
id>/resourceGroups/examplegroup/providers/Microsoft.KeyVault/vaults/<vault-
name>"
            },
        "secretName": "packtsecret"
    }
},
```

This should give you an impression of how to embed secrets in your ARM templates. For a complete tutorial about how to create ARM templates, you can refer to the following article: https://docs.microsoft.com/en-us/azure/azure-resource-manager/resource-manager-keyvault-parameter.

Azure Storage Service Encryption

Azure Storage provides encryption for data at rest by default using Azure Storage Service Encryption (SSE). Data gets secured when it is in transit between the Application and Azure using HTTPS, and it gets encrypted when it is written to the storage account using 256-bit AES encryption. You can use SMB 3.0 or a VPN connection for safely transferring the data to Azure as well. Once the data is accessed again, it get's decrypted, and it is sent back over HTTPS. Azure manages the encryption storage keys inside Azure Key Vault automatically. SSE is used for Table, File, Queue, and Blob Storage, and SSE is available for the Standard and Premium pricing plans, for all redundancy levels, and for all regions.

You can set encryption for your storage account in the Azure Portal, PowerShell, CLI, the REST API, and the Azure Storage SDK. It is enabled by default, so you don't have to set this in your PowerShell scripts manually:

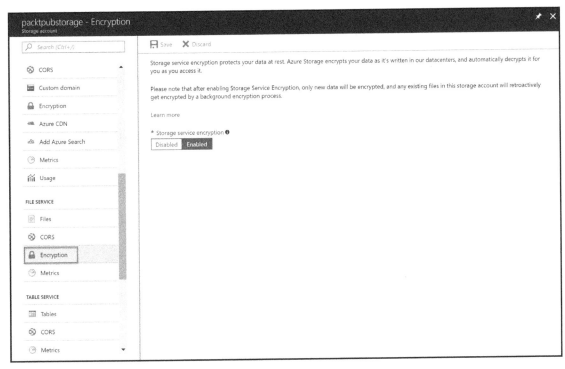

Azure Storage Service Encryption settings

You can use client-side encryption in your custom code as well. The Azure Storage Client Library for .NET supports this. This also works in conjunction with the Azure Key Vault. The SDK creates a Content Encryption Key (CEK), which is used to encrypt the data before it is sent to the storage account. The encryption key is then stored in the Azure Key Vault by default, but you can use a custom provider as well. Using client-side encryption will encrypt your data before it is sent to Azure, and at the moment that it is stored inside the storage account.

SSE has one limitation, that is, only the data that is created when encryption is turned on will get encrypted. So, if you have disabled encryption for your storage account at some point, data that is stored inside the storage account is not encrypted anymore. When you decide to enable encryption again, the data that was stored earlier does not get encrypted automatically, as data is only encrypted at the time of storing the data. You have to remove and upload this data again to get it encrypted.

Azure Disk Encryption

Azure Disk Encryption encrypts Windows and Linux VM disks. For Windows disks, it uses Bitlocker, and for Linux, dm-crypt is used, which are both industry standards. Azure Key Vault is used to manage the encryption keys, just like Azure Storage Encryption.

For all VM types, Azure Disk Encryption is available in all Azure regions and can be set using PowerShell. You can use the following commands to set the encryption:

```
Login-AzureRmAccount
```

If necessary, select the right subscription:

```
Select-AzureRmSubscription -SubscriptionId "********-****-****-****-
***********"
```

We are using the Azure Key Vault to store the encryption keys, which we created earlier. We are using the VM that was created in the first chapter here as well (make sure that the VM is running; otherwise, you get an error running the script). Both are created in the same Resource Group. So, fill in the Key Vault name, the Resource Group of the Key Vault, and the VM and encrypt the VM. It uses an App in Azure AD, which is used to write the secrets in the Key Vault. You need to create the app first and replace the App ID and secret in the script. It may take some time before it is fully encrypted:

```
$RGName = "PacktPub"
$VMName = "W16PacktServer"
$AADClientID = "PacktADApp"
$AADClientSecret = "PacktSecret"
$VaultName= "PacktKeyVault"

$KeyVault = Get-AzureRmKeyVault -VaultName $VaultName -ResourceGroupName
$RGName
$DiskEncryptionKeyVaultUrl = $KeyVault.VaultUri
$KeyVaultResourceId = $KeyVault.ResourceId

Set-AzureRmVMDiskEncryptionExtension -ResourceGroupName $RGName -VMName
$VMName -AadClientID $AADClientID -AadClientSecret $AADClientSecret -
DiskEncryptionKeyVaultUrl $DiskEncryptionKeyVaultUrl -
DiskEncryptionKeyVaultId $KeyVaultResourceId
```

Azure SQL Database Security

Azure SQL Database also offers various features for data security. It offers security for data in transit, data in rest, and data in use. To accomplish this, it is using the following features:

- **HTTPS**: This offers security for data in transit. Data is transferred using a secure connection over HTTPS.
- **Transparent Data Encryption**: This offers security for data at rest. It performs real-time encryption and decryption of the database, backup files, and logs. This is used for Azure Data Warehouse as well. It is using a database encryption key that is stored by Azure by default, but can be stored in Azure Key Vault as well. Newly created databases are encrypted by default. You can disable and enable the encryption inside the settings in the Azure Portal, PowerShell, and the REST API:

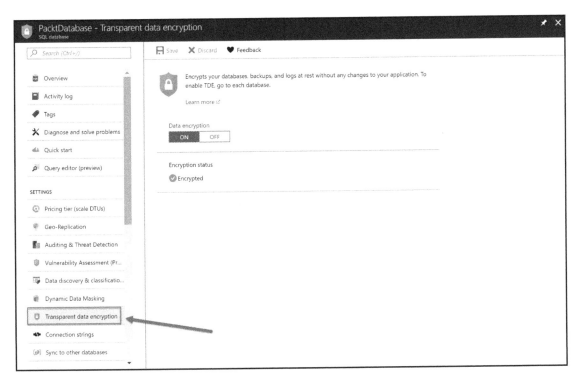

Transparent Data Encryption in the Azure Portal

- **Always Encrypted**: This offers security for data in use. It offers encryption for confidential data inside the database. For instance, social security numbers or credit card numbers are stored encrypted in the database and are decrypted inside the application for those who have permission to access it. You can enable **Always Encrypted** for columns in the database using SQL Server Management Studio or PowerShell. To encrypt sensitive data from the application, you can use the .NET Framework Data Provider for SQL Server.

Azure Active Directory Managed Service Identity

Azure Active Directory Managed Service Identity is, by the time of writing this book, still in preview. It offers a managed identity for all resources in Azure that are using Azure Active Directory.

When you enable MSI on your Azure resource, such as an Azure Virtual Machine, Azure Function, or App, Azure will create a Service Principal and stores the credentials of that Service Principal on to the Azure resource itself. When it is time to authenticate, an MSI endpoint is called, passing your current Azure AD credentials and a reference to the specific resource. MSI then retrieves the stored credentials from the Azure resource, passes it to Azure AD, and retrieves an access token that can be used to authenticate to the Azure resource or service.

 You should note that the Service Principal is only known inside the boundaries of the specific Azure resource where it is stored. If it needs permissions toward other resources as well, you should assign the appropriate role using **Role-Based Access Control** (**RBAC**) in Azure AD.

You can enable MSI for your Azure resources in the Azure Portal, PowerShell, CLI, and ARM templates:

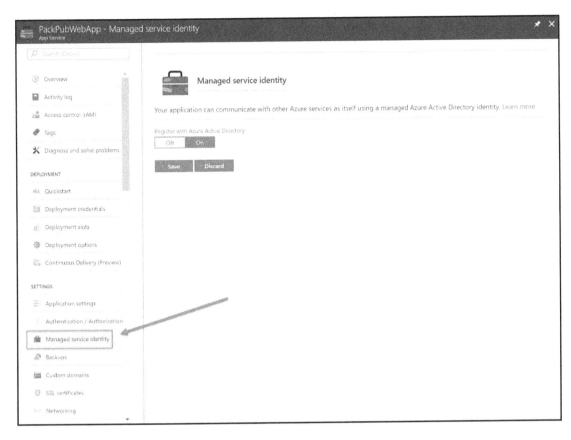

Managed Service Identity Settings for an App Service

From your custom code, you can call the MSI endpoint to get an access token to authenticate the Azure resource as well. For .NET applications, you can use the `Microsoft.Azure.Services.AppAuthentication` library to accomplish this. You can do this by calling the REST API as well, but then you have to create the request manually.

> You can refer to the following GitHub page at `https://github.com/ Azure-Samples/app-service-msi-keyvault-dotnet` for an example of an application that uses MSI.

Summary

In this chapter, we covered how to secure your data using the different services that Azure provides. We covered Azure Key Vault, Azure Storage Service Encryption, Azure Disk Encryption, and more. Now you should know when and how to use these technologies in your solutions.

The next chapter will be the last chapter on this objective, *Governance and Policies*.

Questions

Answer the following questions to test your knowledge of the information in this chapter. You can find the answers in the *Assessments* section at the end of this book.

1. You want to add an additional layer of security to your applications. Credit card numbers need to be stored encrypted inside Azure SQL Database. Should you use Data Masking?
    1. Yes
    2. No

2. You are developing a custom application and don't want to add the App ID and App Secret to your web.config. Can you store these credentials in the Azure Key Vault and retrieve them dynamically when the application is executed?
    1. Yes
    2. No

3. Does Azure Disk Encryption encrypt data at rest and data in transit?
    1. Yes
    2. No

Further reading

You can check the following links for more information about the topics that were covered in this chapter:

- **Key Vault Documentation**: https://docs.microsoft.com/en-us/azure/key-vault/
- **Use Azure Key Vault to pass secure parameter value during deployment**: https://docs.microsoft.com/en-us/azure/azure-resource-manager/resource-manager-keyvault-parameter
- **Use Azure Key Vault to protect application secrets**: https://docs.microsoft.com/en-us/azure/architecture/multitenant-identity/key-vault
- **Get started with Azure Key Vault certificates**: https://blogs.technet.microsoft.com/kv/2016/09/26/get-started-with-azure-key-vault-certificates/
- **Azure Storage Service Encryption for Data at Rest**: https://docs.microsoft.com/en-us/azure/storage/common/storage-service-encryption
- **Securing your SQL Database**: https://docs.microsoft.com/en-us/azure/sql-database/sql-database-security-overview
- **Always Encrypted**: https://docs.microsoft.com/en-us/sql/relational-databases/security/encryption/always-encrypted-database-engine
- **Managed Service Identity (MSI) for Azure resources**: https://docs.microsoft.com/en-us/azure/active-directory/managed-service-identity/overview

11
Governance and Policies

In the previous chapter, we covered how to secure your data using the various technologies that Azure has to offer and when to use them. We covered Azure Key Vault, Azure Storage Service Encryption, Azure Disk Encryption, and more.

In this chapter, we will cover Governance and Policies, such as standard and custom roles in Azure, when to use Azure Role-Based Access Control, Azure Resource Policies, and more.

By the end of this chapter, you will know how to design a mechanism of governance and policies as well as managing security risks.

The following topics will be covered:

- Azure Role-Based Access Control
- Azure Resource Policies
- Azure AD Privileged Identity Management
- Azure AD Identity Protection
- Azure Security Center
- Operations Management Suite - Security and Compliance

Technical requirements

This chapter uses the following tools for the examples:

- Azure PowerShell: `https://docs.microsoft.com/en-us/powershell/azure/install-azurerm-ps?view=azurermps-5.1.1`

The source code for this chapter can be downloaded from the following link:

- `https://github.com/SjoukjeZaal/AzureArchitectureBook/tree/master/Chapter%2011`

Azure Role-Based Access Control

With Role-Based Access Control (RBAC) in Azure, you can implement the principle of least permissions and give users the exact permissions they need to do their jobs properly. Users, groups, and applications are added to roles in Azure, and those roles have certain permissions. You can use the built-in roles that Azure offers or you can create custom roles in RBAC.

The roles in Azure can be added to a certain scope. A Scope can be an Azure Subscription, an Azure Resource Group, or Web App, for instance. Azure then uses access inheritance. Roles added to a parent resource give access to child resources automatically. For instance, a group that is added to an Azure Subscription gets access to all the Resource Groups and underlying resources that are in that subscription as well. A user that is added to a virtual machine only gets access to that particular VM:

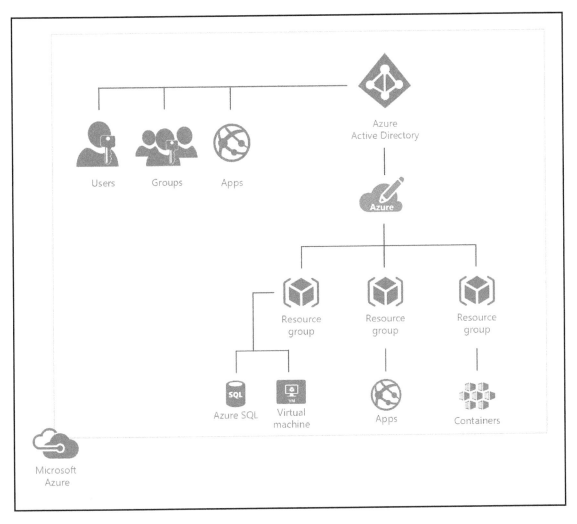

Role-based Access Control inheritance

Within each Azure Subscription, you can grant up to 2,000 role assignments, which can be set from the Azure Portal, PowerShell, CLI, and the REST API.

Built-in Roles

Azure offers various built-in roles that you can use for assigning permissions to users, groups, and applications. RBAC offers the following three standard roles that you can assign to each Azure resource:

- **Owner**: Users in this role can manage everything and can create new resources
- **Contributor**: Users in this role can manage everything just like users in the owner role, but they can't assign access to others
- **Reader**: Users in this role can read everything, but are not allowed to make any changes

Besides the standard roles, each Azure resource also has roles that are scoped to particular resources. For instance, you can assign users, groups, or applications to the SQL Security Manager, where they can manage all security-related policies of the Azure SQL Servers, or you can assign them to the Virtual Machine Contributor role, where they can manage the VMs, but not the VNet or Storage account, which are connected to the VM.

For an overview of all the built-in roles that Azure offers, you can refer to `https://docs.microsoft.com/en-us/azure/active-directory/role-based-access-built-in-roles`.

Custom Roles

You can also create custom roles in RBAC when none of the built-in roles suit your needs. Custom roles can be assigned to the exact same resources as built-in roles and can only be created using PowerShell, CLI, and the REST API. You can't create them in the Azure Portal. In each Azure tenant, there can be up to 2,000 roles which have been created.

Custom roles are defined in JSON, and after deployment, they are stored inside the Azure AD tenant. By storing them inside the Azure AD tenant, they can be used in all the different Azure Subscriptions that are connected to the Azure AD tenant.

Creating a Custom Role

In the next example, we are creating a custom role that can only restart virtual machines in Azure. We are assigning that role to my user account inside the JSON file as well:

1. You can define the custom role using the following JSON code. You should set the Id to null because the custom roles gets an ID assigned at creation. We will add the custom role to two Azure Subscriptions:

```
{
  "Name": "Packt Custom Role",
  "Id": null,
  "IsCustom": true,
  "Description": "Allows for read access to Azure Storage, Network
and Compute resources and access to support",
  "Actions": [
    "Microsoft.Compute/*/read",
    "Microsoft.Storage/*/read",
  "Microsoft.Network/*/read",
  "Microsoft.Resources/subscriptions/resourceGroups/read",
    "Microsoft.Support/*"
  ],
  "NotActions": [
  ],
  "AssignableScopes": [
    "/subscriptions/********-****-****-****-************",
    "/subscriptions/********-****-****-****-************"
  ]
}
```

2. Save the JSON file in a folder named CustomRoles on the C: drive of your computer. Then, run the following PowerShell script to create the role. First, log in to your Azure account:

```
Login-AzureRmAccount
```

3. Then, create the custom role in Azure by importing the JSON file in PowerShell:

```
New-AzureRmRoleDefinition -InputFile
"C:\CustomRoles\PacktCustomRole.json"
```

4. Navigate to the Azure Portal by opening: `https://portal.azure.com/`.
5. Go to **Subscriptions** and select one of the subscriptions where the role was added in the JSON file. Then, click on **Access control (IAM)** | **Add**.
6. Select **Role** in the next blade. The custom role will be in the list:

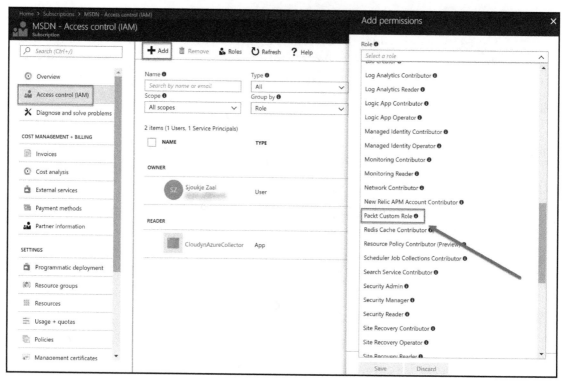

Custom Role in the Azure Portal

Azure Resource Policies

In Azure, you can create policies where you can define and enforce rules and actions for your Azure resources. Azure policies differ from RBAC because this is not about users, groups, or applications that need access, but Azure policies are about applying your organization's governance strategy. Azure can scan your resources, so they stay compliant with company rules and SLAs. For instance, you can create a policy that evaluates all virtual machines that use Managed Disks.

For creating policies, users must be granted the owner role in RBAC, or a custom role needs to be created where the following permissions need to be added to the JSON file:

- **To define policies**: `Microsoft.Authorization/policydefinitions/write`
- **To assign policies**: `Microsoft.Authorization/policyassignments/write`

Policies can be created using the Azure Portal, PowerShell, and CLI.

 To create a policy from the Azure Portal, you can refer to the following tutorial: `https://docs.microsoft.com/en-us/azure/azure-policy/assign-policy-definition`.

Azure AD Privileged Identity Management

Azure AD Privileged Identity Management (PIM) is an Azure AD Premium P2 or Enterprise Mobility + Security E5 feature. With PIM, you can manage and control all access inside the Azure AD tenant, such as access to Azure resources, Office 365, Intune, and Azure AD.

In RBAC, you can grant permanent role access. With PIM, you can grant eligible role access to users. Users that don't need permanent access to resources can request access for a predetermined amount of time when certain type of permissions are needed. For instance, a user can request temporary SharePoint Administrator permissions. This request can be approved by the Delegated Approver, and the permissions are deactivated when the user is done.

PIM uses the following flow:

- **User Request**: The users requests access using an online form for specific permissions for a predefined amount of time
- **Request Review**: The request gets reviewed by administrators inside the PIM Portal
- **Approval**: The request can be approved, and the user is added to the required role
- **Notification**: The user gets notified by email
- **User performs the action**: User signs in to Azure resource using MFA and Azure AD Privileged Identity Management elevates their privileges for a specific time-bound duration

- **Monitoring**: The monitoring team can track all the elevations in the PIM Portal

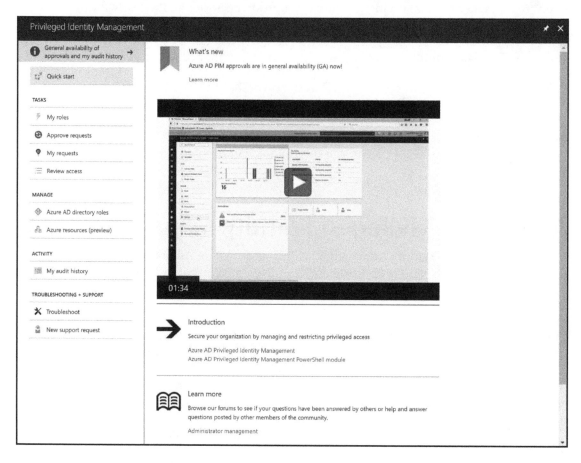

Azure AD Privileged Identity Management overview

Azure AD Identity Protection

Azure AD Identity Protection is a feature that is included in the Azure AD Premium P2 license. It offers premium protection for your identities in Azure by offering detection of identity-based security issues. It helps discovering compromised identities, offers conditional access policies, remediation of security events, and support for investigating security events. Azure uses machine learning algorithms for detection and generates reports and alerts to resolve threats.

Azure AD Identity Protection offers the following policies:

- **MFA Registration**: Here, you can assign the MFA policy where you can enforce your users to log in using MFA.
- **User Risk Policy**: This policy allows you to block users from signing in or enforce them to change their password to a more secure password.
- **Sign-in Risk Policy**: This policy offers protection when users sign in from unfamiliar locations. You can enforce them to use MFA when signing in from that particular location.

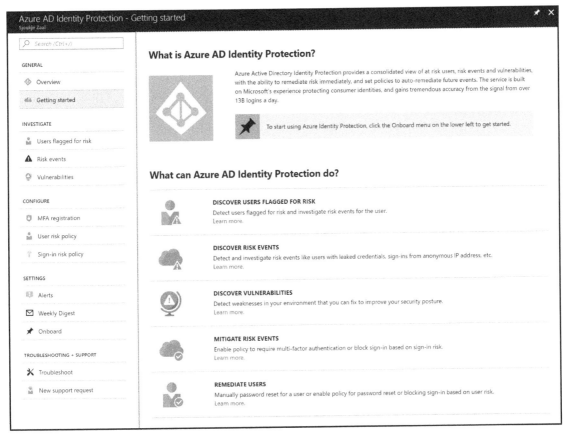

Azure AD Identity Protection overview

Azure Security Center

Azure Security Center provides Advanced Threat Protection and Security management for all the Azure resources that are available inside an Azure AD tenant and on-premises resources in a hybrid environment. It is integrated in the Azure Portal, and it offers the following features:

- **Centralized Policy Management**: You can manage all security policies for resources in the hybrid environment from a central place. Azure Resource Policies are integrated with Azure Security Center.
- **Continuous Security Assessment**: This offers a security monitoring solution for all virtual machines, Apps, VNets, and Storage accounts.
- **Actionable Recommendations**: This offers recommendations to remediate vulnerabilities and potential threats from the Azure Portal.
- **Advanced Cloud Defenses**: This offers JIT access to ports and whitelisting applications deployed on VMs.
- **Prioritized alerts and incidents**: This offers prioritized alerts to focus on the biggest vulnerabilities and threats first.
- **Integrated security solutions**: You can integrate Azure Security Center with third-party solutions to collect data from various resources.

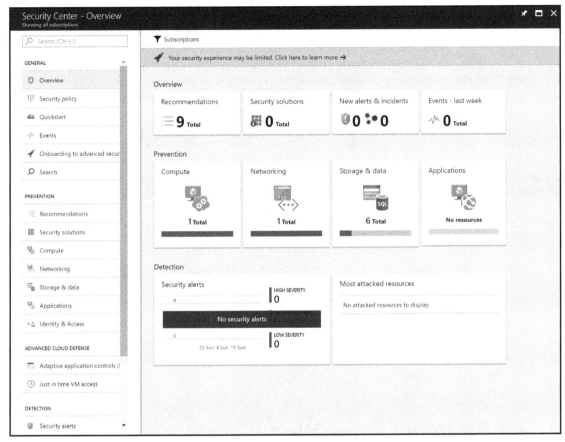

Azure Security Center overview

Azure Security Centers offers two different pricing tiers:

- **Free**: All Azure Subscriptions get the free access tier out of the box. It offers security policies, continuous security assessments, and actionable security recommendations.
- **Standard**: This offers all the features from the **Free** plan, but now for hybrid environments. It also offers Advanced Threat Detection, which will be covered later in this chapter, and Advanced Cloud Defenses.

 For a complete tutorial on how to create security policies, you can refer to `https://docs.microsoft.com/en-us/azure/security-center/security-center-azure-policy`. Note that Azure Policies are still in preview by the time of writing this book.

Advanced Threat Detection

Advanced Threat Detection monitors the security information of all the Azure resources that are inside an Azure Subscription, hybrid environments, and connected third-party solutions. It analyzes the data to detect potential threats, and when it identifies a threat, it will create a security alert. This security alert provides detailed information about the threat, and it provides suggestions about how to solve the threat.

Azure uses machines learning algorithms to help detect threats. These algorithms are used inside the entire Azure Cloud fabric and can be leveraged for all type of accounts, such as enterprise accounts and accounts for smaller organizations and personal accounts. They can all benefit from all the data that Microsoft has analyzed in the past decade.

Azure Security Center provides three types of threat reports that are generated using Advance Threat Detection. These reports can vary according to the attack:

- **Activity Group Report**: This provides information about the attackers, such as the identities or associations, the objectives and the tactics, and tools and procedures of the attackers.
- **Campaign Report**: This provides information about the current and historical attack campaigns.
- **Threat Summary Report**: This combines all the information from the previously mentioned reports.

Azure Endpoint Protection

Azure Endpoint Protection is a feature that enables anti-malware protection for your Azure VMs and on-premises VMs that are connected to Azure Security Center. In Azure Security Center, you can monitor the status of anti-malware protection for your VMs.

To enable Endpoint Protection for your VMs, you have to do this from the Azure Security Center.

Follow these steps to create VM from the Azure Portal:

1. Navigate to the Azure Portal by opening: `https://portal.azure.com/`.
2. Click on **Security Center** in the left menu. Make sure that the **Overview** page is opened. Under the **Prevention** tab, click on **Compute**:

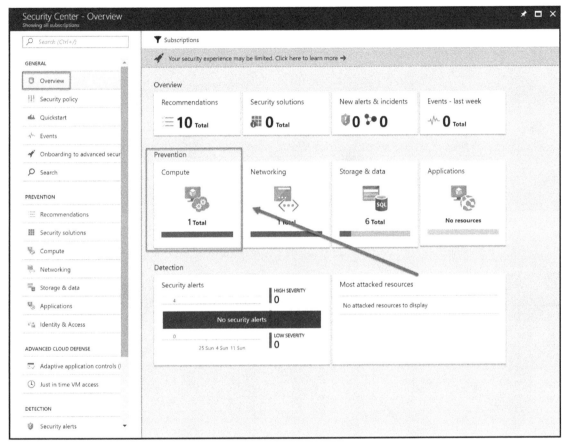

Endpoint Protection in Azure Security Center

3. When Endpoint Protection is not installed on your VMs, you will see a recommendation inside the reporting tool. Click on the **RECOMMENDATIONS**:

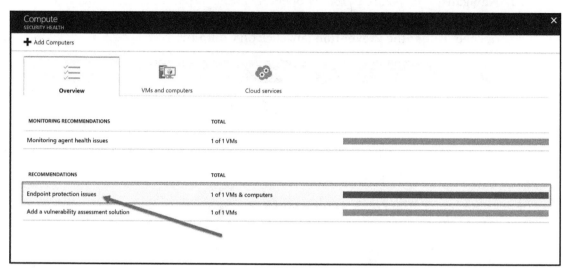

Endpoint Protection recommendation in the Azure Security Center

4. In the next blade, click on **Endpoint Protection not installed on Azure VMs**:

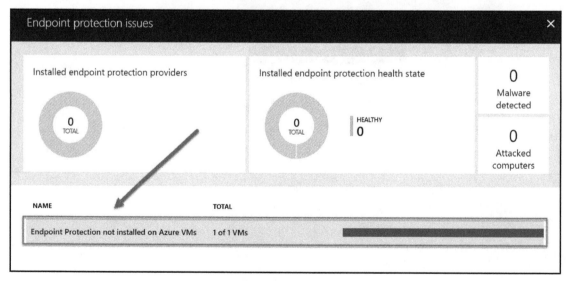

Endpoint Protection settings

5. You can now select the VM on which you want to install Endpoint Protection, and select the **Microsoft Antimalware** solution to install it:

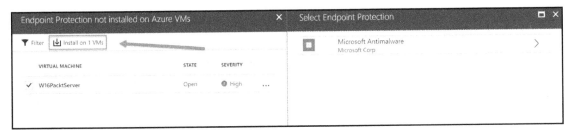

Installing Endpoint Protection on the VM

6. Click on **Create**, and now you can set some additional settings, such as excluding files and location, files and extensions, and processes. Leave the default settings in here and click on **OK** and then **Create** to install Endpoint protection on your VM:

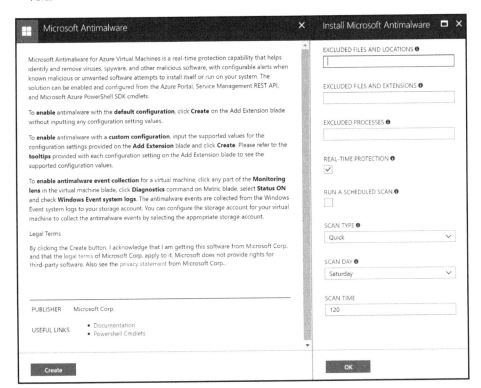

Install Endpoint Protection on the VM

Operations Management Suite - Security and Compliance

Operations Management Suite (**OMS**) is a hybrid cloud and data management tool from Microsoft, hosted in Azure, to manage your on-premises and Azure infrastructure from one single place. With OMS, you can manage large hybrid environments easily. Besides Azure, OMS can also manage and protect AWS, Windows Server, Linux, VMWare, and OpenStack environments and machines. OMS offers different management solutions, and one of them is the Security and Compliance Solution.

To manage and protect VMs and servers, an agent needs to be installed, which collects all the data for OMS. To collect data from Azure, you need to create a **Log Analytics Workspace**. This workspace is created automatically when you associate your Azure Subscription with OMS.

 You can associate OMS with your Azure Subscription from: `https://www.microsoft.com/en-us/cloud-platform/operations-management-suite`. You can create a Log Analytics Workspace from the Azure Portal as well. For more information about how to create this, you can refer to: `https://docs.microsoft.com/en-us/azure/log-analytics/`.

To install the agent and connect Azure VMs to OMS, you can open the Log Analytics Workspace from the Azure Portal, click on **Virtual machines** in the left menu, and connect your VM to the workspace:

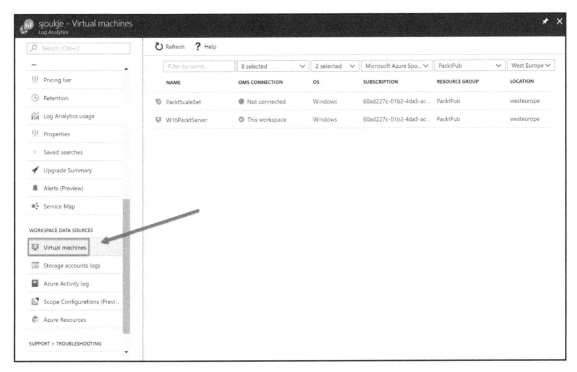

Connect VM to OMS

The data will now be displayed in the OMS Portal. OMS offers a **Security and Audit** dashboard, which provides the following areas of information:

- **Security Domains**: This will provide information about security records, such as malware assessments, network security, identity, and access information
- **Notable Issues**: This will give information about current threats and issues
- **Detections (Preview)**: This helps identify attack patterns by visualization of alerts

- **Threat Intelligence**: This visualizes the total number of servers with different threats and a map that shows from which IP address the threats are coming

OMS Security and Audit dashboard

Summary

In this chapter, we covered how to design a mechanism of governance and policies for administering Azure resources and how to manage security risks using an appropriate security solution.

This concludes the Design Security and Identities objective. In the next chapter, we will be looking at the Design Solutions using Platform Services objective. The first chapter will be about Artificial Intelligence, IoT, and Azure Media Services.

Questions

Answer the following questions to test your knowledge of the information in this chapter. You can find the answers in the *Assessments* section at the end of this book.

1. Can you grant eligible role access to users with Azure AD Privileged Identity Management?
    1. Yes
    2. No

2. Can you manage your on-premises and Azure infrastructure with the Operations Management Suite?
    1. Yes
    2. No

3. You want to check whether all virtual machines inside your Azure Subscription use Managed Disks. Can you use Azure Resource Policies for this?
    1. Yes
    2. No

Further reading

You can check the following links for more information about the topics that were covered in this chapter:

- **Get started with Role-Based Access Control in the Azure portal**: https://docs.microsoft.com/en-us/azure/active-directory/role-based-access-control-what-is
- **Use Role-Based Access Control to manage access to your Azure Subscription resources**: https://docs.microsoft.com/en-us/azure/active-directory/role-based-access-control-configure
- **Create custom roles for Azure Role-Based Access Control**: https://docs.microsoft.com/en-us/azure/active-directory/role-based-access-control-custom-roles
- **What is Azure Policy?**: https://docs.microsoft.com/en-us/azure/azure-policy/azure-policy-introduction

- **What is Azure AD Privileged Identity Management?**: `https://docs.microsoft.com/en-us/azure/active-directory/active-directory-privileged-identity-management-configure?toc=%2fazure%2factive-directory%2fprivileged-identity-management%2ftoc.json`

- **Azure Security Center Documentation**: `https://docs.microsoft.com/en-us/azure/security-center/`

- **Azure Security Center Threat Intelligence Report**: `https://docs.microsoft.com/en-us/azure/security-center/security-center-threat-report`

- **Manage endpoint protection issues with Azure Security Center**: `https://docs.microsoft.com/en-us/azure/security-center/security-center-install-endpoint-protection`

- **What is Operations Management Suite (OMS)?**: `https://docs.microsoft.com/en-us/azure/operations-management-suite/operations-management-suite-overview`

12
Artificial Intelligence, IoT, and Media Services

In the previous chapter, we covered Governance and Policies, such as standard and custom roles in Azure, when to use Azure Role-based Access Security, and Azure Resource Policies.

In this chapter, you will learn about the various features and capabilities that Azure offers for Artificial Intelligence, IoT, and for streaming media content. By the end of this chapter, you will know how to design state-of-the-art solutions using Azure Cognitive Services, the Azure Bot Service, IoT Hub, Azure Media Services, and more.

The following topics will be covered:

- Azure Cognitive Services
- Azure Bot Service
- Azure Machine Learning
- IoT Hub, Event Hubs, and IoT Edge
- Azure Stream Analytics
- Azure Time Series Insights
- Azure Media Services

Technical requirements

This chapter uses the following tools for the examples:

- Visual Studio 2017: `https://www.visualstudio.com/downloads/`

The source code for this chapter can be downloaded from the following link:

- `https://github.com/SjoukjeZaal/AzureArchitectureBook/tree/master/Chapter%2012`

Azure Cognitive Services

With Azure Cognitive Services, you can create modern and intelligent applications. It offers various AI and machine learning APIs and SDKs, which can be used in applications to make them more intelligent, such as speech and facial recognition, speech and language understanding, and more.

Cognitive Services is part of the AI offering of Azure. It offers APIs that can be consumed *as-is* and APIs that need training and can be used to create your own custom AI solutions.

The APIs are split up into multiple categories, such as vision, speech, language, knowledge, and search APIs. These categories with the available APIs are covered in more detail in the upcoming sections.

Cognitive Services offers a set of APIs and SDKs that are still in the experimental stage as well. These services are added to the labs category. By the time of writing this book, the Labs section offers a gesture, event tracking, academic knowledge, local insights, knowledge exploration service, and entity linking service.

Available services and APIs

Azure Cognitive Services offers the following APIs and services:

- **Vision**:
    - **Computer Vision API**: This API provides image processing and recognition. You can use this API for categorizing images, tagging images based on content, recognizing handwritten text, flagging adult content, cropping images, detecting human faces, and more.

- **Content Moderator**: The content moderator offers automatic moderator capabilities such as detecting possible adult and racy content in videos. It offers review tooling where automatic moderation can be used in conjunction with human involvement as well.
- **Custom Vision Service**: This API offers a tool in order to build custom image classifiers. This can be used to identify images, such as certain flowers or dogs for instance. This API needs to be trained by uploading images to it.
- **Face API**: This API can detect human faces in an image. It can extract information from the images, such as pose, facial hair, glasses, gender, age, and head pose. You can use this API for face verification, face grouping, face identification, and finding similar faces.
- **Emotion API**: This API is part of the Face API and can be used as a standalone API as well. You can use it to detect the emotion of people in images.
- **Video Indexer**: This API can extract insights from your videos using various artificial intelligence technologies. This API is used inside Azure Media Services as well and will be covered in more detail later in this chapter.

- **Speech**:

  - **Microsoft Speech API**: This API provides speech-enabled features, such as voice command control and speech transcription and dictation. It offers speech to text, where human speech is converted into text, which can be used to control applications by speech and text to speech, where text is converted to audio streams, which can be played back in applications.
  - **Custom Speech Service**: This enables you to create customized language models and acoustic models aimed at a specific user population or used for applications in a particular environment. You can train the API to learn product names or jargon.
  - **Speaker Recognition API**: This API provides speaker verification, which can be used to identify a person using voice commands for authentication. It provides speaker identification, where it can recognize a person in a group of speakers by their voice.

- **Translator Speech API**: This API offers a service that translates conversational speech from one language into the text of another language.

- **Language**:

  - **Language Understanding (LUIS)**: LUIS can extract meanings from text. It uses machine learning to train the API.
  - **Bing Spell Check API**: This offers a spell checker and a contextual grammar tool. It is based on all the web searches in Bing and uses machine learning to dynamically train the API.
  - **Linguistic Analysis API**: This API offers three different tools for natural language processing, such as sentence separation and tokenization, part-of-speech tagging, and constituency parsing.
  - **Text Analytics API**: This API provides natural language processing over raw text and includes the features mentioned here. One of the features is language detection for up to 120 languages. It returns a language code and a score indicating the strength of the analyzation. It also provides Key Phrase Extraction, where it extracts key phrases to identify the main points in sentences, and it offers sentiment analysis, which you can use to find out what people think of certain things by analyzing text.
  - **Translator Text API**: This API can be used to provide text-to-text language translation in more then 60 different languages.
  - **Web Language Model API**: This offers a variety of standard natural language processing tasks. The models are trained using Bing data at web-scale.

- **Knowledge**:

  - **Custom Decision Service**: You can use this API to create a personal experience for your users. It can personalize content or videos on a website or portal. You can use it for ad placement and ranking items in shops.
  - **QnA Maker**: This offers a web API that trains an AI model to respond to user's questions in a more natural, conversational way. It can be trained using FAQ, URLs/documents, and more.

- **Search:**

  - **Bing Search APIs**: This API consists of multiple APIs and functions. It includes all Bing search APIs, such as the Bing web search API, Bing image search API, Bing video search API, and Bing news search API.
  - **Bing Autosuggest API**: This offers suggestions when you are typing the first few characters of a word. You can use it to populate a drop-down box under search boxes.
  - **Bing Custom Search API**: This offers tailored search experiences. You can tailor results based on interests. So, instead of letting users go through pages to search for relevant content, you can filter irrelevant content before providing it to your users.
  - **Bing Entity Search API:** This API provides search results that includes entities and places that can be used for tourist attractions, for instance.

For a complete overview of all the Cognitive Services APIs, you can refer to: `https://docs.microsoft.com/en-us/azure/#pivot=productspanel=ai`. Want to get started with Cognitive Services? You can refer to the following page to obtain free trial API keys for the various APIs that Cognitive Service offers: `https://azure.microsoft.com/en-us/try/cognitive-services/`. These trial plans have rate limits. The Azure Portal has paid offerings. You can create Cognitive Services APIs in there as well.

Using the Computer Vision API

In this example, we are going to create an application that uses the Computer Vision API to analyze some pictures.

First, you need to obtain an API subscription key from `https://docs.microsoft.com/en-us/azure/cognitive-services/Computer-vision/Vision-API-How-to-Topics/HowToSubscribe`.

Next you have to open up Visual Studio 2017.

1. Click on **File** | **New** | **Project**, and in the **New Project** window, select **Console App**. Name the project and click on **OK**:

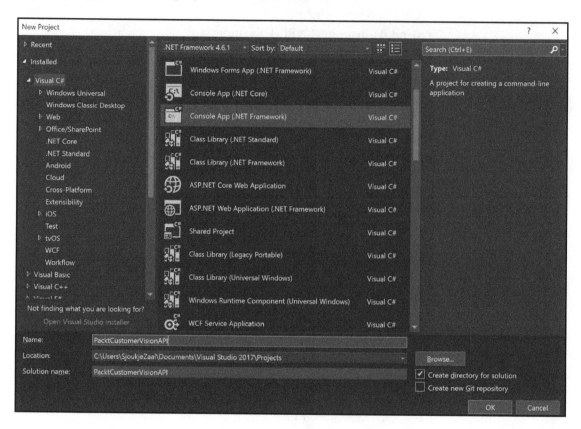

Creating Console application

2. Create a new class, named Extensions.cs, and replace the code with the following:

```
using System;
using System.Collections.Generic;

namespace PacktCustomerVisionAPI
{
    static class Extensions
    {
        public static void ForEach<T>(this IEnumerable<T> ie,
```

```
Action<T> action)
        {
            foreach (var i in ie)
            {
                action(i);
            }
        }
    }
}
```

3. Add the following namespaces to the `Main.cs`:

```
using System;
using System.Collections.Generic;
using System.IO;
using System.Linq;
using System.Net.Http;
using System.Net.Http.Headers;
using System.Text;
```

4. Add the following variables to the `Main.cs`. Replace the `subscriptionKey` value with your valid subscription key:

```
// Fill in the subscription Key
    const string subscriptionKey =
"7c98f3e0aa3a4a729f69b20583a0bc18";

    //API Url in West Central US Region
    const string uriBase =
"https://westcentralus.api.cognitive.microsoft.com/vision/v1.0/mode
ls/celebrities/analyze";
```

5. Replace the `Main` method with the following:

```
static void Main(string[] args)
    {
        Console.Write("Enter the path to an celebrity image: ");
        string imageFilePath = Console.ReadLine();

        MakeAnalysisRequest(imageFilePath);

        Console.WriteLine("\nPlease wait a moment for the results to
appear. Then, press Enter to exit ...\n");
        Console.ReadLine();
    }
```

6. Add the following method for creating a request and send it to the customer service API of the class:

```
static async void MakeAnalysisRequest(string imageFilePath)
{
    HttpClient client = new HttpClient();

    client.DefaultRequestHeaders.Add("Ocp-Apim-Subscription-Key",
subscriptionKey);
        string requestParameters = "model=celebrities";
        string uri = uriBase + "?" + requestParameters;
        HttpResponseMessage response;
        byte[] byteData = GetImageAsByteArray(imageFilePath);
        using (ByteArrayContent content = new
ByteArrayContent(byteData))
        {
            content.Headers.ContentType = new
MediaTypeHeaderValue("application/octet-stream");
            response = await client.PostAsync(uri, content);
            string contentString = await
response.Content.ReadAsStringAsync();
            Console.WriteLine("\nResponse:\n");
            Console.WriteLine(JsonPrettyPrint(contentString));
        }
}
```

7. Add the following method to import the celebrity image below the previous method:

```
static byte[] GetImageAsByteArray(string imageFilePath)
{
    FileStream fileStream = new FileStream(imageFilePath,
FileMode.Open, FileAccess.Read);
    BinaryReader binaryReader = new BinaryReader(fileStream);
    return binaryReader.ReadBytes((int)fileStream.Length);
}
```

8. Add the last method in order to display the JSON results in the Console below the previous method:

```
static string JsonPrettyPrint(string json)
    {
        if (string.IsNullOrEmpty(json))
            return string.Empty;

        json = json.Replace(Environment.NewLine,
"").Replace("\t", "");
```

```
            string INDENT_STRING = " ";
            var indent = 0;
            var quoted = false;
            var sb = new StringBuilder();
            for (var i = 0; i < json.Length; i++)
            {
                var ch = json[i];
                switch (ch)
                {
                    case '{':
                    case '[':
                        sb.Append(ch);
                        if (!quoted)
                        {
                            sb.AppendLine();
                            Enumerable.Range(0,
++indent).ForEach(item => sb.Append(INDENT_STRING));
                        }
                        break;
                    case '}':
                    case ']':
                        if (!quoted)
                        {
                            sb.AppendLine();
                            Enumerable.Range(0, --
indent).ForEach(item => sb.Append(INDENT_STRING));
                        }
                        sb.Append(ch);
                        break;
                    case '"':
                        sb.Append(ch);
                        bool escaped = false;
                        var index = i;
                        while (index > 0 && json[--index] == '\\')
                            escaped = !escaped;
                        if (!escaped)
                            quoted = !quoted;
                        break;
                    case ',':
                        sb.Append(ch);
                        if (!quoted)
                        {
                            sb.AppendLine();
                            Enumerable.Range(0,
indent).ForEach(item => sb.Append(INDENT_STRING));
                        }
                        break;
                    case ':':
```

```
                sb.Append(ch);
                if (!quoted)
                    sb.Append(" ");
                break;
            default:
                sb.Append(ch);
                break;
        }
    }
    return sb.ToString();
}
```

9. Now, download a celebrity image, run the application, and provide the full image path.

 For a detailed overview of all the capabilities of the Computer Vision API, you can refer to: https://docs.microsoft.com/en-us/azure/cognitive-services/computer-vision/home#Categorizing.

Azure Bot Service

Azure Bot Service offers a complete environment to build and deploy Bots. A Bot is an app that can interact with users in a conversational way. It can communicate with users using speech, text, and cards. You can create Bots that communicate with users using a freeform approach, where a users asks a question in a chatbox, for instance, and gets an answer back from the Bot, or you can use a more guided approach, where you provide choices to the users and take actions based on the choice they make.

You can integrate Bots in all types of applications, such as custom web applications and Azure Functions. You can create bots that integrate in Azure SaaS applications as well. Azure Bot Service offers different channels to connect your Bot to Skype, Facebook, Teams, Slack, SMS, and more. Bots can be created using .NET or Node.js, and there are five different templates provided to get you up to speed with developing them. You can choose from a Basic Bot, a Form Bot that collects user input, a language understanding Bot, which leverages LUIS, a Bot to use for FAQs, and a Bot that alerts users about events.

Azure Bot Service offers the following two different pricing tiers:

- **Free**: This offers unlimited messages for Standard channels and 10,000 messages per month on Premium Channels (such as Microsoft Teams and Skype).
- **Standard S1**: This offers unlimited messages for Standard channels, and you pay a certain amount for 1,000 messages at a time on Premium channels. This pricing tier offers SLA as well.

You can use Bots from the Azure Portal or from Visual Studio 2017. Microsoft offers a complete solution for building and deploying Bots, which is included in the Bot Builder SDK for .NET. You need to download templates that can be installed inside the Visual Studio `Template` folder. This template will then be a starting point for developing Bots.

Creating a Bot from the Azure Portal

In this example, we are going to create a Bot that can be deployed in a Web App from the Azure Portal:

1. Navigate to the Azure Portal by opening: `https://portal.azure.com/`.
2. Click on **New** and type `Web App Bot` in the search bar.

3. Enter the following settings:

Web App Bot settings

4. Click on **Bot template**, select the **Form** template, and click on **Select**:

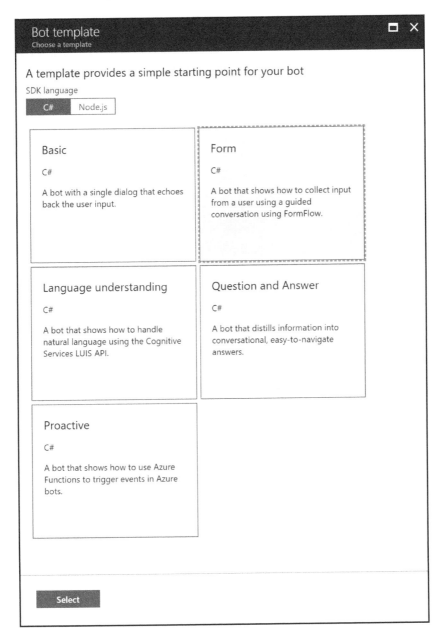

Selecting Bot template

5. When created, you can navigate to the Bot in the Azure Portal. When you click on **Build** in the left menu, you can make changes to the code in the online code editor. There are a couple of tools integrated in the online editor, such as Git, Kudu, and more. You can download the ZIP file to make changes in Visual Studio, and you can configure Continuous Deployment as well:

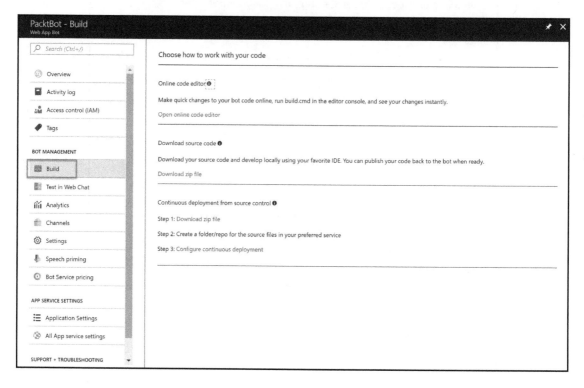

Bot Build settings

6. To test the Bot, click on **Test in Web Chat** in the left menu. This Bot provides an example of a sandwich ordering service, using a guided approach. So, if you type anything in the message box, you get a set of options for sandwiches to order. Pick one, and you can select the length of your sandwich:

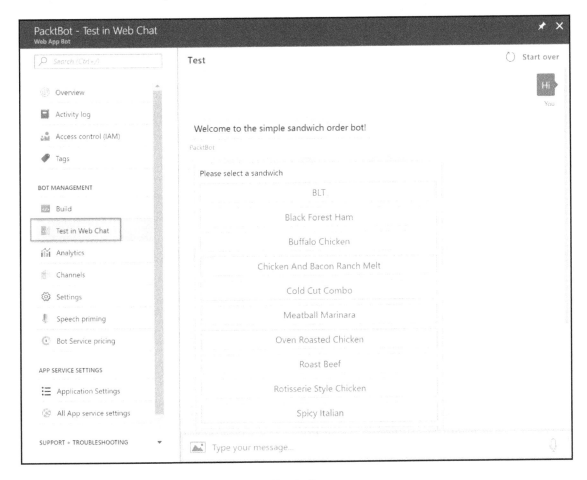

Example of bot

7. For channel registration, you can click on **Channels** in the left menu. Here, you can register the different channels that you want your Bot to connect to:

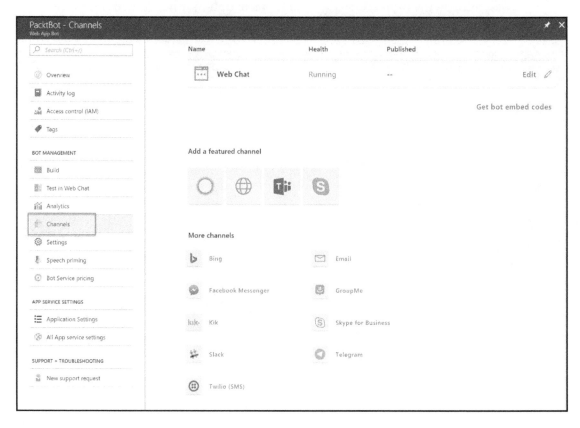

Different bot channels

For more information about how to create Bots using Visual Studio 2017, you can refer to https://docs.microsoft.com/en-us/bot-framework/dotnet/bot-builder-dotnet-quickstart.

Azure Machine Learning

We all produce massive amounts of data these days. Data created in the past can give us valuable insights into the future.

Machine learning provides a set of algorithms that can apply complex mathematical calculations to big data automatically and can eventually learn from this data. It is a data science technique, which can be used to predict the future by forecasting outcomes and trends. Applications using this technique can learn from data and experiences without being explicitly programmed. Machine learning models can be trained using large amounts of historical data which applications can act upon.

Fraud detection, self-driving vehicles, and personal recommendations on websites are all examples of applications that use machine learning. Artificial intelligence and machine learning possibilities are endless and will have an enormous impact on our daily lives in the near future.

Azure Machine Learning provides a set of tools and capabilities for data scientists and developers to leverage machine learning in their applications. The following tools and capabilities are offered:

- **Machine Learning Studio**: Machine Learning Studio is a drag and drop tool, which you can use to create predictive models. You can use it to deploy and test your solutions as well. You can create **Experiments** on which you can drag and drop datasets and data analyzation activities, named **Modules**. You can train the **Experiments** using parts of the data from the datasets, and when the models are trained properly, you can convert them into **Predictive** experiments and publish them as web services.
- **Azure Machine Learning Workbench**: At the time of writing this book, this tool is still in preview. It offers an integrated end-to-end data science solution for data scientists to prepare data, develop experiences, and deploy models to Azure.
- **Azure AI Gallery**: The AI Gallery provides various community-driven solutions built with different AI features of Azure. You can use these solutions for learning purposes or as a resource for developing your custom solutions.

- **Machine Learning Modules**: You can use out-of-the box machine learning models in your experiments for analyzing data. There are machine learning algorithms, data input and output modules, data transformation modules, text analytics modules, and Microsoft-specific modules with algorithms from Bing and Xbox.

- **Data Science Virtual Machines**: Azure offers virtual machines that are configured for data science workloads. There are Windows and Linux Data Science VMs and Deep Learning VMs. You can deploy containers for data science workloads as well:

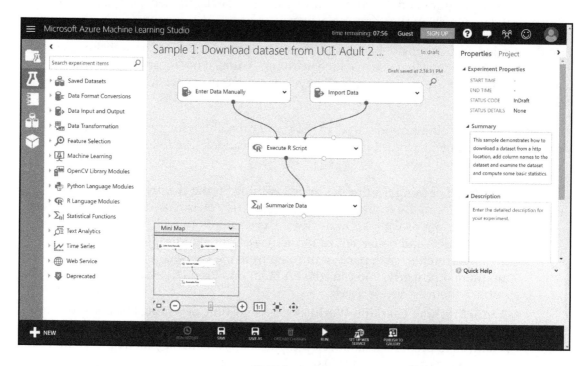

Machine Learning studio

Data science is a specialization; however, Microsoft offers a series of videos that can give some basic understanding of data science. For these series of videos, you can refer to: `https://docs.microsoft.com/en-us/azure/machine-learning/studio/data-science-for-beginners-the-5-questions-data-science-answers#other-videos-in-this-series`.

Azure IoT Hub

In an Internet of Things (IoT) solution, devices send massive amounts of data to Azure for further processing. The IoT Hub is used to connect these devices securely and route the messages from those devices to different resources in Azure for further processing.

The IoT Hub offers the following capabilities:

- **Bi-directional communication**: It provides bi-directional communication between devices and Azure, such as one-way messaging, file transfer, and request-reply messaging. Devices can send data to Azure IoT Hub, but the IoT Hub can send data to the devices as well. It supports various communication protocols, such as HTTPS, AMQP, and MQTT. It provides built-in declarative message routing to other Azure services.
- **Secure Connectivity**: Communication between devices and the IoT Hub can be secured using per-device security keys or X.509 certificates. Azure IoT Hub does not open any connections, only connected devices initiate all the connections. IoT Hub stores the messages inside a per device queue for two days and waits for the device to connect. It uses Azure AD for user authentication and authorization.
- **Scaling**: IoT Hub offers massive scaling because it can scale up to millions of simultaneously connected devices and millions of events per second.
- **Monitoring**: It offers a monitoring solution in Azure. IoT Hub is integrated with Azure Monitor, which gives you detailed information about device management operations and connectivity events.

Azure IoT Hub offers the Azure IoT SDK, which consists of Device SDKs and can be used to create apps that run on IoT devices and send data to the IoT Hub. The SDK also offers Service SDKs, which can be used to manage the IoT Hub, and it offers the Azure IoT Edge, which is covered in more detail later in this chapter.

IoT Hub comes in the following pricing tiers:

- **Free**: This offers total 8,000 messages per unit a day. This tier is most suitable for testing scenarios.
- **Standard S1**: This offers up to 400,000 messages per day across all connected devices. This is must suitable for scenarios that generate small amounts of data.
- **Standard S2**: This offers up to 6 million messages per unit a day across all connected devices. This is suitable for scenarios with large amounts of data.

- **Standard S3**: This offers up to 300 million messages per unit a day across all connected devices. This is suitable for scenarios with large amounts of data as well.

Next to the IoT Hub, Azure offers the Azure Event Hub. The Azure Event Hub offers similar capabilities such as the Azure IoT Hub, except that the IoT Hub offers more advanced capabilities. If your architecture demands cloud-to-device communication or per device security and performance management, the IoT Hub is the best solution.

The Event Hub is covered in more detail in the next section. Azure also offers IoT Edge, which offers additional functionality and will be covered in the next section as well:

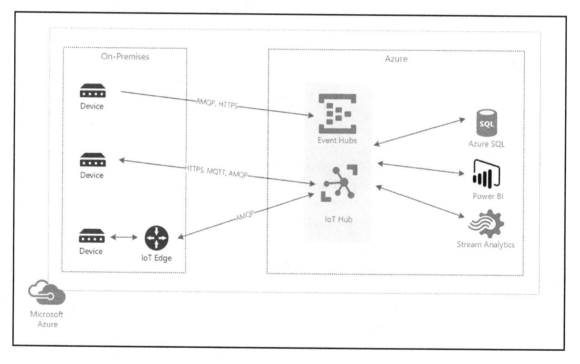

IoT architecture overview

Azure Event Hub

Azure Event Hub is designed for high throughput ingress of data streams generated by devices and services. It provides a telemetry ingestion service that can collect, transform, and store millions of events.

It offers similar capabilities such as the IoT Hub, but there are differences as well. When to use which solutions depends on the scenario. If your solution demands high throughput data ingestion only, Azure Event Hubs is a more cost-effective solution than the IoT Hub. However, if your solution needs bi-directional communication, such as communicating from the cloud to your devices, IoT Hub is a better solution.

To make the right decision on which solution to use for your IoT architecture, you can look at the following differences:

- **Device Protocol Support**: Azure Event Hub supports HTTPS, AMQP, and AMQP where the IoT Hub supports MQTT, MQTT over WebSockets, AMQP, AMQP over WebSockets, and HTTPS, MQTT, MQTT over WebSockets, AMQP, AMQP over WebSockets. IoT Hub supports file upload as well.
- **Communications Patterns**: The Event Hub only supports event ingress where the IoT Hub supports device-to-cloud communications and cloud-to-device communications as well.
- **Security**: The Event Hub supports Shared Access Policies, where the IoT Hub supports per device identity and revocable access control.
- **Monitoring**: The IoT Hub offers a complete set of monitoring capabilities, where the Event Hub only offers aggregate metrics.
- **Scale**: IoT Hub can scale up to millions of simultaneously connected devices and millions of events per second, where the Event Hub can scale up to 5,000 AMQP connections per namespace.
- **SDKs**: Event Hubs supports .NET and C, where IoT Hub supports .NET, C, Node.js, Java, and Python.

For a complete overview of the differences between the Event Hub and the IoT Hub, you can refer to: `https://docs.microsoft.com/en-us/azure/iot-hub/iot-hub-compare-event-hubs`.

Azure Event Hub offers the following three different pricing tiers:

- **Basic**: This offers a maximum of 20 throughput units with 1 MB/s ingress and 2 MB/s egress per unit. Maximum message size is 256 KB. A message retention of 1 day, 1 consumer group, and 100 brokered connections.

- **Standard**: On top of the basic features, the standard plan offers lower costs for throughput units and messages. It offers 20 consumer groups and 1,000 brokered connections.
- **Dedicated**: This offers a dedicated environment for customers. Offers a maximum message size of 1 MB and 50 throughput units, a retention period of 7 days and 25,000 brokered connections.

Azure IoT Edge

Azure IoT Edge is an additional feature of Azure IoT Hub, which is installed at the edge of the on-premises network, inside a DMZ or inside the corporate network. Instead of sending messages to Azure, the messages can be sent to Azure IoT Edge, which takes less time because it doesn't have to be sent beyond the on-premises network. Data can be stored and analyzed on the device as well.

You can register the IoT Edge inside the IoT Hub settings page in the Azure Portal. The IoT Edge runtime can then be installed on the IoT Edge device. Devices can be a Windows or Linux machine, a container, or a Raspberry Pi, for instance. This IoT Edge device can then connect to the Azure IoT Hub, collect the data from the devices, and send it to the IoT Hub.

Azure Stream Analytics

Azure Stream Analytics is part of Azure's IoT Suite and offers a pipeline for event processing and real-time analytics for the data that is streaming from various sources. You can use it for scenarios that require real-time analytics on data, such as stock analysis, fraud detection, and analyzing data that comes from a massive amount of sensors, for instance.

Data can come from various sources, such as custom applications, sensors, Azure IoT Hub, and Azure Event Hubs. It can come from Blob Storage as well. Stream Analytics can handle an ingest of data up to 1 GB per second. You can create a Stream Analytics **Job**, where you configure the data source. You can create a **Transformation**, where you can query the data for patterns or relationships using a SQL-like language.

You can create filter, sort, or aggregate the data from the data sources. Finally, the data is sent to an output source, which can be Azure Data Lake, Power BI for creating dashboards, using machine learning, or storing it in a SQL Data Warehouse:

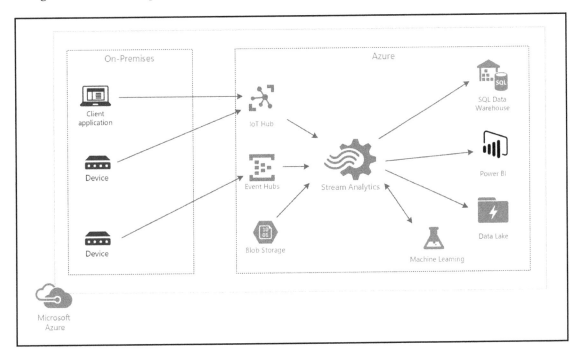

Azure Stream Analytics

Azure Time Series Insights

Time Series Insights offers a portal that can be used to get valuable insights in your IoT data. It offers database storage for a massive amount of data sent from IoT Hub and Event Hubs. It can join different types of data easily, such as metadata and telemetry, and then visualize this data.

Time Series Insights offers the following features:

- **Integration**: It offers out-of-the-box integration with Azure IoT Hub and Event Hub.
- **Data Storage**: Time Series Insights stores your data on SSDs and in memory for up to 400 days.
- **Visualization**: This offers a dedicated portal that offers visualization of your data using the TSI Explorer.
- **Query Service**: Time Series insights offers a query service inside the TSI Explorer and APIs that can be called from your custom applications. By integrating Time Series Insights in your applications, you can leverage it as a backend for indexing, storing, and aggregating data. You can then build your custom visualization tool on top of it.

Azure Time Series Insights TSI Explorer

Azure Media Services

Azure Media Services offers a secure and high-quality service in order to stream content to all sorts of devices. It can stream videos or audio files and offers REST APIs to upload, store, and encode package content. Audios and videos can be delivered to clients, such as TVs, computers, and mobile devices using both on-demand streaming and live streaming.

Azure Media Services supports the following flow:

- **Upload**: You can upload your videos using the Azure Portal, .NET SDK, REST API, and you can copy files from Blob Storage.
- **Encode**: AMS offers two different encoding tiers, such as Media Encoder Standard and Media Encoder Premium Workflow. The former offers an encoding service which encodes video and audio files, which are suitable for playback on a variety of devices, such as smartphones and PCs. The latter offers encoding for video and audio files that require a more complex workflow. It offers a Workflow Designer tool, which can be used for combining multiple input files or to create decision-based workflows with dynamic values using parameters. It also supports formats that are required for broadcasting and movies.
- **Secure**: You can secure your media using dynamic encryption using the Advanced Encryption Standard (AES-128) or other major digital rights management (DRM) systems. It offers AES keys and DRM licenses to authorized clients as well. You can secure your Media Services Channels with IP restrictions, so users can only upload media content from allowed IP addresses, and you can access the Azure Media Services API with Azure AD authentication. AMS still supports the Azure Access Control service authentication model using tokens. However, this will be deprecated in the near future, so Azure AD authentication is the preferred authentication method now.
- **Analyze**: AMS offers Media Analytics in order to extract insights from media content. It offers a collection of speech and computer vision APIs from Azure Cognitive Services. This is described in the following section in more detail.

Azure Media Analytics

Azure Media Analytics uses various Cognitive Services APIs to analyze media content. It offers the following capabilities:

- **Indexer**: Using the Indexer, you can create closed-captioning tracks and make the media file searchable. By the time of writing, the Indexer offers two different versions of the service, where the Azure Media Indexer 2, which is still in preview, has faster indexing and broader language support.
- **Hyperlapse**: This offers time lapse capabilities and capabilities to create stable videos from first person or action camera content.
- **Motion Detector**: This offers motion detection, which can be used on static camera footage to identify parts in the video where motion occurs. It generates a metadata file with timestamps of when the motion occurred. This is very useful for security camera footage.
- **Video Summarization**: This can create summaries for videos by generating snippets from different sections of the video. These snippets can be placed as an overview of all the different sections of the video.
- **Optical Character Recognition**: Azure Media optical character recognition (OCR) offers converting text content in videos into editable and searchable digital text. For instance, you can use this for making the content of videos of PowerPoint presentations searchable in search engines.
- **Scalable Face Redaction**: You can use scalable face redaction for blurring faces of individuals on video content automatically.
- **Content Moderation**: Azure Content Moderator offers automatic moderator capabilities such as detecting possible adult and racy content in videos. It offers review tooling where automatic moderation can be used in conjunction with human involvement as well.

Using the Azure Media Analytics Indexer

In the following example, we are going to create closed caption files for a video using the Azure Media Analytics Media Indexer. Microsoft recommends using Azure Media Analytics over the Video API from Cognitive Services, so that's what we are going to use here. We are going to use the speech to text feature of the Azure Media Indexer 2 Preview media processor (MP) to create subtitles for the video from a Console Application.

For this example, you need to create a Media Service Account in the Azure Portal. For a complete walkthrough on how to create this, you can refer to: `https://docs.microsoft.com/en-us/azure/media-services/media-services-portal-create-account`.

When the Azure Media Service account is created, you can copy the `PacktIndexer` folder from GitHub to your `C:` drive. You can download the video from the following website and put it inside the `InputFiles` folder together with the JSON file: `https://peach.blender.org/download/`. These files will be used for the example. Create a new folder named `OutputFiles` in the `PacktIndexer` folder as well.

Next, open up Visual Studio 2017 and create a new project.

1. Click on **File** | **New** | **Project**, and in the **New Project** windows, select **Console App**. Name the project and click on **OK**:

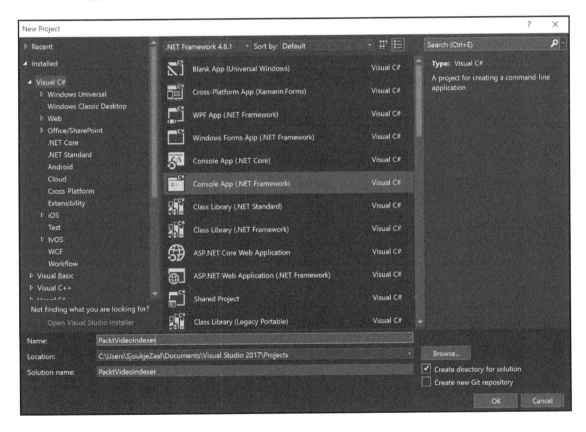

Create a new Console Application

2. Install the `windowsazure.mediaservices.extensions` and the `windowsazure.mediaservices` NuGet packages.

3. The first step is adding Azure AD authentication to the project. For this demo, we are using **Service principal authentication**. You can set this up easily in the Azure Portal in the access blade of the **Azure Media Service Account** settings:

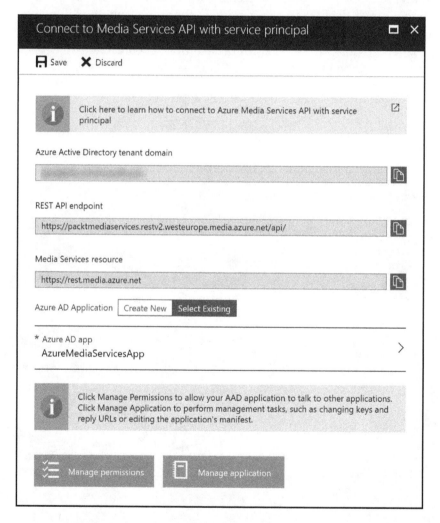

Creating a App Service Principal

4. Copy the Azure AD tenant name, the API URL, client ID, and client secret from the Azure Portal and add them to the following code:

```
var tokenCredentials = new AzureAdTokenCredentials("{YOUR Azure AD
TENANT DOMAIN HERE}", new AzureAdClientSymmetricKey("{YOUR CLIENT
ID HERE}", "{YOUR CLIENT SECRET}"),
AzureEnvironments.AzureCloudEnvironment);

             var tokenProvider = new
AzureAdTokenProvider(tokenCredentials);
```

5. Add the following code to the `Main` method below the authentication code:

```
_context = new CloudMediaContext(new
Uri("https://packtmediaservices.restv2.westeurope.media.azure.net/a
pi/"), tokenProvider);

             var video =
@"C:\PacktIndexer\InputFiles\BigBuckBunny.mp4";
             var config = @"C:\PacktIndexer\InputFiles\config.json";
             var asset = RunIndexingJob(video, config);

             DownloadAsset(asset, @"C:\PacktIndexer\OutputFiles");
```

6. Add the following method for creating and running the `Index Job`:

```
static IAsset RunIndexingJob(string inputMediaFilePath, string
configurationFile)
        {
             IAsset asset =
CreateAssetAndUploadSingleFile(inputMediaFilePath,
                 "Packt Indexing Input Asset",
                 AssetCreationOptions.None);

             IJob job = _context.Jobs.Create("Packt Indexing Job");

             string MediaProcessorName = "Azure Media Indexer 2
Preview";

             var processor =
GetLatestMediaProcessorByName(MediaProcessorName);
             string configuration =
File.ReadAllText(configurationFile);

             ITask task = job.Tasks.AddNew("Packt Indexing Task",
                 processor,
                 configuration,
```

```
                    TaskOptions.None);

            task.InputAssets.Add(asset);
            task.OutputAssets.AddNew("Packt Indexing Output Asset",
AssetCreationOptions.None);

            job.StateChanged += new
EventHandler<JobStateChangedEventArgs>(StateChanged);
            job.Submit();

            Task progressJobTask =
job.GetExecutionProgressTask(CancellationToken.None);

            progressJobTask.Wait();

            if (job.State == JobState.Error)
            {
                ErrorDetail error =
job.Tasks.First().ErrorDetails.First();
                Console.WriteLine(string.Format("Error: {0}. {1}",
                                            error.Code,
                                            error.Message));

                return null;
            }

            return job.OutputMediaAssets[0];
        }
```

7. Add the following method in order to create the `Asset`:

```
static IAsset CreateAssetAndUploadSingleFile(string filePath,
string assetName, AssetCreationOptions options)
        {
            IAsset asset = _context.Assets.Create(assetName,
options);

            var assetFile =
asset.AssetFiles.Create(Path.GetFileName(filePath));
            assetFile.Upload(filePath);

            return asset;
        }
```

8. Add the following method for downloading the `Asset` after indexing:

```
static void DownloadAsset(IAsset asset, string outputDirectory)
  {
    foreach (IAssetFile file in asset.AssetFiles)
    {
      file.Download(Path.Combine(outputDirectory, file.Name));
    }
  }
```

9. Add the following code for obtaining the `MediaProcessor` that processes the video:

```
static IMediaProcessor GetLatestMediaProcessorByName(string
mediaProcessorName)
        {
            var processor = _context.MediaProcessors
              .Where(p => p.Name == mediaProcessorName)
              .ToList()
              .OrderBy(p => new Version(p.Version))
              .LastOrDefault();
            if (processor == null)
            throw new ArgumentException(string.Format("Unknown
media processor",
mediaProcessorName));
            return processor;
        }
```

10. At last, add the following code in order to display the process inside the console:

```
  static private void StateChanged(object sender,
JobStateChangedEventArgs e)
    {
        Console.WriteLine("Job state changed event:");
        Console.WriteLine(" Previous state: " + e.PreviousState);
        Console.WriteLine(" Current state: " + e.CurrentState);
          switch (e.CurrentState)
          {
              case JobState.Finished:
Console.WriteLine();
              Console.WriteLine("Job is finished.");
              Console.WriteLine();
              break;
               case JobState.Canceling:
               case JobState.Queued:
               case JobState.Scheduled:
               case JobState.Processing:
```

```
                    Console.WriteLine("Please wait...\n");
                    break;
              case JobState.Canceled:
              case JobState.Error:
                    IJob job = (IJob)sender;
                    break;
              default:
                    break;
        }
    }
```

11. Run the App, and after indexing, you should have a `WebVtt` and `ttml` file in the `output` folder according to the values in the JSON input files.

> In this example, we have created closed caption files. You can call other methods for indexing the video as well. The following website provides you with some more examples for the other capabilities that are described earlier: `http://azuremedialabs.azurewebsites.net/demos/Analytics. html`.

Summary

In this chapter, we covered how to design solutions using the various AI services that Azure offers. We covered Azure Machine Learning, IoT features, and Azure Media Services.

In the next chapter, we are going to cover the different messaging capabilities that Azure provides and how to design effective messaging architectures.

Questions

Answer the following questions to test your knowledge of the information in this chapter. You can find the answers in the *Assessments* section at the end of this book.

1. You are designing an IoT Solution using the IoT Hub that needs to process 5 million events a day. Does the Standard S1 tier suit your needs?
    1. Yes
    2. No

2. Does Azure Media Services use various Azure Cognitive Services APIs underneath?

    1. Yes
    2. No

3. Should you use Azure Event Hubs in scenario where bi-directional communication between Azure and devices is required?

    1. Yes
    2. No

Further reading

You can check the following links for more information about the topics that were covered in this chapter:

-   **Cognitive Services Directory**: https://azure.microsoft.com/en-us/services/cognitive-services/directory/lang/
-   **About Bot Service**: https://docs.microsoft.com/en-us/bot-framework/bot-service-overview-introduction
-   **Introduction to Machine Learning in the Azure Cloud**: https://docs.microsoft.com/en-us/azure/machine-learning/studio/what-is-machine-learning
-   **What is Azure Machine Learning Studio?**: https://docs.microsoft.com/en-us/azure/machine-learning/studio/what-is-ml-studio
-   **Share and discover resources in the Azure AI Gallery**: https://docs.microsoft.com/en-us/azure/machine-learning/studio/gallery-how-to-use-contribute-publish
-   **Azure Machine Learning WorkBench**: https://blogs.msdn.microsoft.com/uk_faculty_connection/2017/09/29/azure-machine-learning-workbench/
-   **Azure Machine Learning Studio Algorithm and Module Reference**: https://docs.microsoft.com/en-us/azure/machine-learning/studio-module-reference/index
-   **Azure IoT Suite**: https://azure.microsoft.com/en-us/suites/iot-suite/
-   **Overview of the Azure IoT Hub service**: https://docs.microsoft.com/en-us/azure/iot-hub/iot-hub-what-is-iot-hub
-   **Event Hubs Documentation**: https://docs.microsoft.com/en-us/azure/event-hubs/

- **Azure IoT Edge**: https://docs.microsoft.com/en-us/azure/iot-edge/
- **Stream Analytics Documentation**: https://docs.microsoft.com/en-us/azure/stream-analytics/
- **Azure Time Series Insights**: https://docs.microsoft.com/en-us/azure/time-series-insights/
- **Media Services Documentation**: https://docs.microsoft.com/en-us/azure/media-services/

13
Implementing Messaging Solutions

In the previous chapter, we covered how to design solutions using the various artificial intelligence services that Azure offers. We covered Azure Machine Learning, IoT features, and Azure Media Services.

In this chapter, you will learn how to design effective messaging architectures using the Azure Service Bus, Azure Queues, Notification Hubs, Azure Event Grid, and services that were covered throughout the previous chapters, such as Logic Apps and Event Hubs.

The following topics will be covered:

- Azure Storage Queues
- Azure Service Bus
- Azure Event Grid
- Notification Hubs
- Designing an effective messaging architecture

Technical requirements

This chapter uses the following tools for the examples:

- Azure PowerShell: `https://docs.microsoft.com/en-us/powershell/azure/install-azurerm-ps?view=azurermps-5.1.1`

The source code for this chapter can be downloaded from the following link:

- `https://github.com/SjoukjeZaal/AzureArchitectureBook/tree/master/Chapter%2013`

Azure Queue Storage

We've briefly discussed Azure Queue Storage in `Chapter 7`, *Using Storage Solutions*, in the *Storage* section. Queue Storage offers asynchronous processing of messages. It provides a reliable and persistent messaging mechanism. It offers a REST API, which supports GET/PUT/PEEK operations. The message queue can be used to decouple applications, which enables independent scaling between the different application components.

Azure Queue Storage offers the following capabilities:

- Single queue messages can be up to 64 KB in size. The maximum time that a message can remain in the queue is 7 days.
- A Message can become invisible for other readers when it is requested from the queue. The message is locked for other applications and can't be processed by other applications during the time that it is invisible. By default, this will last for 30 seconds.
- Messages should be deleted from the queue when they are processed. If the message is not deleted from the application that requested the message, it will be visible again after the 30 seconds of invisibility.

Azure Service Bus

Azure Service Bus is a highly reliable, brokered messaging system for integration scenarios and IoT solutions. It is aimed at enterprise applications, and it offers middleware technologies such as message queueing and publish/subscribe messaging. It decouples the communication between applications and services.

Azure Service Bus offers the following key capabilities:

- **Queues**: This offers asynchronous, decoupled message communication between applications and services. It offers First In, First Out (FIFO) message delivery, and each message is received by one consumer. Messages are stored in the queue, so senders and consumers don't have to be connected to the queue at the same time. Service Bus Queues also offers **Sessions**, where messages can be grouped using a session ID. This way, the messages can be isolated and processed by dedicated clients.
- **Topics and Subscriptions**: This offers the same functionalities as Queues, except there can be multiple consumers. This uses the publish/subscribe pattern, where the message is sent to a **Topic**. Applications don't connect to that topic directly, but they connect to the **Subscription**. The Subscription then connects to the Topic. These subscriptions can have filters that only subscribe to a subset of messages, named **Filter Expressions**.
- **WCF Relays**: WCF Relays offers a gateway to connect your on-premises WCF Services to Azure, without having to open a firewall connection on your network. Azure Relay Services has already been covered in detail in `Chapter 6`, *Connecting Hybrid Applications*.

 For an overview of examples of the capabilities of Azure Service Bus, you can refer to the following GitHub page: `https://github.com/Azure/azure-service-bus/tree/master/samples`.

Across the different key capabilities, Azure Service Bus offers transaction capabilities. This offers the ability for all operations against messages to either succeed or fail.

Azure Service Bus offers the following tiers:

- **Basic**: This offers Queues and scheduled messages. The message size can be up to 256 KB.
- **Standard**: On top of the Basic offering, the Standard tier offers Topics and Subscriptions; Transactions, Sessions, and De-duplication are included.
- **Premium**: On top of the Standard tier, the Premium tier offers a maximum message size of 1 MB.

Azure Event Grid

Azure Event Grid is a service in Azure that enables event management across different Azure resources. Instead of creating a polling mechanism in your application that polls for changes, the apps get notified when an event happens automatically.

Azure Event Grid offers throughput of millions of events per second and a 24-hour retrying mechanism. You can filter events based on publishing paths, so you can receive only the events that are relevant for your application or resource. Events can be created without using code and are named built-in events by configuring them in the Azure Portal. You can create custom events as well, which can be created in your custom applications, PowerShell, or CLI.

Azure Event Grid offers the following built-in publishers: Azure Subscriptions, Event Hubs, Custom Topics, IoT Hub, Azure Resources Groups, Blob Storage, Service Bus, and V2 Storage accounts. For Event Handlers, Event Grid currently offers Webhooks, Azure Automation, Azure Functions, Logic Apps, Event Hubs, and Microsoft Flow:

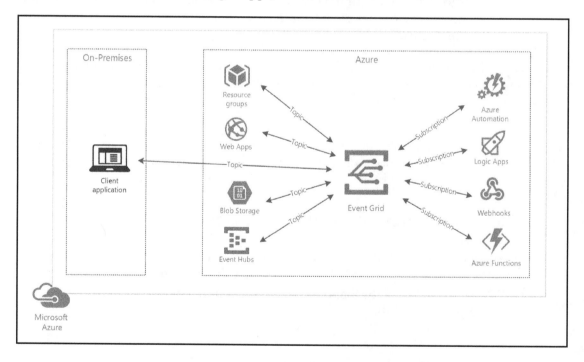

Azure Event Grid

New publishers and event handlers are added rapidly to Azure Event Grid, so keep an eye on `https://docs.microsoft.com/en-us/azure/event-grid/overview`.

Routing Events with Azure Event Grid

In this example, we are going to route events from Event Grid to an Azure Function.

First, we need to create a new Event Grid Topic in Azure. To create this, follow these steps:

1. Navigate to the Azure Portal by opening `https://portal.azure.com/`.
2. Click on **New** and type `Event Grid Topic` in the search bar. Create a new Event Grid Topic.
3. Enter the following settings and click on **OK**:

Creating the Event Grid Topic

4. Next, create a new Azure Function with the following configurations:

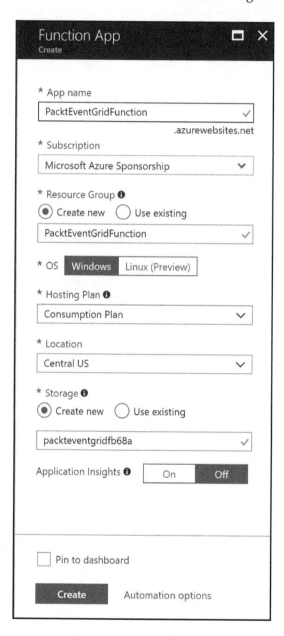

Creating Azure Function

5. When the Azure Function is created, navigate to the settings and click on the Function file:

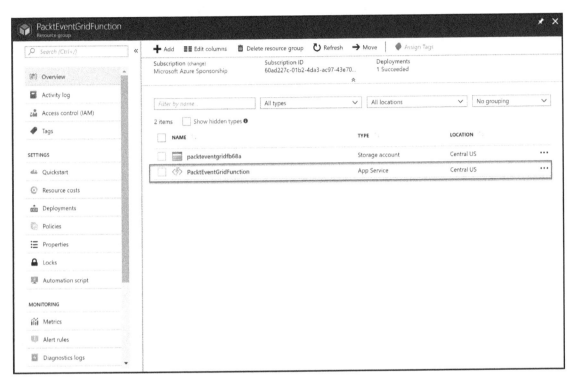

Selecting Azure Function file

6. Click the + button and select **Custom function**:

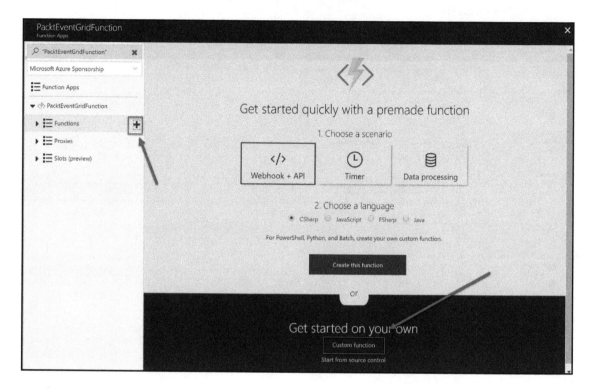

Creating Custom Function

7. In the next blade, scroll down and select **Event Grid trigger**:

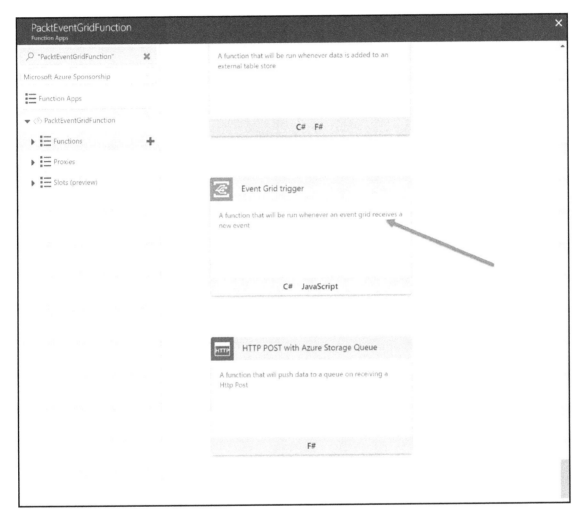

Selecting the Event Grid trigger template

8. Add the following settings and click on **Create**:

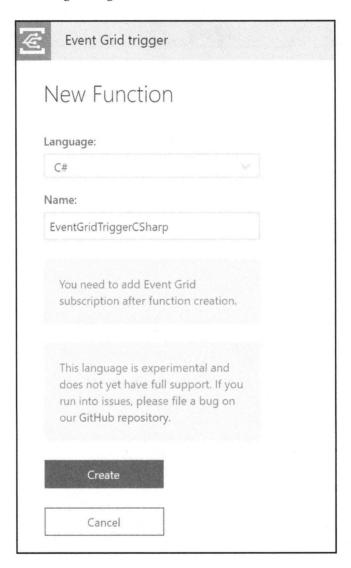

Creating trigger

9. When the trigger is created, the `run.csx` file is opened by default. Click on the **Add Event Grid subscription** link in the top menu:

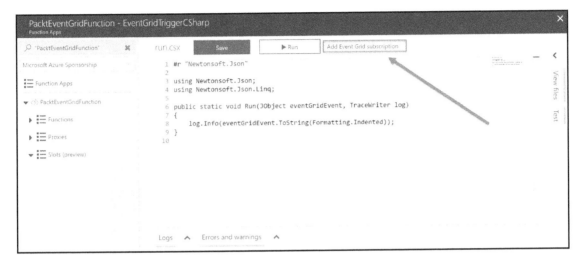

Selecting Event Grid subscription

10. Name the Event Subscription and select the Event Grid, which we created earlier:

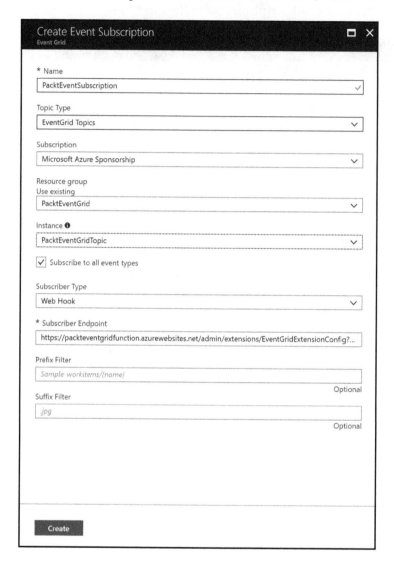

Creating Event Subscription

11. Click on **Create**; this will create a new event subscription that subscribes to the Event Grid Topic.

12. Open PowerShell and run the following script from your desktop. This will create a custom event. You can check the Azure Function logs for the result:

```
Login-AzureRmAccount
Select-AzureRmSubscription -SubscriptionId "********-****-****-
****-***********"

$endpoint = (Get-AzureRmEventGridTopic -ResourceGroupName
PacktEventGrid -Name PacktEventGridTopic).Endpoint
$keys = Get-AzureRmEventGridTopicKey -ResourceGroupName
PacktEventGrid -Name PacktEventGridTopic

$eventID = Get-Random 99999

#Date format should be SortableDateTimePattern (ISO 8601)
$eventDate = Get-Date -Format s

#Construct body using Hashtable
$htbody = @{
    id= $eventID
    eventType="recordInserted"
    subject="myapp/packtpub/books"
    eventTime= $eventDate
    data= @{
        title="Architecting Microsoft Solutions"
        eventtype="Ebook"
    }
    dataVersion="1.0"
}

#Use ConvertTo-Json to convert event body from Hashtable to JSON
Object
#Append square brackets to the converted JSON payload since they
are expected in the event's JSON payload syntax
$body = "["+(ConvertTo-Json $htbody)+"]"

Invoke-WebRequest -Uri $endpoint -Method POST -Body $body -Headers
@{"aeg-sas-key" = $keys.Key1}
```

Notification Hubs

Notification Hubs in Azure offers a push notification service to send notifications from backends to mobile devices. Push notifications on mobile devices are usually displayed to a user in a popup or a dialog box. Users can then decide if they want to view or dismiss the message. You can use push notifications for various scenarios, such as sending codes for MFA, sending notifications from social media, and sending news.

Notification Hubs offers cross-platform notifications by offering a set of SDKs and APIs for IoS, Android, and Windows devices. Normally, applications will use Platform Notification Systems (PNSes), which are dedicated infrastructure platforms. Apple has the Apple Push Notification Service and Windows has the Windows Notification Service, for instance. Notification Hubs removes all the complexity that comes with calling the different PNSes manually in your applications because it offers platform independency by offering a single API, massive scaling, various delivery patterns, rich telemetry, and more.

Notification Hubs offers the following tiers:

- **Free**: This offers a maximum of 1 million push messages per month and 100 namespaces with 500 active devices per namespace and total 100 hubs.
- **Basic**: In addition to the Free tier, the Basic tier offers a maximum of 10 million push messages per month and 100 namespaces with 200,000 active devices per namespace. SLA is covered for this plan, and it also offers limited telemetry.
- **Standard**: In addition to the Basic tier, the Standard tier offers a maximum of 10 million push messages per month, unlimited namespaces with 10,000,000 active devices per namespace. It also offers rich telemetry, scheduled push capabilities, bulk import, and multitenancy.

Designing an effective messaging architecture

Azure offers various features and capabilities in order to design and implement messaging solutions. In order to create successful application and solution architectures on the Azure platform, an effective messaging architecture is key. This will result in robust solutions and applications, that can fully benefit from the scaling capabilities that the Azure platform has to offer. It will also result in high performance for your applications and decoupled applications.

Throughout this book, multiple Azure resources are described and you should know by now what each resource is capable of. In the following section, some of them will be covered again from a messaging and integration perspective. This will give an overview and help you make the right decision when designing your messaging and IoT solutions on the Azure platform:

- **Azure Functions versus Logic Apps**: You can think of Logic Apps as workflows that are triggered by an event and Azure Functions as code that is triggered by an event. So, when your solution requires custom code or custom transformations, choose Azure Functions. Use Logic Apps when your solution needs to connect to other SaaS solutions, such as Office 365, Azure Storage, and SalesForce. It offers a huge amount of connectors to connect using HTTPS out-of-the-box. Also, when a graphical editor is required, choose Logic Apps.
- **Azure IoT Hub versus Azure Event Hubs**: Azure IoT Hub offers two-way communication from devices to Azure and Azure to devices. It can process millions of events per second and supports multiple device protocols, such as MQTT, MQTT over WebSockets, AMQP, AMQP over WebSockets, and HTTPS, MQTT, MQTT over WebSockets, AMQP, AMQP over WebSockets and file upload. So, if your solution requires massive event processing and bi-directional communication, choose Azure IoT Hub. Event Hubs only allow one-way communication from devices to Azure. So, when your solution requires only data ingest, Event Hubs can be a more appropriate and cost-effective solution.

- **Azure Service Bus versus Azure Storage Queues**: Azure Service Bus is a brokering message solution at enterprise scale. It offers more enterprise messaging capabilities, such as transactions and sessions. It also provides support for bigger messages. Azure Service Bus supports messages up to 1 MB for the premium tier. Azure Queue Storage supports messages up to 64 KB.

Summary

In this chapter, we covered the different messaging solutions that Azure provides for various types of applications and solutions. You have also learned, when to use the right messaging solutions in your applications. This concludes the last chapter of the design solutions for platform services objective.

Next, we will look at the Design for Operations Objective, which will be the last objective of this book. It will start with the different application monitoring and alerting strategies.

Questions

Answer the following questions to test your knowledge of the information in this chapter. You can find the answers in the *Assessments* section at the end of this book.

1. You are designing a global mobile application for your organization that needs to process approximately 10 million push messages per month. Your administrators have a monitoring requirement. Is the Basic tier the appropriate tier for your application?
   1. Yes
   2. No

2. You are designing a serverless solution for your organization and need to call an external SDK in your solution for image processing. Is Azure Logic Apps the appropriate solution for this?
   1. Yes
   2. No

3. You are designing a messaging solution for your organization and have a requirement for messages that are approximately 1 MB big. Should you use Azure Storage Queue for this solution?
   1. Yes
   2. No

Further reading

You can check the following links for more information about the topics that were covered in this chapter:

- **Notification Hubs Documentation**: `https://docs.microsoft.com/en-us/azure/notification-hubs/`
- **Azure Event Grid Documentation**: `https://docs.microsoft.com/en-us/azure/event-grid/`
- **Azure Logic Apps Documentation**: `https://docs.microsoft.com/en-us/azure/logic-apps/`
- **Get started with Azure Queue storage using .NET**: `https://docs.microsoft.com/en-us/azure/storage/queues/storage-dotnet-how-to-use-queues`
- **Add push notifications to your Android app**: `https://docs.microsoft.com/en-us/azure/app-service-mobile/app-service-mobile-android-get-started-push`
- **Add Push Notifications to your iOS App**: `https://docs.microsoft.com/en-us/azure/app-service-mobile/app-service-mobile-ios-get-started-push`
- **Azure Logic Apps Documentation**: `https://docs.microsoft.com/en-us/azure/logic-apps/`
- **Azure Functions Documentation**: `https://docs.microsoft.com/en-us/azure/azure-functions`

14
Application Monitoring and Alerting Strategies

In the previous chapter, we covered how to design effective messaging solutions, by covering the Azure Service Bus and Azure Queue Storage and combining different Azure resources in an effective messaging architecture.

In this chapter, we are introducing the Design for Operations objective by covering application and platform monitoring and alerting strategies by giving an overview of the available solutions that Azure has to offer. By the end of this chapter, you should know when to use the different types of solutions when issues occur on the Azure platform in general and inside your custom solutions and configurations.

The following topics will be covered:

- Azure Log Analytics
- Azure Monitor
- Application Insights
- Azure Service Health
- Azure Advisor
- Azure Network Watcher

Azure Log Analytics

Azure Log Analytics is a service that collects and analyzes log files from various Azure resources and on-premises resources. It can collect all the data into a single workspace and offers a query language to query the data.

You can integrate various resources in Log Analytics, such as data from VMs, by installing an agent on Windows and Linux VMs, or you can connect to System Center Operations Manager to collect telemetry from existing agents. Most Azure resources are already integrated in Log Analytics. You only need to create a workspace from the Azure Portal to collect the data from them. You can then query the data from the workspace directly using the query language, or you can use analysis tools that can analyze the data. Some examples of analysis tools are Operations Management Suite, Azure Security Center, and Application Insights. You can import the data in Power BI as well to create data visualizations.

When the data is collected, it is organized in data tables separated by the data type. It can collect data from the following resources:

- Data from Azure Monitor can be collected in Log Analytics and searched using the query language
- Agents can be installed on Windows and Linux machines to send data to Log Analytics
- A System Center Operations Manager management group can be connected to Log Analytics to collect data from agents
- Application Insights and Azure Security Center use Log Analytics by default to store data
- Log Analytics offers cmdlets that can be used from PowerShell and can be used in Azure Automation Runbooks
- It offers a HTTP Data Collector API that can be leveraged in custom applications to send log data to Log Analytics

Creating a Log Analytics Workspace

To create a Log Analytics Workspace, take the following steps:

1. Navigate to the Azure Portal by opening: `https://portal.azure.com/`.
2. Click on **New** and type in `Log Analytics` in the search bar. Create a new workspace.

3. Enter the following settings and click on **OK**:

Creating a Log Analytics Workspace

4. The workspace has now been created.
5. You can now connect the Azure resources to the workspace. For example, pick the **PacktPub** resource group, which was created in the first chapter, and open the settings in the Azure Portal. Click on **Activity log** in the left menu:

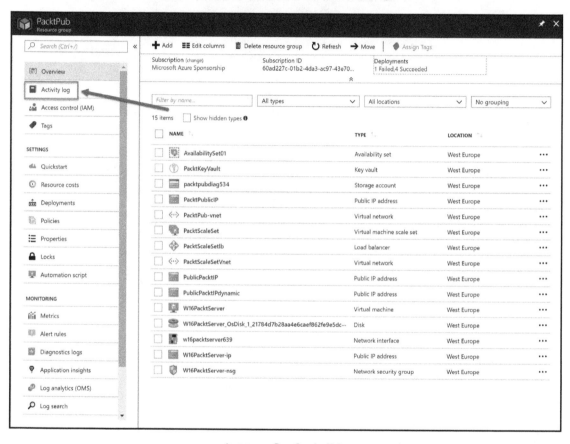

Azure resource Group Overview blade

6. Click on **Log Analytics** in the top menu, click on the **Add** button, and select the workspace that was created in the previous steps and click on **OK**:

Selecting workspace

7. Logging for this Resource Group is now sent to the Log Analytics Workspace.
8. When you navigate back to the Log Analytics Overview blade and click on **View Designer**, a blade opens where you can create views for your data:

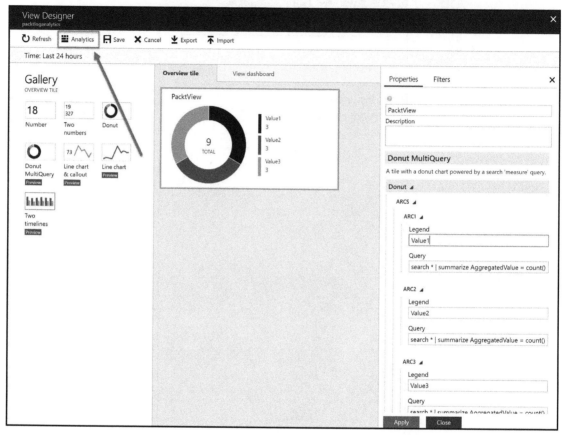

Log Analytics Designer

9. You can also click on the **Analytics** button in the top menu, which will open the Log Analytics portal. Here, you can use predefined and create custom queries. In there, you can open a new tab and create a new query. You can add the following query to create a bar chart with the alert count by severity, per day (for the past 7 days):

```
Alert
| where TimeGenerated > ago(7d)
| summarize count() by AlertSeverity, bin(TimeGenerated, 1d)
| render barchart kind=unstacked
```

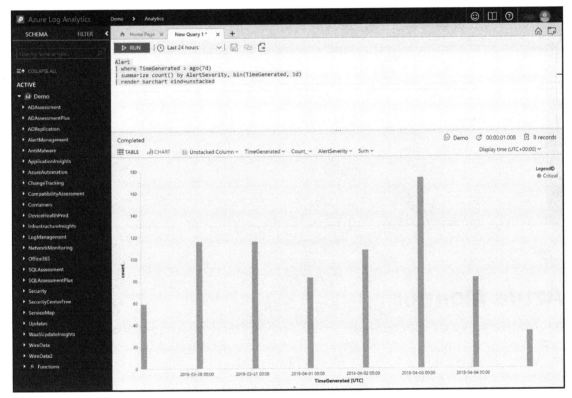

Query result in the Log Analytics Portal

10. When you navigate back to the Log Analytics Overview blade in the Azure Portal and click on **OMS Portal**, Microsoft Operations Management Suite should be open, where you can check all the logs and other activities as well:

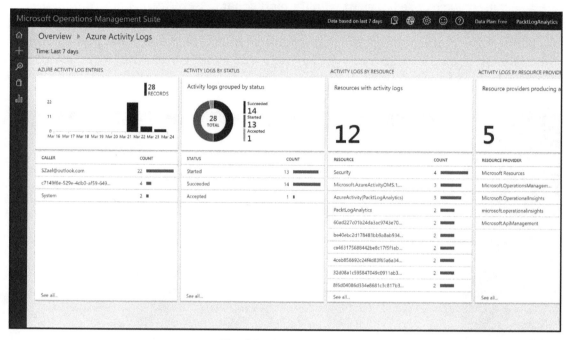

Microsoft Operations Management Suite

Azure Monitor

Azure Monitor is a monitoring solution in the Azure Portal, which provides infrastructure metrics and logs for mostly all services in Microsoft Azure. Not all Azure resources have been added to Azure Monitor by the time of writing this book, but in the future, more will be added.

Azure Monitor offers the following capabilities:

- **Activity Log**: The activity log provides information about all types of events that are occurring inside an Azure Subscription. This can be activities such as stopping or starting VMs and maintenance activities. It offers different event categories, such as administrative, security, service health, autoscale, alerts, recommendations, policies, and resource health events. The events are stored for a retention period of 90 days. Queries can be saved and pinned to the Azure Dashboard, and they can be exported to a storage account for storing them for a larger period of time. They can also be exported to an Event Hub for real-time streaming or sent to Log Analytics as well.

- **Diagnostic Settings**: This provides information about events that happen inside a particular resource inside an Azure Subscription, for instance, an event for retrieving a secret from the Azure Key Vault. These events are not collected by default; they need to be enabled for the resources manually inside the Azure Portal, inside an ARM template when the resources are created, or using PowerShell or calling the REST API. These events can be stored inside a storage account or Event Hub or sent to Log Analytics as well, just like the events in the Activity log.

- **Metrics**: Metrics offers time-based metric points for your resources, just as performance counters in Windows Server. Metrics are available by default, and they have a retention period of 93 days. You can check the performance of an Azure resource and track the used and available credits, for instance. They can be sent to Event Hubs, Azure Stream Analytics, and you can retrieve and query data using the REST API and PowerShell.

- **Alerts:** The Alerts section offers a single place to view and manage all Azure alerts. It displays alerts coming from the Activity Log, Metrics, Application Insights, and Log Analytics. You can create Alert Rules, which can send out an email or SMS, Webhook, send data to a third-party IT Service Management application, or call an Automation Runbook.

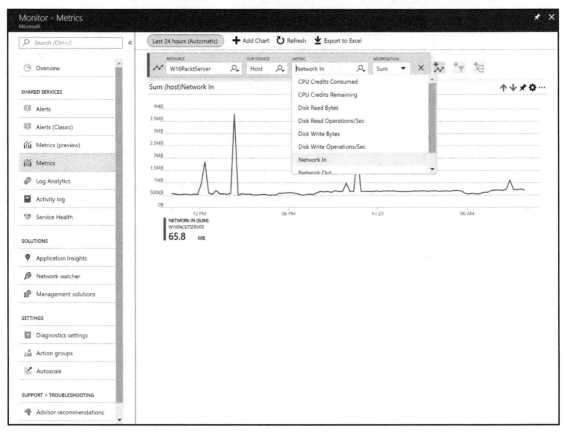

Azure Monitor Metrics

Application Insights

Application Insights offers a monitoring solution for cross-platform Apps that are hosted in Azure and for on-premises apps. It is aimed at developers and can be used in order to monitor the performance and detect issues, and it helps improve usability of your apps. It can be integrated in DevOps processes and development tools, such as Visual Studio.

Developers can set up an Application Insights Resource inside Azure and install a package inside their application. This can be an Azure application or an on-premises application; they can both connect to the resource in Azure. This package is responsible for sending telemetry data to Azure. You can add performance counters, Docker logs, and diagnostic logs as well.

It collects the following types of application events:

- **Rate data**: Different types of rate data can be sent to Application Insights, such as request and dependency rates and response times and user session counts.
- **Exceptions**: Exceptions that occur inside an application can be sent to Application Insights.
- **Page views and performance**: It can give information about page views and load performance of the application.
- **Diagnostic Logs**: This sends Docker Host diagnostic information to Application Insights and trace logging from applications.
- **AJAX calls**: This is the performance of AJAX calls and failed requests and response time.
- **Custom Events**: You can create custom events in your applications as well.
- **Integration**: It can integrate with Visual Studio App Center and HockeyApp to analyze telemetry data from mobile applications as well.

Once the data is sent to Azure, it can be viewed in the Azure Portal. The Azure Portal offers different capabilities to display and analyze the data. It offers an **Application map** blade, a **Live Metrics Stream**, **Metrics Explorer** blades, a **Performance** blade, and more:

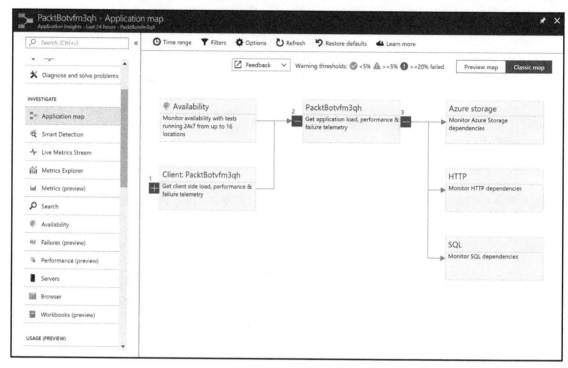

Application Insights in the Azure Portal

Azure Service Health

Azure Service Health offers a dashboard in the Azure Portal where issues regarding the different Azure resources are displayed. This can give you insights about maintenance schedules, which are platform issues that can effect the availability of the resources in Azure.

It offers the following views from the Azure Portal:

- **Service Issues**: This provides an overview of all the global issues on Azure that currently occur in all the different Azure Regions. It also offers a health history where you can review or download summaries of historical events.
- **Planned Maintenance**: This provides an overview of all the maintenance events that are scheduled.
- **Resource Health**: An overview of the current and historical health of the different resources inside the Azure Subscription. When you are having issues, you can run a troubleshoot tool from there as well.
- **Health Alerts**: You can create Health Alerts from there as well so that you are notified when maintenance activities are scheduled and service issues occur.

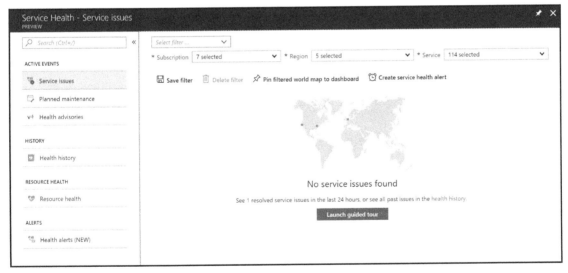

Azure Service Health in the Azure Portal

Azure Advisor

Azure Advisor is a tool that helps you follow best practices for deployments in Azure. It analyzes the current configuration of all the Azure resources, and based on that, it can make recommendations about them. For most recommendations, you can address them from inside the Azure Advisor portal directly.

It offers the following categories:

- **High Availability**: This provides several recommendations to improve the continuity of your applications and other Azure resources, such as enabling backups and creating Availability Sets.
- **Security**: This provides recommendations to improve security of Azure resources. It integrates with Azure Security Center.
- **Performance**: This provides recommendations for the overall performance of the different Azure resources, such as database performance and App Service performance.
- **Costs**: This section provides recommendations for being more cost-effective, such as resizing or shutting down virtual machines, or reducing costs by eliminating unprovisioned ExpressRoute circuits.

Address Recommendation from Azure Advisor

To address a recommendation from Azure Advisor directly, take the following steps:

1. Navigate to the Azure Portal by opening: `https://portal.azure.com/`.
2. Select **Azure Advisor** from the left menu.

3. You get an overview of all the different recommendations, categorized into four sections:

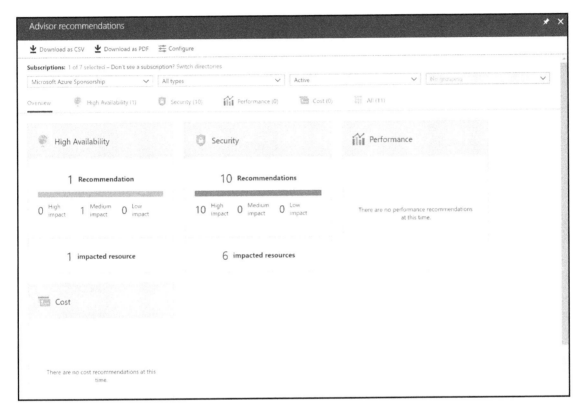

Azure Advisor overview

4. These recommendations are based on all the different services that we've created for this book. So, if you have followed along, your recommendations will be the same. For this example, we select the **Security** section and then **Follow Security Center Recommendations**. Pick a high severity recommendation:

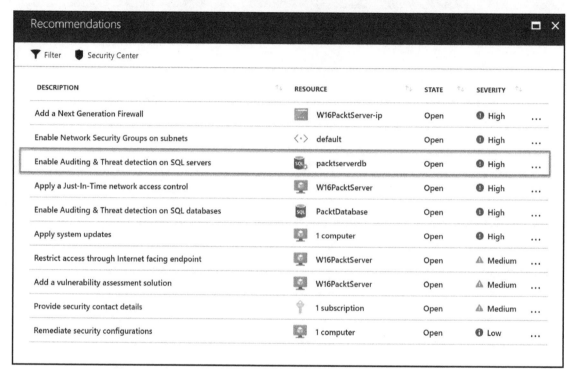

Security recommendations

5. A new blade opens where you can select the database. Here, you can enable **Auditing & Thread Detection** for the selected database directly.

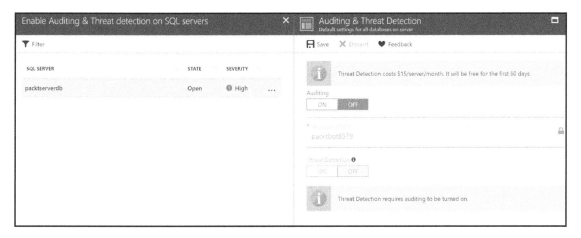

Auditing & Thread Detection settings

Azure Network Watcher

Azure Network Watcher offers a network monitoring solution on the Azure resources level for all network communication. This includes VNets, ExpressRoute circuits, Application Gateway traffic, Load Balancers, and more. It can be accessed from the Azure Portal and offers monitoring tools, diagnostic tools, and logs from the network level.

It offers the following capabilities:

- **Topology**: This provides an overview of all the network resources in a VNet by offering a Graph. From the Azure Portal, it provides a subset of all the network parts. To view a full list of the resources, you can use PowerShell or the REST API.
- **IP flow verify**: This offers an overview of allowed or denied packages for a network interface of a virtual machine. This helps administrators to solve connectivity issues quickly.
- **Next Hop**: This provides an overview of the destination routes of packages. This is useful for determining connectivity issues and checking whether packages arrive at the destination, such as to on-premises virtual machines.

- **Security Group View**: This provides an overview of all the configured NSGs and rules that are associated with it from two different levels, the network interface level, and the subnet level.
- **VPN Diagnostics:** This offers a troubleshooting solution for VPN gateways and connections. Connections and gateways can be called and return the result from the Azure Portal, PowerShell, Azure CLI, or REST API.
- **Packet Capture:** You can capture network traffic packets to diagnose network anomalies. It requires an extension that needs to be installed on virtual machines to capture the data packages. Packages can be stored locally on the virtual machines or on Azure Blob Storage for further analysis.
- **Connection Troubleshoot**: This offers a troubleshooting solution that checks TCP connections from VMs to VMs, IPv4 addresses, URIs, and fully qualified domain names (FQDNs). This helps with detecting connectivity issues by collecting all the configurations. It uses the same extension as the Packet Capture feature and connectivity can be checked from PowerShell, CLI, and the REST API as well.

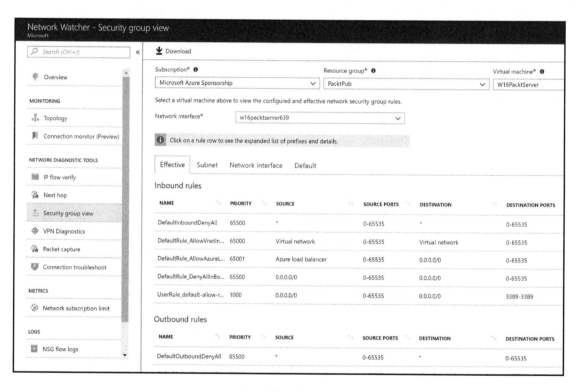

Network Watcher Overview

Summary

In this chapter, we've covered the different monitoring solutions Azure provides from a platform and application's perspective, such as Application Insights, Network Watcher, and Azure Log Analytics.

The next chapter will be the last chapter of this objective and the final chapter of this book, `Chapter 15`, *Exploring Operations Automation Strategies*.

Questions

Answer the following questions to test your knowledge of the information in this chapter. You can find the answers in the *Assessments* section at the end of this book:

1. You are designing an IoT Solution and want to provide a real-time monitoring tool for your administrators. Should you use Azure Log Analytics for this?
    1. Yes
    2. No

2. Is Azure Network Watcher a separate application that needs to be installed on your computer?
    1. Yes
    2. No

3. You want to get an overview of all the maintenance events that are scheduled for the Azure platform. Can you retrieve this information from Azure Service Health?
    1. Yes
    2. No

Further reading

You can check the following links for more information about the topics that were covered in this chapter:

- **What is Azure Log Analytics?**: https://docs.microsoft.com/en-us/azure/log-analytics/log-analytics-overview
- **Create custom views using View Designer in Log Analytics**: https://docs.microsoft.com/en-us/azure/log-analytics/log-analytics-view-designer
- **Azure Monitor Documentation**: https://docs.microsoft.com/en-us/azure/monitoring-and-diagnostics/
- **Overview of Azure Monitor**: https://docs.microsoft.com/en-us/azure/monitoring-and-diagnostics/monitoring-overview-azure-monitor
- **Application Insights Documentation**: https://docs.microsoft.com/en-us/azure/application-insights/
- **Azure Service Health Documentation**: https://docs.microsoft.com/en-us/azure/service-health/
- **Introduction to Azure Advisor**: https://docs.microsoft.com/en-us/azure/advisor/advisor-overview
- **Azure Network Watcher Documentation**: https://docs.microsoft.com/en-us/azure/network-watcher/

15
Exploring Operations Automation Strategies

In the previous chapter, we introduced the Design for Operations objective by covering Application and platform monitoring and alerting strategies.

This chapter covers how to design an operations automation strategy using Azure Automation, Chef, Puppet, PowerShell, Desired State Configuration (DSC), Event Grid, Azure Logic Apps, and how to define an autoscaling strategy.

The following topics will be covered:

- Designing an operations automation strategy
- Designing an autoscaling strategy

Designing an Operations Automation Strategy

Automating steps in Azure is a great solution to ensure consistency in your deployments and save time. It reduces errors when applications need to be deployed between different environments in a Development, Testing, Acceptance, and Production (DTAP) architecture. It also saves a lot of time when resources need to be deployed repeatedly, such as multiple development VMs for a team of developers.

Azure offers different solutions and methods in order to design a successful automation strategy, which are described in the following sections.

Azure PowerShell

Azure PowerShell can be used to create Azure resources, manage and configure your resources, and for automation as well.

Azure PowerShell is used for several examples throughout this book to automate different tasks, such as creating virtual machines and creating network interfaces. It can be used from your local machine, as well as from Azure Cloud Shell. You can use PowerShell for almost everything in Azure that can be done from the Azure Portal and even for some Azure resources, PowerShell offers additional capabilities that can't even be configured from the Azure Portal.

Desired State Configuration

DSC is the process of forcing a configuration on a system. It uses configuration files that consist of PowerShell scripts. These scripts are responsible for making the required configurations to the system and for ensuring that these systems stay in sync. So for example, when you have created a DSC file to configure IIS on a Windows Server and this is removed by an administrator, the DSC file will reinstall and configure IIS again.

DSC uses three key features to configure the machines:

- **Configurations**: A set of PowerShell scripts that configure the resources. These scripts also ensure that the systems remain configured in the desired state. It uses **Nodes** to define the resources that are being configured.
- **Resources**: These are the different building blocks that need to be configured on the machine. For example, this can be a WindowsFeature Resource or a Environment Resource.
- **Local Configuration Manager (LCM)**: This is the engine that deploys the scripts to the machines. LCM regularly polls the different machines to ensure that the desired state of the machines is maintained. If systems are out of sync, LCM runs the scripts to reinstall and configure the systems according to the resources in the scripts.

See the following example of a DSC file:

```
Configuration PacktDscConfiguration {
    param(
        [string[]]$ComputerName="PacktMachine"
    )
    Node $ComputerName {
        WindowsFeature PacktFeatureInstance {
            Ensure = "Present"
            Name = "RSAT"
        }
        WindowsFeature PacktFeatureInstance2 {
            Ensure = "Present"
            Name = "Bitlocker"
        }
    }
}
PacktDscConfiguration -ComputerName $ComputerName
```

Azure Automation

Azure Automation is a service in Azure that offers complete control over the deployment and management operations in on-premises and in Azure environments. It offers support for Windows and Linux machines, and it offers a community gallery with predefined configurations and automation runbooks, which can be used as a starting point.

To manage these types of workloads, Azure Automation offers the following features and capabilities:

- **Process Automation**: You can use Process Automation in order to automate management tasks and repeatable configuration tasks in Azure and your on-premises environments. Various Azure services and resources can be integrated when automating processes. It uses **Automation Runbooks**, which automate the different steps. Azure offers a graphical editor in order to create runbooks from the Azure Portal, or you can create them from PowerShell. You can create different types of runbooks, such as Graphical, Graphical PowerShell Workflow, PowerShell, PowerShell Workflow, and Python Runbooks. Those workflows can then be exported from the automation account and imported in other automation accounts. However, automation runbooks in Azure cannot access the on-premises infrastructure and other cloud environments by default. You should install the Hybrid Runbook Worker feature of Azure Automation to run the runbooks on these environments.

- **Configuration Management**: For configuration management, Azure Automation offers a DSC server for PowerShell DSC scripts. This server can be used to write, manage, and compile PowerShell DSC. It provides a Desired State Configuration Pull Service to send configurations to nodes automatically. You can get insights about installed applications and other configuration items as well.
- **Update Management**: This provides information and visibility about update compliance across your Azure, on-premises and other cloud environments. It offers capabilities for orchestrating and scheduling update deployments.
- **Shared Capabilities**: Azure Automation offers various shared resources that can be used for automating and configuring your environments, such as Role-based Access Control. You can store credentials and certificates for security, create connection strings, schedules, source-control integration, and PowerShell modules.

 For more information about Windows PowerShell Desired State Configuration, you can refer to `https://docs.microsoft.com/en-us/powershell/dsc/overview`. For more information about the Desired State Configuration Pull Service, you can refer to `https://docs.microsoft.com/en-us/powershell/dsc/pullserver`.

Creating an Azure Automation Runbook

In this example, we are going to create an Azure Runbook with DSC Configurations. We should first create an Automation Account before the Azure Automation Runbook can be created.

To create an Azure Automation Account, take the following steps:

1. Navigate to the Azure Portal by opening `https://portal.azure.com/`.
2. Type `Automation` in the search bar and create a new account. Add the following properties and click on **Create**:

Create Azure Automation Account

3. When created, navigate to the Automation Account. From there you can open the Graphical Editor to create an Automation Runbook. This example uses a preconfigured Graphical Runbook, which can be imported. This Runbook can be downloaded from the source code provided for this book on the GitHub page.

4. To import the runbook file, select **Runbooks** from the left menu and **Add a runbook**:

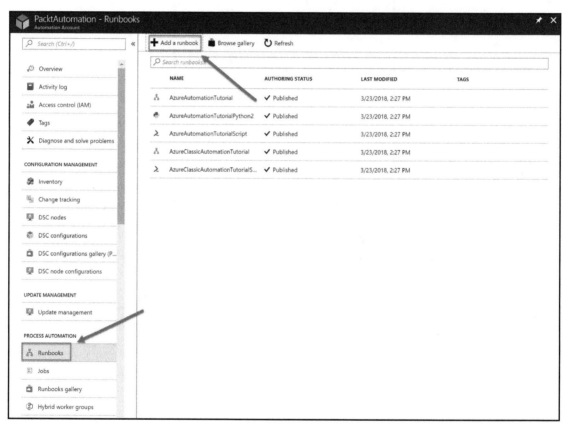

New Runbook

5. Select **Import**, select the Runbook file, and the following properties are automatically added:

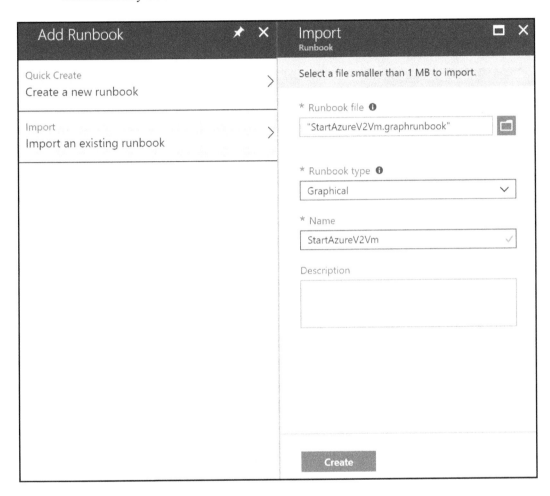

Import runbook

6. Click on **Create.** You can now select the newly added runbook to make changes
to it. Select it and click on **Edit** in the top menu. This will open the graphical
editor where you can see the different steps in the workflow and make changes to
it. You can select the different steps and configure parameters, configure retry
behavior, and so on.

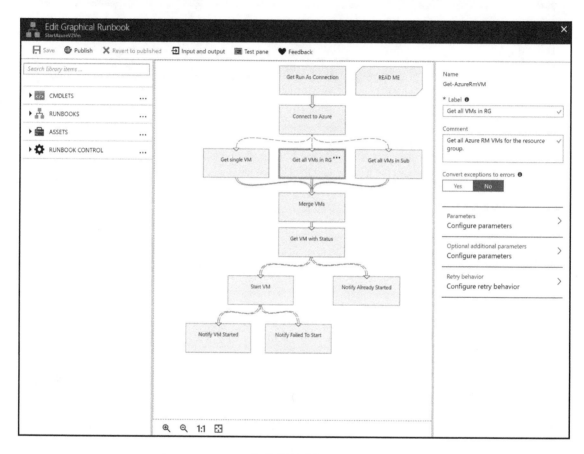

Graphical Runbook Editor

7. When you are done changing the settings according to your own environment, you can publish and schedule the Runbook.

Chef

Chef is a third-party solution that offers a DevOps automation platform for Linux, Windows, and Mac devices. It can be used for virtual and physical server configurations. It requires an agent to be installed on the virtual machines or servers, which connects to the Chef server to check whether there are available updates and other configurations for the machines. You can use the Chef Automate Platform to package and deploy applications as well.

To connect an Azure VM with the Chef Server, a publish settings file needs to be downloaded from Azure and imported in the Chef Server and an agent needs to be installed on your connected devices to communicate with Chef. You can then create Chef Cookbooks on the server, which consists of scripts and instructions to manage the devices and automate deployments.

Puppet

Puppet is a third-party solution as well, and it has similar capabilities as Chef. You can enable support for Puppet when you create a virtual machine from the Azure Portal automatically. You can add it as an extension when you create a new virtual machine. It will install the Puppet Agent, which connects to the Puppet Master Server.

You will have to provide the name of the Puppet Master Server, and the VM will be integrated when it is created:

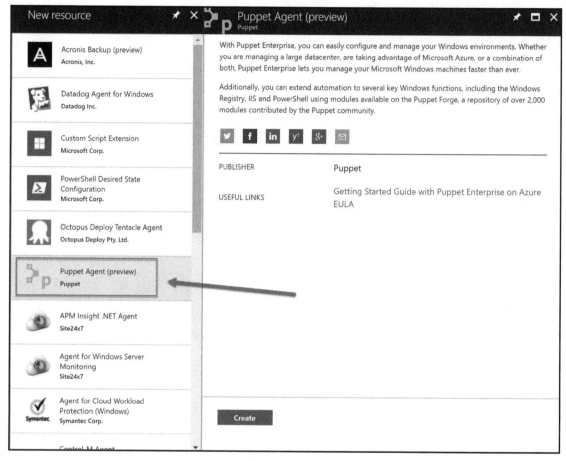

Install Puppet Agent

Azure Event Grid

Azure Event Grid provides support to automate tasks as well. Azure Event Grid offers an Azure Automation Subscriber that can act upon different events that are sent to Azure Event Grid. So when an Azure resource is created, it can call an Automation Runbook to automatically perform a sequence of steps. For instance, when a virtual machine is created in Azure, it can call an Automation runbook via Event Grid to create a schedule for starting and stopping virtual machines at a certain time.

For an complete walkthrough of integrating Azure Automation with Azure Event Grid and Microsoft Teams, you can refer to `https://docs.microsoft.com/en-us/azure/event-grid/ensure-tags-exists-on-new-virtual-machines`.

Azure Logic Apps

Azure Logic Apps offers support to call Automation Runbooks as well. It offers **Actions** that can be called from your Logic Apps to create automation jobs, collect output or get the status of jobs inside an Logic App. This can be used to create automations from within all types of workflows and can be integrated with various Azure resources.

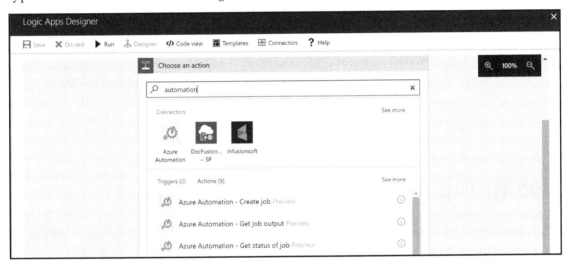

Azure Logic Apps Automation Actions

Visual Studio Team Services

Visual Studio Teams Services offers a Continuous Integration and Delivery (CI/CD) solution for your custom applications. It consist of a collection of DevOps services that can be used from Azure, and it can be installed on your on-premises servers as well by installing Team Foundation Server (TFS).

VSTS offers the following features and capabilities:

- **Version Control**: The starting point of continuous integration, delivery, and testing is a version control server. VSTS offers two different forms of version control, Git, and Team Foundation Version Control. It offers support for various version control repositories such as Subversion, Bitbucket, and GitHub.
- **Continuous Integration**: When CI is configured in VSTS, any code changes that are checked in are automatically built and validated. To configure CI, you have to create a new build definition, which consists of tasks that build and test your source code. It offers support in order to build .NET, Java, Node, Android, Xcode, and C++ applications. You can use continuous testing to automatically validate the code that is checked in, in VSTS. It offers support for various testing frameworks, such as unit tests and Selenium. You can run PowerShell, CLI, and command-line scripts in your automation as well.
- **Continuous Deployment:** The next step is to create a release definition. You can use to deploy your application automatically on one or more environments. The release definition also consists of a set of tasks. Both VSTS and TFS supports deploying applications to PaaS Services, such as Web Apps and Azure Functions for instance. You also deploy your code to virtual machines, containers, on-premises and other cloud platforms and publish mobile apps to the store.

Designing an autoscaling strategy

Autoscaling offers a solution to match performance requirements and meet SLAs for Azure resources and Applications. It can add additional resources such as adding VMs and CPUs to VMs and other Azure resources, and when those resources are no longer needed, they can be removed to minimize costs. This process is handled by Azure.

Autoscaling is one of the key benefits of cloud technologies because you add and remove additional resources easily and even automatically without the need to manage those resources. Autoscaling can be done in the following two different ways:

- **Vertical Scaling**: This is also called scaling up and down. You can move applications to a different VM size. By changing the VM size, applications become unavailable for a short period of time, so this type of scaling is normally not executed automatically.

- **Horizontal Scaling**: This is also called scaling in and out. You scale horizontally, when you add additional resources, such as adding or removing containers to Azure Container Services for instance. This type of scaling is mostly done automatically because it doesn't require resources to become unavailable.

To design an effective autoscaling strategy, you can use the following approaches and services:

- **Monitoring and alerting**: Use the monitoring and alerting capabilities that are available from the different monitoring solutions in Azure. These solutions are covered in more detail in the previous chapter. Next to the monitoring solutions, different Azure resources offer autoscaling as well, such as virtual machines, Azure Service Fabric, Azure Functions, Azure App Services, and other cloud services. These resources can be configured from the setting pages in the Azure Portal.
- **Decision Making Logic**: Make use of decision-making logic that helps deciding whether a resource needs to be scaled. This can be done dynamically inside Azure Logic Apps by calling Automation Runbooks or using predefined schedules at times where the system is heavily used.
- **Azure Monitoring Scale**: This is a service integrated in Azure Monitor that offers autoscaling for VMs, VM Scale Sets, Azure App Services, and Azure Cloud Services. You can use this for scheduling instances, scale-out when a certain CPU usage is met and when a certain number of messages are added to a queue.
- **Application Architectures**: Architect custom applications accordingly, so that they can be scaled horizontally. This applies to Azure Service Fabric applications, applications that run inside containers, or batch applications. For this, the Throttling Pattern and the Competing Consumers Pattern can be used.

Summary

In this final chapter, we covered how to design an operations automation strategy using the different solutions and tools that Azure provides as well as how to design an autoscaling strategy.

With the knowledge gained throughout the, chapters, you should be able to pass the 70-535 exam. Don't forget to look at the *Further reading* sections because there is a lot of extra information there that could be covered on the exam as well.

I hope you enjoyed reading this book as much I enjoyed writing it and good luck on your exam!

Questions

Answer the following questions to test your knowledge of the information in this chapter. You can find the answers in the *Assessments* section at the end of this book.

1. Your company uses Windows, Linux, and Mac devices. Is Azure Automation the best solution for your automation strategy?
    1. Yes
    2. No

2. You are designing a standardized deployment solution for your virtual machines. You also have a requirement to configure and keep VMs in sync after deployment. Should you use Azure PowerShell Desired State Configuration (DSC) for this?
    1. Yes
    2. No

3. Can you use Azure Event Grid for automation tasks?
    1. Yes
    2. No

Further reading

You can check the following links for more information about the topics that were covered in this chapter:

- **An introduction to Azure Automation**: https://docs.microsoft.com/en-us/azure/automation/automation-intro
- **Windows PowerShell Desired State Configuration Overview**: https://docs.microsoft.com/en-us/powershell/dsc/overview
- **Azure Automation DSC Overview**: https://docs.microsoft.com/en-us/azure/automation/automation-dsc-overview
- **Chef on Azure**: https://docs.microsoft.com/en-us/azure/chef/

- **Azure Event Grid Documentation**: `https://docs.microsoft.com/en-us/azure/event-grid/`
- **Azure Logic Apps Documentation**: `https://docs.microsoft.com/en-us/azure/logic-apps/`
- **Visual Studio Team Services: Build and release**: `https://docs.microsoft.com/en-us/vsts/build-release/?view=vsts`
- **Autoscaling Guidance**: `https://docs.microsoft.com/en-us/azure/architecture/best-practices/auto-scaling`

Appendix A – Assessments

Chapter 1, Working with Azure Virtual Machines

The answers to the questions are:

1. Correct answer: Yes: Managed Disks is the default disk type.
2. Correct answer: Yes: They should be added to Availability Sets.
3. Correct answer: No: By default, they are added to two Fault Domains and five Update Domains.

Chapter 2, Configuring Compute-Intensive Applications

The answers to the questions are:

1. Correct answer: No: You should use HPC Pack for this.
2. Correct answer: Yes: They are aimed at High Performance.
3. Correct Answer: No: Azure Batch has its own JSON templates that look like ARM templates.

Chapter 3, Designing Web Applications

The answers to the questions are:

1. Correct answer: Yes: Redis Cache is a on-memory key value data store.
2. Correct answer: 2: The Basic tier is best suited for development environments, not production environments.
3. Correct answer: 2: Azure B2C is the one you can leverage in your custom applications, not Azure B2B.

Chapter 4, Implementing Serverless and Microservices

The answers to the questions are:

1. Correct answer: Yes: You can use API Management as a stateless gateway for your microservices.
2. Correct answer: Yes: You can deploy Kubernets on Azure Container Instances.
3. Correct answer: Yes: Azure Service Fabric offers a full Devops environment for building Microservices.

Chapter 5, Robust Networking Implementations

The answers to the questions are:

1. Correct answer: No: When a custom Routing Table is created, Azure prefers the custom one over the System Route Table. It is not deleted.
2. Correct answer: No: NSG rules are processed from low to high.
3. Correct answer: Yes: A firewall is a well-known security solution to host in the DMZ.

Chapter 6, Connecting Hybrid Applications

The answers to the questions are:

1. Correct answer: 2: This is one of the constraints. To secure your App from outside access, you have to create an App Service Environment with a Internal Load Balancer.
2. Correct answer: No: You need Azure AD Connect to sync the on-premises accounts with Azure Active Directory.
3. Correct answer: Yes: You can use Azure App Service Virtual Network Integration for this.

Chapter 7, Using Storage Solutions

The answers to the questions are:

1. Correct answer: Yes: CosmosDB is globally distributed by default, so it offers low latency, which is most suited for gaming applications.
2. Correct answer: No: Azure Search can only be used with Azure SQL Database, Azure CosmosDB, and Azure Blob Storage.
3. Correct answer: No: MongoDB API doesn't offer support for graphs; for this, you should use the Gremlin API.

Chapter 8, Scalable Data Implementations

The answers to the questions are:

1. Correct answer: Yes: You can do a deleted database restore for restoring databases that are deleted.
2. Correct answer: Yes: You can use SQL Server Stretch database to mark tables to archive data from your on-premises SQL Server to Azure SQL database.
3. Correct answer: No: Azure Data Analytics uses U-SQL.

Chapter 9, Securing Your Resources

The answers to the questions are:

1. Correct answer: Yes: The Microsoft Graph provides a set of APIs that connects multiple Azure Services, such as Office 365 and Azure AD together, and provides a single endpoint for developers to use in their custom applications.
2. Correct answer: No: For a single sign-on experience accross on-premises and cloud applications, you should use ADFS.
3. Correct answer: Yes: You can use Azure B2B for giving controlled access to external users.

Chapter 10, Securing Your Data

The answers to the questions are:

1. Correct answer: No: You should use Always Encrypting. This enables storing encrypted data in the database. Encryption and decryption is handled from the client's side. Data Masking enables hiding sensible information for certain roles.
2. Correct answer: Yes: This is a feature of Azure Key Vault. You can use it to store the App Id and App secret and retrieve these values dynamically at runtime.
3. Correct answer: No: Azure Storage Service Encryption encrypts data at rest and data in transit. Not Azure Disk Encryption.

Chapter 11, Governance and Policies

The answers to the questions are:

1. Correct answer: Yes: With Azure AD Privileged Identity Management, you can grant eligible role access to users.
2. Correct answer: Yes: You can manage your on-premises and Azure infrastructure with Operations Management Suite.
3. Correct answer: Yes: You can use Azure Resource Policies for evaluating if your Azure Resources meet certain criteria, like if all Virtual Machines use Managed Disks.

Chapter 12, Artificial Intelligence, IoT, and Media Services

The answers to the questions are:

1. Correct answer: 2: You should use the Standard S2 service tier to process 5 million events a day.
2. Correct answer: 1: Yes: Media Services uses various Cognitive Services APIs underneath.
3. Correct answer: 2: No: For bidirectional communication between Azure and devices, you should use the IoT Hub. For data ingress scenarios, the Event Hub is a more suitable and cost-effective solution.

Chapter 13, Implementing Messaging Solutions

The answers to the questions are:

1. Correct answer: 2: No: you should use the Standard service tier; The Basic and Standard tier both offer 10 million push messages per month, but the Standard tier offers rich telemetry capabilities on top of the Basic tier.
2. Correct answer: 2: No, Azure Logic Apps doesn't provide a solution for calling external SDKs. Azure Functions does, so this is the best solution.
3. Correct answer: 2: No Azure Storage Queues can only handle messages with sizes up to 64 KB. You should use Azure Service Bus Queues for this.

Chapter 14, Application Monitoring and Alerting Strategies

The answers to the questions are:

1. Correct answer: 1: Yes, Azure Log Analytics offers real-time monitoring for your IoT solutions.
2. Correct answer: 2: No, you can open Azure Network watcher from the Azure Portal.
3. Correct answer: 1: Yes, Azure Service Health is the place where you retrieve information about scheduled maintenance events for the Azure platform.

Chapter 15, Exploring Operations Automation Strategies

The answers to the questions are:

1. Correct answer: 2: No, Chef is the best solution for this, as it can be used on Windows, Linux, and Mac devices.
2. Correct answer: 1: Yes, with Azure PowerShell Desired State Configuration (DSC), you can deploy and configure VMs after deployment.
3. Correct answer: 1: Yes. Azure Event Grid offers an Azure Automation Subscriber that can be used for automation tasks.

Appendix B – Mock Test Questions

Answer the following questions to test your knowledge of the information in this chapter. You can find the answers in the *Mock Test Answers* section at the end of this book.

Chapter 1, Working with Azure Virtual Machines

1. You need to recommend an appropriate strategy for development environments. Which VM series would you choose?
    1. F-series
    2. B-series
    3. L-series
    4. N-series

2. You have a set of applications that are deployed on a VM. You need to ensure that applications are still accessible when the VM is updated. What should you do?
    1. Create an availability set for each application
    2. Implement autoscaling
    3. Create a resource group
    4. Create an availability set with two or more virtual machines

3. When placing your VMs inside an availability set, how many fault domains are provided by Azure?
    1. 2
    2. 4
    3. 5
    4. 7

4. When a Azure VM is provisioned in Azure, is it created with managed disks or not?
    1. Yes
    2. No

5. How can VM Scale Sets be deployed?
    1. Using the Azure portal
    2. Using CLI
    3. Using PowerShell
    4. Using ARM templates

6. After deployment, can you access your VMs inside a VM Scale Set directly using SSH or RDP, using their public IP address?
    1. Yes
    2. No

7. You deploy an Azure VM to the East US region. You need to design a solution that will recover as quickly as possible in case of a data center outage. To which region would you deploy the VM?
    1. East US 2
    2. West Europe
    3. West US
    4. West US 2

Chapter 2, Configuring Compute-Intensive Applications

1. You are designing a graphically intensive application. Which VM series will you choose?
    1. B series
    2. N series
    3. A series
    4. G series

2. Your organization wants to run intensive scientific calculations only once a year. What is the cheapest solution?
    1. Azure Batch
    2. HPC Pack
    3. Azure VMs
    4. Azure HDInsight

3. Your company needs to run large-scale computation workloads. The core requirements of the implementation is to add and remove compute nodes from a central point, such as a management environment. What do you advise?
    1. Use Azure Batch
    2. Use Azure VMs
    3. Use Azure VM H-series
    4. Use HPC Pack

Chapter 3, Designing Web Applications

1. What are the benefits of a CDN?
    1. Reduce response time
    2. Reduce traffic to the original service
    3. Enable faster upgrades
    4. Improve Security

2. Which of the following programming languages does Azure Web Apps support?
    1. .NET Core
    2. Java
    3. Node.js
    4. Python

3. What are the available routing methods for Azure Traffic Manager?
    1. Geographic
    2. Scaling
    3. Caching
    4. Priority

4. You are creating an application that uses Redis Cache. You should recommend a pricing tier. Which one should you recommend?
    1. Basic
    2. Standard
    3. Premium
    4. Free

5. You are creating a custom application and have a requirement for users logging in with their Facebook account. Which solution would you choose?
    1. Azure AD B2C
    2. Microsoft Graph
    3. Azure Active Directory Connect
    4. Azure AD B2B

Chapter 4, Implementing Serverless and Microservices

1. You are designing an application that needs to trigger a BizTalk Server Electronic Data Interchange (EDI) Service. Which technical implementation is most suitable for this functionality?
    1. Azure API Management
    2. Azure Logic Apps
    3. Azure Functions
    4. Azure Container Instances

2. Azure Service Fabric offers full support for the application life cycle of your microservice application. Which roles does Azure Service Fabric provide?
    1. Service developer
    2. Application developer
    3. Operator
    4. Contributer

3. What is API management?
    1. An add-on for Visual Studio 2017, which you can use to deploy your APIs to Azure
    2. An API Gateway for your custom APIs
    3. A management tool for your Azure Logic apps
    4. A orchestrator for your containers

Chapter 5, Robust Networking Implementations

1. What VPN types are supported by Azure?
    1. VNet-to-VNet
    2. Site-to-Site
    3. Point-to-Site
    4. OpenVPN

2. What is the maximum bandwith that can be provided by ExpressRoute?
    1. 100 Mbps
    2. 1 Gbps
    3. 10 GBps
    4. 2 Gbps

3. You are designing an application that needs to be available to thousands of consumers around the world. You have performance and response time concerns for users that are located in distant geographies. What should you do?
    1. Set up a VPN gateway
    2. Deploy the application in multiple regions
    3. Deploy Traffic Manager
    4. Deploy a Load Balancer

4. You have two Virtual Machines, VM1 and VM2. All external traffic must be routed through VM1. What solution should you use?
    1. DNS
    2. A System Route
    3. A User-defined Route
    4. A Network Security Group

Chapter 6, Connecting Hybrid Applications

1. You want to connect your on-premises application to the cloud, but you aren't allowed to open up a firewall port. Which Azure Service do you use?
    1. Azure Active Directory Domain Services
    2. Azure Data Factory
    3. Azure Data Management Gateway
    4. Azure Relay Services

2. Your application is deployed on an on-premises virtual machine in your own data center. You want to leverage the Azure AD credentials inside your application. What is the easiest way to achieve this?
    1. Set up a hybrid environment and synchronize the user accounts and credentials with the cloud using Azure AD connect.
    2. Configure Azure AD Domain Services
    3. Use Azure On-Premises Data Gateway
    4. Use Azure VNet integration

Chapter 7, Using Storage Solutions

1. You are developing an application and need to store Microsoft Word and Excel documents. Which storage type do you choose?
    1. Blob Storage
    2. StorageV2
    3. Storage
    4. Table Storage

2. You are developing an application for a multinational and need to store datasets. Which replication type do you choose?
    1. Geo-redundant
    2. Zone-redundant
    3. Locally-redundant

3. Your organization uses an on-premises SharePoint 2013 farm with a lot of archiving data that is stored on SAN Storage and that is reaching the storage limitations of the current device. They need a more cost-effective storage option for the archive in the feature. What would you recommend?
    1. Adding new SAN storage devices inside the on-premises data center
    2. Using StorSimple Virtual Array
    3. Using Office 365 with SharePoint Online for storing data in the Cloud
    4. Using StorSimple 8000 Series

4. You want to use CosmosDB for a financial application. Which API is the best for this?
    1. Graph API
    2. SQL API
    3. Cassandra API
    4. DocumentDB API

5. You are planning to deploy Azure Search inside your organization for searching content from the company website, mobile applications, and other applications. You have the following requirements: Store up to 100 million documents, support multitenant scenarios, and support over 1,000 indexes. Which Service tier do you choose?
    1. Standard S1
    2. Standard S2
    3. Standard S3
    4. Standard HD

Chapter 8, Scalable Data Implementations

1. You have an on-premises SQL Server 2012 database and want to migrate as quickly as possible. You need to recommend a migration solution. What do you choose?
    1. Stretch Database
    2. Azure Database for MySQL
    3. Mongo DB
    4. Azure SQL Database

2. You want to implement Geo-replication for a Azure SQL Database. Where can you configure this?

    1. PowerShell

    2. Transact SQL

    3. The REST API

    4. The Azure portal

3. Which type of restoring scenarios are there for Azure SQL Database Backups?

    1. Point in time restore

    2. Standard restore

    3. Deleted database restore

    4. Geo-restore

4. You have five Azure SQL Databases that all use the Standard Service Tier. You are designing a backup strategy for the databases and the backups must be stored for a minimum of 5 years to meet legal requirements. Databases must be restored to a specific point in time. What should you do?

    1. Change the service tier from Standard to Premium

    2. Configure Azure Recovery Services and add a long-term backup retention policy

    3. Configure a Geo-restore

    4. Export the automated backups and store them as blobs

5. You are migrating an SQL Server on-premises database to Azure SQL Database, which has approximately 100 GB of data stored on it. You have the following requirements: 99.99% garanteed uptime, support multiple concurrent queries, and minimize the costs. Which service tier and level should you choose?

    1. Standard S1

    2. Standard S2

    3. Premium P1

    4. Premium P2

Chapter 9, Securing Your Resources

1. You are creating a mobile application hosted in Azure where external users can log in using their LinkedIn credentials. Which Azure Service do you use?
    1. The Microsoft Graph
    2. Azure B2B
    3. Azure AD REST APIs
    4. Azure B2C

2. How do you implement that in your mobile app?
    1. By adding a third-pary authentication SDK
    2. By adding built-in policies to the web.config
    3. By registering the app in Azure Active Directory
    4. By creating a new solution in Visual Studio 2017

3. You work for an organization that wants to integrate the on-premises AD with Azure AD. A requirement is that they can keep using their current login page, which has custom notifications and helpdesk information for their users. Which solution do you advise using?
    1. Deploy Azure AD Connect
    2. Use password sync with Azure AD
    3. Deploy ADFS
    4. Migrate the current active directory to Azure VMs

4. Your organization wants to gives controlled access to external users in Office 365, and they want to let external administrators manage the users. What is the best solution?
    1. Enable external sharing in Office 365 and let the users decide with whom they want to share documents
    2. Deploy ADFS
    3. Use Azure B2B
    4. User Azure B2C

Chapter 10, Securing Your Data

1. You want to enable Azure Storage Service Encryption on your storage account. Which storage type will get encrypted automatically?
    1. Blobs
    2. Files
    3. Queues
    4. Tables

2. You want to encrypt the data disks of your Virtual Machines. Which technology do you use?
    1. Azure Storage Service Encryption
    2. Always Encrypted
    3. Azure Key Vault
    4. Azure Disk Encryption

3. What is Always Encrypted?
    1. A place to store certificates
    2. A database setting for data in transit
    3. A database settings for data in use
    4. A key to encrypt and decrypt data

4. You are designing a new application, and for security reasons, you don't want to store any credentials in code and in web.config files. Which technology do you choose?
    1. Azure Active Directory Managed Service Identity
    2. Azure Key Vault
    3. Transparent Data Encryption
    4. App Service Principal

Chapter 11, Governance and Policies

1. You need to grant limited access to a team of adminstrators. Two of them need access to manage the Azure Subscription. To which role do you add the admins?
    1. Contributor
    2. Admin
    3. Reader
    4. Owner

2. You are monitoring your Compute Resources inside the Azure Security Center. A recommendation is displayed to install Endpoint Protection. What kind of protection does this provide?
    1. Anti-malware protection for your API Endpoints
    2. Anti-malware protection for your Virtual Machines
    3. Identity Protection for your API Endpoints
    4. Identity Protection for your Virtual Machines

3. There are several users inside your organization who need temporary access to administrator resources for Exchange Online. However, from a security perspective, you don't want them to be added to the Exchange Admin role inside RBAC. What solution would you advise using?
    1. Azure Active Directory Managed Service Identity
    2. Add them to the Contributor role in RBAC
    3. Use Azure AD Privileged Identity Management
    4. Add them to the Owner role and remove them manually when the users are done

4. You are working for a global company that is combining solutions from different Cloud Providers and has a number of on-premises data centers. You need to monitor and protect all of these environments from a single solution. Which solution do you advise using?
    1. Azure Security Center
    2. Operations Management Suite Security & Compliance
    3. Azure AD Identity Protection
    4. Advanced Threat Protection

5. You need to grant limited access to a team of adminstrators. One of them only needs permissions to restart virtual machines. To which role do you add the admin?
    1. Create a custom role
    2. Reader
    3. Owner
    4. Contributor

Chapter 12, Artificial Intelligence, IoT, and Media Services

1. You are creating a website where users can upload photographs of cultural landmarks. These pictures need to be categorized automatically based on the image. Which Cognitive Services API would you use?
    1. Face API
    2. Computer Vision API
    3. AMS Media Analytics
    4. LUIS API

2. You are designing a solution for collecting a large amount of data generated by sensor devices. The data needs to be processed locally inside the on-premises network. Which solution would you choose?
    1. Azure Time Series Analytics
    2. Azure IoT Hub
    3. Azure Event Hubs
    4. Azure IoT Edge

3. You are designing a solution for processing millions of events per second generated by various IoT devices. Which solution would you choose?
    1. Azure Time Series Analytics
    2. Azure IoT Hub
    3. Azure Event Hubs
    4. Azure IoT Edge

4. You are designing a solution using the Azure IoT Hub that processes more than 100 million events per day. Which pricing tier would you choose?
    1. Standard S1
    2. Standard S2
    3. Standard S3
    4. Standard S4

5. You are designing a solution that needs to ingest data from IoT devices to Azure. You need to choose the most cost-effective solution. Which solution would you choose?
    1. Azure IoT Hub
    2. Azure IoT Edge
    3. Azure Functions
    4. Azure Event Hubs

Chapter 13, Implementing Messaging Solutions

1. You are designing an application with the following requirements. The User Interface layer needs to be decoupled from multiple processing layers. The message size will be around 1 MB. This is an application that has scaling requirements in the future, and some processing layers will only receive a subset of the messages. Which solution would you choose?
    1. Azure Service Bus Queues
    2. Azure Service Bus Topics
    3. Azure Queue Storage
    4. Azure Functions

2. You are designing a solution that can monitor and respond to device events. You want to be able to multicast device events to multiple endpoints and create custom topics and Azure Functions. Which solution would you choose?
    1. Azure Event Grid
    2. Azure IoT Hub
    3. Azure Event Hubs
    4. Azure IoT Edge

3. You are designing an application with the following requirements. The User Interface layer needs to be decoupled from the processing layer. The message size will not exceed 50 KB. This is a small application that only has 1 processing layer, and there is no need for future upgrades. Which solution would you choose?
    1. Azure Service Bus Queues
    2. Azure Service Bus Topics
    3. Azure Queue Storage
    4. Azure Functions

Chapter 14, Application Monitoring and Alerting Strategies

1. You are creating a monitoring and alerting solution for your Azure Resources. You have the following requirements: send an alert when a VM is deleted and write events to Event Hubs and Log analytics. Which solution would you use?
    1. Azure Security Center
    2. Azure Health
    3. Azure Activity Log
    4. Azure Application Insights

2. You are creating a monitoring and alerting solution. Administrators want to query all available logs inside an Azure Subscription. Which solution would you use?
    1. Azure Security Center
    2. Azure Log Analytics
    3. Azure Health
    4. Azure Network Watcher

3. You are creating a Web Application, which can be hosted on-premises and in Azure in Docker Containers. You want to get more insights in page views and API calls. Which monitoring solution would you use?
    1. Azure Application Insights
    2. Azure Service Health
    3. Azure Activity Log
    4. Azure Network Watcher

4. You want to know when maintenance activities will occur on Azure Resources by Microsoft. Which monitoring solution will provide this type of information?
    1. Azure Application Insights
    2. Azure Service Health
    3. Azure Activity Log
    4. Azure Network Watcher

Chapter 15, Exploring Operations Automation Strategies

1. You are designing a standardized deployment and configuration of Virtual Machines. You need to publish a configuration library that can be used to automate the setup of roles and the feature installation on the new VMs. Which solution should you use for your automation strategy?
    1. Chef
    2. Puppet
    3. Graphical Runbooks
    4. Azure PowerShell Desired State Configuration (DSC)

2. You need to design a strategy for shutting down all VMs at 7:00 PM and restart them at 8:00 AM. The solution should run completely in Azure. Which solution would you choose?
    1. Chef
    2. Azure Automation
    3. Puppet
    4. PowerShell scripts that are configured as scheduled tasks on the VMs.

3. Your company uses Windows, Linux, and Mac devices. You are designing an automation strategy. Which solution would you choose?
    1. PowerShell
    2. Azure Automation
    3. Chef
    4. Puppet

Appendix C – Mock Test Answers

You can find the answers to the questions as follows:

Chapter 1, Working with Azure Virtual Machines

1. Correct answer: 2
    1. Incorrect: F-series are typically used for Compute-optimized VMs. They are used for gaming servers, web servers, and batch processing, not development.
    2. Correct: B-series are good for testing and development, small to medium databases, and low to medium traffic web servers.
    3. Incorrect: L-series are typically used data for storage scenarios like Big Data.
    4. Incorrect: N-series are specialized VMs targeted for heavy graphics rendering and video editing.

2. Correct answer: 4
    1. Incorrect: There is no such thing as creating availability sets for applications that are deployed on a virtual machine.
    2. Incorrect: Autoscaling is for the performance of your applications and virtual machine, not for high availability.
    3. Incorrect: A resource group will not help you here.
    4. Correct: By creating at least two virtual machines and place them in a availability set, your application will still be accessible if one virtual machine fails or needs to be updated.

3. Correct answer: 3
4. Correct answer: 1
5. Correct answer: 1, 2, 3, 4
    1. Correct: You can deploy a VM Scale Set using the Azure portal.
    2. Correct: You can deploy a VM Scale Set using CLI.
    3. Correct: You can deploy a VM Scale Set using PowerShell.
    4. Correct: You can deploy a VM Scale Set using ARM Templates.

6. Correct answers: 1

7. Correct answer: 1: The West US region is paired with the East US region. This means that in case of an outage, recovery of at least one region out of every pair is prioritized.

Chapter 2, Configuring Compute-Intensive Applications

1. Correct answer: 2
    1. Incorrect: B-series are good for testing and development, small to medium databases, and low to medium traffic web servers.
    2. Correct: N-series are specialized VMs targeted for heavy graphic rendering and video editing.
    3. Incorrect: Some VMs from the A-series are designed for HPC computing, but the N series is primarily designed for images rendering.
    4. Incorrect: X-Series do not exist.

2. Correct answer: 1: Azure Batch can scale up to hundreds of cores easily, and you pay only for the compute power you use. For the rest of the year, you don't have to pay anything. This cannot be accomplished using VMs or HPC Pack, which is installed on VMs or on-premises servers as well.

3. Correct answer: 4: Only Microsoft HPC Pack offers a management tool for adding and removing additional nodes. Azure Batch doesn't provide this.

Chapter 3, Designing Web Applications

1. Correct answers: 1, 2
    1. Correct: A CDN reduces response time. The content is stored on different servers from other locations.
    2. Correct: With the static content coming from other servers, the traffic to the original server reduces.
    3. Incorrect: A CDN has nothing to do with updates.
    4. Incorrect: A CDN has nothing to do with security.

2. Correct answers: 1, 2, 3, 4
3. Correct answers: 1, 4

    1. Correct: Geographic is a routing method for Azure Traffic Manager. The routing is based on the geographic location of the user.
    2. Incorrect: This is not a routing method.
    3. Incorrect: This is not a routing method.
    4. Correct: Priority is a routing method for Azure Traffic Manager. Using this method, the routing uses one endpoint as the primary endpoint for all traffic and provides backups in case the primary or the backup endpoints are unavailable.

4. Correct answer: 2. The Standard tier is best suited for production applications and is the most cost-effective one.
5. Correct answer: 1. Azure B2C is the one you can leverage in your custom applications when you want your users to log in with their Facebook credentials.

Chapter 4, Implementing Serverless and Microservices

1. Correct answer: 2

    1. Incorrect: API Management serves as a gateway for your custom APIs. On its own, it is not used to call on-premise BizTalk services.
    2. Correct: Azure Logic Apps consists of an out-of-the-box connector, which you can leverage to easily call a BizTalk service. It handles authentication as well.
    3. Incorrect: You can use a function for this and write code to access the service. This is, however, not the advised approach.
    4. Incorrect: A container is a package and deployment mechanism for applications.

2. Correct answers: 1, 2, 3: Azure Service Fabric provides the service developer role, the application developer role, and the operator role.
3. Correct answer: 2

Chapter 5, Robust Networking Implementations

1. Correct answers: 1, 2, 3: Only OpenVPN is not supported by Azure.
2. Correct answer: 3: 10 Gbps is the maximum bandwith.
3. Correct answer: 3: You should deploy Traffic Manager and configure it to use the performance method route. This will route traffic across the world based on the latency.
4. Correct answer: 3: You should use a UDR to force all traffic to go through VM1.

Chapter 6, Connecting Hybrid Applications

1. Correct answer: 4: You should use Azure Relay Services.
2. Correct answer: 2: Using Azure AD Domain Services, you can join a VM easily with Azure without installing a DC or syncing user accounts with the cloud.

Chapter 7, Using Storage Solutions

1. Correct answers: 2: StorageV2 is the recommended storage account by Microsoft.
2. Correct answers: 1: Geo-redundant. Multinationals use globally distributed data for high performance and high availability.
3. Correct answers: 4: StorSimple 8000 series provides a physical device that can store cold data, like archiving data easily in Azure Storage. This will be a more cost-effective solution compared to buying an on-premises storage device.
4. Correct answers: 2: The SQL API provides ACID transactions, which is most suitable for financial applications.
5. Correct answers: 4 Standard HD is the only pricing tier that can store up to 1,000 indexes.

Chapter 8, Scalable Data Implementations

1. Correct answer: 4: Azure SQL Database is the right solution here. Since you already have a SQL Server 2012 database, which is a relational database and already hosted on Microsoft technology this will be the quickest solution.
2. Correct answers: 1, 2, 3, 4: All answers are correct here.
3. Correct answers: 1, 3, 5: You can restore backups using a Point in Time restore, Deleted Database restore, and a Geo-restore.
4. Correct answer: 2: Azure Recovery Services with a long-term backup retention policy. Using an LTR policy, backup can be stored up to 10 years and restored using a Point in Time restore to restore the database.

5. Correct answer: 2: You should pick Standard S2. Using this tier and service level lets you store databases up to 250 GB and you can also manage 1,200 concurrent connections. You can use the Premium tier for this as well, since this can store databases larger then 250 GB and manage 2,400 concurrent connections, but this is more expensive than the Standard service tier.

Chapter 9, Securing Your Resources

1. Correct answer: 4: Azure Business to Consumer is the service that you can use to authenticate to LinkedIn. It provides a number of external authentication providers that you can leverage inside your custom applications.
2. Correct answer: 2: Azure B2C uses built-in policies, which needs to be added to the web.config in your code. By adding them, you can use them to sign-in, sign-up, read profile data, and more. These policies are linked to the various identity providers in Azure B2C.
3. Correct answer: 3: Using ADFS, the users logs on and the request is sent back to the on-premises environment and is validated against the on-premises Active Directory. It uses the on-premises login page, which can be fully customized to the needs of the organization.
4. Correct answer: 3: This is a feature of Azure that you can use for controlled external sharing. Administrators can manage external users from an dedicated portal and create groups and policies for them as well.

Chapter 10, Securing Your Data

1. Correct answers: 1, 2, 3, 4: Azure Storage Service Encryption will encrypt all four storage types automatically.
2. Correct answer: 4. You use Azure Disk Encryption for encrypting VM disks.
3. Correct answer: 3. database settings for data in use. You can enable this for Azure SQL databases, and it is used to store data encrypted in the database.
4. Correct answer: 1. Using Azure Active Directory Managed Service Identity, you can call an endpoint that uses your Azure AD credentials to obtain an access token. Credentials are not needed anymore.

Chapter 11, Governance and Policies

1. Correct answer: 4: The admins need to be added to the owner role to be able to manage everything.
2. Correct answer: 2: Endpoint Protection offers anti-malware protection for your Virtual Machines. It can only be enabled from the Azure Security Center.

3. Correct answer: 1: For only restarting the VM, you need to create a custom role. The built-in roles don't suit this.

4. Correct answer: 3: Operations Management Suite Security & Compliance is the solution that can monitor large hybird environments, including servers and solutions from different cloud providers.

5. Correct answer: 3: You can grant eligible role access to users using Azure AD Privileged Identity Management.

Chapter 12, Artificial Intelligence, IoT, and Media Services

1. Correct answer: 2: You should use the Computer Vision API. This can categorize cultural landmarks automatically based on the content of the image.

2. Correct answer: 4: Azure IoT Edge can be installed on the edge of the on-premises network and can store and process the data locally.

3. Correct answer: 2: IoT Hub is the only solution that can process millions of events per second.

4. Correct answer: 2: Standard S2 offers support for up to 6 million messages per day, so this will be the best solution.

5. Correct answer: 4: Azure Event Hubs is the most cost-effective solution for this scenario because it only requires one way communication from the devices to Azure.

Chapter 13, Implementing Messaging Solutions

1. Correct answer: 2: For an application this size, with this message size and multiple subscribers that need filtering capabilities, Azure Service Bus Topics is the appropriate solution.

2. Correct answer: 1: Azure Event Grid is the right solution here. This can push events to multiple Azure Resources, such as Azure Functions.

3. Correct answer: 3: For a small application with only one processing layer and maximum message sizes of 50 KB, Azure Queue storage is the right solution.

Chapter 14, Application Monitoring and Alerting Strategies

1. Correct answer: 3: You should use Azure Activity Log, which is integrated in Azure Monitor.
2. Correct answer: 2: In Azure Log Analytics, the administrator can create queries to query data.
3. Correct answer: 1: Application Insights is the appropriate monitoring solution for custom applications. They can be hosted on Azure and on-premises.
4. Correct answer: 2: Azure Platform maintenance activities and schedules are provided via Azure Service Health.

Chapter 15, Exploring Operations Automation Strategies

1. Correct answer: 4: You should use Azure PowerShell Desired State Configuration (DSC). This provides support for machine configuration and application deployment on initial startup of the Virtual Machines.
2. Correct answer: 2: You should use Azure Automation for this. This solution runs completely in Azure, and you can create a runbook that is scheduled to stop and start the VMs daily.
3. Correct answer: 3: Chef offers support for Windows, Linux, and Mac devices.

Other Books You May Enjoy

If you enjoyed this book, you may be interested in these other books by Packt:

Azure for Architects
Ritesh Modi

ISBN: 978-1-78839-739-1

- Familiarize yourself with the components of the Azure Cloud platform
- Understand the cloud design patterns
- Use enterprise security guidelines for your Azure deployment
- Design and implement Serverless solutions
- See Cloud architecture and the deployment pipeline
- Understand cost management for Azure solutions

Azure Serverless Computing Cookbook
Praveen Kumar Sreeram

ISBN: 978-1-78839-082-8

- Develop different event-based handlers supported by serverless architecture supported by Microsoft Cloud Platform – Azure
- Integrate Azure Functions with different Azure Services to develop Enterprise-level applications
- Get to know the best practices in organizing and refactoring the code within the Azure functions
- Test, troubleshoot, and monitor the Azure functions to deliver high-quality, reliable, and robust cloud-centric applications
- Automate mundane tasks at various levels right from development to deployment and maintenance
- Learn how to develop statefulserverless applications and also self-healing jobs using DurableFunctions

Leave a review - let other readers know what you think

Please share your thoughts on this book with others by leaving a review on the site that you bought it from. If you purchased the book from Amazon, please leave us an honest review on this book's Amazon page. This is vital so that other potential readers can see and use your unbiased opinion to make purchasing decisions, we can understand what our customers think about our products, and our authors can see your feedback on the title that they have worked with Packt to create. It will only take a few minutes of your time, but is valuable to other potential customers, our authors, and Packt. Thank you!

Index

A

Access Control Lists (ACLs) 202
access tiers
  about 163
  archive storage tier 163
  cool access tier 163
  hot access tier 163
Active Directory Federation Services (ADFS)
  about 72
  features 212
API gateway 102
API management
  about 102
  administrators 103
  developer portal 103
  developers 103
  guests 103
  portal 102
App Service plans
  about 45
  basic 46
  free and shared 45
  isolated 49
  premium 48
  standard 47
Application Delivery Controller (ADC) 120
Application Insights
  about 335
  application events 335
Application Service Environment (ASE)
  about 49, 76, 150
  creating 50
  reference link 150
application solutions
  designing, Azure Functions used 78, 82, 84, 86
  designing, Logic Apps used 89, 92, 94, 95

approaches and services, autoscaling strategy
  alerting 357
  application architectures 357
  Azure monitoring scale 357
  decision making logic 357
  monitoring 357
Artificial Intelligence (AI) 273
assets migration
  Cloud DevOps-ready 104
  cloud infrastructure-ready 104
  cloud-optimized 104
  versus cloud-native deployments 103
Atomicity, Consistency, Isolation, Durability (ACID)
  202
autoscaling strategy
  designing 356
  horizontal scaling 357
  vertical scaling 356
Azure Active Directory (Azure AD)
  about 208
  pass-through authentication 211
  password hash synchronization 211
  pricing plans 208
Azure Active Directory Business to Business
  about 215
  features 216
Azure Active Directory Business to Consumer
  about 217
  authentication providers 217
  leveraging, in application 217, 219, 220, 222,
    223, 225, 227, 228, 229, 230
  reference 217
Azure Active Directory Library (ADAL) 208
Azure Active Directory Managed Service Identity
  about 248
  reference 249
Azure AD Application Proxy

about 150
  connector 150
  external endpoint 151
Azure AD Connect
  about 210
  reference 210
Azure AD Domain Services
  enabling 151, 154
Azure AD Identity Protection
  about 260
  policies 261
Azure AD Privileged Identity Management
  about 259
  flow 259
Azure Advisor
  about 338
  categories 338
  recommendation, addressing 338, 340
Azure Analysis Services 192
Azure app service hybrid connections 146
Azure App Service on Linux
  reference 54
Azure app service virtual network integration 148, 149
Azure application gateway
  about 120
  reference 121
Azure Audit Logs content pack, for Power BI
  reference 119
Azure Automation Runbook
  creating 348, 351
Azure Automation
  about 347
  configuration management 348
  process automation 347
  shared capabilities 348
  update management 348
Azure Autoscale 63
Azure Backup Service
  components 25
Azure Batch
  about 34
  containers 41
  service, creating 36, 37, 39
  stateless components 39

Azure blob storage
  about 160, 161, 162
  access tiers 163
  account types 160
  General-purpose v1 (GPv1) 160
  General-purpose v2 (GPv2) 161
  replication types 160, 161
Azure Bot Service
  about 282
  bot, creating from Azure Portal 283, 286, 288
Azure CDN custom domain, HTTPS configuring
  reference 59
Azure CDN endpoint, custom domain adding
  reference 59
Azure CLI 2.0
  URL 98
Azure Cognitive Services
  about 274
  APIs 274
  computer vision API, using 277, 282
  services 274
Azure Container Instances (ACI) 97
Azure container instances
  used, for designing serverless computing 97
Azure Cosmos DB
  reference 174
Azure Data Catalog
  about 180
  free 180
  reference 180
  standard 180
Azure Data Factory
  about 181
  features, for composing data into data-driven workflows 181
  reference 182
Azure Data Lake Analytics
  about 183, 185
  data, analyzing 185, 187, 188, 189, 190
  price packages 185
Azure Data Lake Store 184
Azure Data Management Gateway
  for data factory 144
  reference 144
Azure database for MySQL

features 202
pricing tiers 203
Azure database for PostgreSQL
features 203
pricing tiers 204
Azure Disk Encryption 246
Azure disk storage
about 169
premium disk storage 170
standard disk storage 169
unmanaged disks, versus managed disks 170
Azure Event Grid
about 310, 354
events, routing 311, 313, 316, 318, 319
reference 310
Azure Event Hub
about 292
Azure IoT Edge 294
versus Azure IoT Hub 321
Azure file storage 169
Azure Functions
consumption App Service plan 78
Durable Functions 87
reference 76
used, for designing application solutions 78, 82,
84, 86
used, for event-driven actions 76
versus Logic Apps 321
Azure HDInsight
about 191
cluster types 191
Azure IoT Edge 294
Azure IoT Hub
versus Azure Event Hub 321
Azure Key Vault
about 236
creating, in Azure portal 236, 238, 240, 242,
243
premium tier 236
secrets, using in ARM templates 244
standard tier 236
Azure Load Balancer
about 117
probes 119
versions 118

Azure Log Analytics 326
Azure Logic Apps 355
Azure Logic Apps, connectors
reference 87
Azure machine learning
about 289
tools 289
Azure Marketplace
reference 30
Azure Media Analytics Indexer
using 298, 301
Azure Media Analytics
about 298
content moderation 298
hyperlapse 298
indexer 298
motion detector 298
optical character recognition 298
scalable face redaction 298
video summarization 298
Azure Media Services
about 297
analyze 297
Azure Media Analytics 298
Azure Media Analytics Indexer, using 298, 301
encode 297
secure 297
upload 297
Azure Monitor
about 332
activity log 333
Alerts section 334
capabilities 333
diagnostic settings 333
metrics 333
Azure Network Watcher
about 341
capabilities 341
connection troubleshoot 342
IP flow verify 341
next hop 341
packet capture 342
security group view 342
topology 341
VPN diagnostics 342

Azure on-premises data gateway 145
Azure portal
  Multi-Factor Authentication, enabling 213
  virtual machines, creating 13
  VM scale sets, creating 22
Azure queue storage 168
Azure Queue Storage
  about 308
  capabilities 308
Azure relay hybrid connections protocol
  reference 143
Azure relay service
  about 142
  Hybrid connections 143
  WCF Relays 144
Azure Relay WCF Relays
  reference 144
Azure Resource Policies 258
Azure resources, for cloud-native HPC architecture
  ARM templates 32
  HPC compute nodes 31
  HPC head node 31
  storage 31
  Virtual Machine Scale Set (VMSS) 31
  virtual network 31
Azure resources, Hybrid HPC architecture
  ExpressRoute 33
  HPC compute nodes 33
  HPC head node 32
  storage 33
  Virtual Machine Scale Sets 33
  virtual network 33
  VPN Gateway 33
Azure Role-Based Access Control 254
Azure search
  about 175
  basic 176
  free tier 176
  Standard HD 176
  standard S1 176
  standard S2 176
  standard S3 176
Azure Security Center
  about 262
  advanced threat detection 264

Endpoint Protection 264, 266
  features 262
Azure Service Bus
  about 308
  basic tier 309
  capabilities 309
  premium tier 309
  queues 309
  reference 309
  relays 309
  standard tier 309
  subscriptions 309
  topics 309
  versus Azure Storage Queues 322
  WFC 309
Azure Service Fabric, life cycle features
  reference 101
Azure Service Fabric
  about 99, 100
  life cycle management 101
  reference link 101
Azure Service Health
  about 337
  views, from Azure portal 337
Azure Site Recovery Services
  features 26
Azure SQL Data Warehouse 182
Azure SQL Database Security
  about 247
  Always Encrypted 248
  HTTPS 247
  transparent data encryption 247
Azure SQL database
  about 193
  backup 201
  elastic database pools 193
  high availability 194
  individual databases 193
  recovery 201
  reference 193
  SQL Server Stretch Database 194
Azure Storage pricing
  reference 161
Azure Storage Queues
  versus Azure Service Bus 322

Azure Storage Service Encryption (SSE) 244
Azure Stream Analytics 294
Azure table storage, .NET used
  reference 168
Azure table storage
  about 164
  account, creating 164
  data, uploading 165, 168
Azure Time Series Insights 295
Azure Traffic Manager 119
Azure virtual machines
  availability sets 10
Azure Virtual Network (VNet)
  about 108
  creating, with two subnets 113, 114, 115, 116
  DNS 112
  external connectivity 122
  IP addresses 109
Azure VPN
  about 122
  basic 122
  ExpressRoute 125
  point-to-site (P2S) VPN 124
  site-to-site (S2S) VPN 123
  VNet-to-VNet VPN 124
  VpnGw1 122
  VpnGw2 122
  VpnGw3 122
Azure web apps 44
Azure
  built-in roles 256

B

basic Load Balancer 118
block blobs 162
built-in roles, Azure
  contributor 256
  owner 256
  reader 256
  reference 256
Business to Consumer (B2C) 72

C

Chef 353

cloud-native deployments
  versus assets migration 103
cloud-native HPC architecture
  required Azure resources 31
cloud-native HPC solution 31
cluster types, Azure HDInsight
  Apache Hadoop 191
  Apache HBase 191
  Apache Interactive Query (Preview) 191
  Apache Kafka 191
  Apache Spark 191
  Apache Storm 191
  Microsoft R Server 191
computer vision API
  using 277
connection models, ExpressRoute
  any-to-any (IPVPN) 125
  co-located at Cloud Exchange 126
  point-to-point Ethernet 125
consumption App Service plan 78
consumption plan 78
container orchestrations
  about 98
  affinity/anti-affinity 99
  application upgrades 99
  failover 99
  health monitoring 99
  networking 99
  scaling 99
  scheduling 99
  service discovery 99
containers, on Batch Shipyard
  reference 41
Content Delivery Network (CDN)
  about 58
  using 58
Content Encryption Key (CEK) 245
Continuous Integration and Delivery (CI/CD) 355
Cosmos DB storage
  about 173
  Cassandra API 174
  Gremlin (Graph) API 174
  MongoDB API 174
  SQL API 174
  Table API 174

custom roles
  about 256
  creating 257, 258

D

Data Catalog REST API
  reference 180
data sources, in Azure Analysis Services
  reference 145
data
  analyzing, Azure Data Lake Analytics used 185,
    187, 188, 189, 190
Database Transaction Units (DTUs)
  reference 193
demilitarized zone (DMZ) 127
Desired State Configuration (DSC) 345
Desired State Configuration
  about 346
  configuration 346
  Local Configuration Manager (LCM) 346
  resources 346
Developer Finder 54
Development, Testing, Acceptance, and Production
  (DTAP) 345
digital rights management (DRM) 297
disaster recovery 25
DNS 112
Docker Hub
  reference 54
Durable Functions 87
dynamic addresses 110

E

elastic Database Transaction Units (eDTUs)
  about 193
  reference 193
Event Grid
  reference 354
event-driven actions
  Azure Functions, used 76
events
  routing, with Azure Event Grid 311, 313, 316,
    318, 319
ExpressRoute

about 125
  connection models 125
external connectivity, Azure virtual networks
  about 122
  Azure VPN 122

F

fault domains 11
First In, First Out (FIFO) 309
fully qualified domain name (FQDN) 112, 342

G

Geo-redundant Storage (GRS) 161
Graph API
  reference 209
guest agent probe 119

H

Hadoop YARN, solutions
  Azure Data Lake Analytics 185
  Azure Data Lake Store 184
  Azure HDInsight 191
Hadoop YARN
  reference 183
Hardware Security Modules (HSMs) 236
hardware specification, N-series virtual machines
  reference 30
high availability, Azure SQL database
  active geo-replication, configuring 195, 196
  failover groups 194
  failover groups, configuring 195, 196
  geo-replication, activating 194
high availability, web apps
  Azure Traffic Manager, used 61
  CDN, used 58
  Redis Cache, used 59
high-performance computing (HPC)
  about 29
  virtual machines 29
high-performance VMs
  reference 30
highly available virtual machines
  creating 13
  creating, from Azure portal 13

creating, from PowerShell 18
hybrid connections 143
Hybrid HPC architecture
  about 32
  required Azure resources 32

I

Internal Load Balancer (ILB)
  about 150
  reference 150
Internet Key Exchange (IKE) 123
Internet of Things (IoT)
  about 291
  Azure Event Hub 292
  bi-directional communication 291
  monitoring 291
  scaling 291
  secure connectivity 291
Internet Protocol Security (IPSec) 123
IP address
  public IP address 110
IP addresses
  dynamic addresses 110
  private IP address 111
  static IP addresses 110

L

life cycle management, Azure Service Fabric
  application administrator 101
  application developer 101
  operator 101
  service developer 101
line of business (LOB) applications 208
Linux VM sizes
  reference 10
Locally Redundant Storage (LRS) 161
Log Analytics workspace
  creating 326, 328, 329, 330, 331, 332
Logic Apps
  application solutions, designing 89, 92
  used, for designing application solutions 94, 95
  used, for workflow-driven applications 87
  versus Azure Functions 321

M

managed disks 13
Massively Parallel Processing (MPP) 182
media processor (MP) 298
Message Passing Interface (MPI) 34
messaging architecture
  designing 321
Microsoft Authentication Library (MSAL) 208
Microsoft Graph 209
Microsoft HPC Pack
  about 30
  features 31
Microsoft Management Console (MMC) 172
Multi-Factor Authentication
  about 212
  enabling, in Azure portal 213
  enabling, in Office 365 214
multi-instance tasks 39
multiversion concurrency control (MVCC) 204
MyApps portal
  URL 151

N

network interfaces (NIC) 127
Network Security Group (NSG)
  about 107, 127
  creating 128, 129, 130, 131, 132
network security strategies
  about 126
  demilitarized zone (DMZ) 127
  Network Security Group (NSG) 127
  User Defined Routes (UDRs) 132
  virtual network service tunneling 137
  Web Application Firewall (WAF) 138
Notification Hubs
  about 320
  basic tier 320
  free tier 320
  standard tier 320
NuGet packages
  Microsoft Windows Azure Configuration Manager 166
  Windows Azure Storage 166

O

Office 365
  Multi-Factor Authentication, enabling 214
on-premises MFA Server
  reference 213
operations automation strategy
  Azure Automation 347
  Azure Event Grid 354
  Azure Logic Apps 355
  Azure PowerShell 346
  Chef 353
  designing 345
  Desired State Configuration 346
  Puppet 353
  Visual Studio Team Services 355
Operations Management Suite (OMS)
  about 268
  compliance 268
  security 268
optical character recognition (OCR) 298

P

page blobs 162
performance, web apps
  CDN, used 58
  Redis Cache, used 59
point-to-site (P2S) VPN 124
policy, Azure Portal
  reference 259
PowerShell
  highly available virtual machines, creating from 18
price packages, Azure Data Lake Analytics
  monthly commitment 185
  pay-as-you-go 185
  reference 185
pricing plans, Azure Active Directory (Azure AD)
  basic 208
  free 208
  Premium P1 208
  Premium P2 208
  reference 208
private IP address 111
public IP address

about 110
  creating 111
Puppet 353

R

read-access geo-redundant storage (RA-GRS) 201
Redis Cache
  basic tier 59
  premium tier 59
  standard tier 59
  using 59
Reliable Actor programming model
  reference 101
replication types, Azure blob storage
  Geo-redundant Storage 162
  Locally Redundant Storage (LRS) 162
  Zone Redundant Storage 162
Role-Based Access Control (RBAC) 97, 248
Routing and Remote Access Service (RRAS) 123
routing methods, Azure Traffic Manager
  geographic 62
  performance 62
  priority 62
  weighted 62
rule set, OWASP
  reference 138

S

scalability, web apps
  scaling out 63
  scaling up 65
Secure Socket Tunneling Protocol (SSTP) 124
Security Assertion Markup Language (SAML) 212
security policies, Azure
  reference 263
Server Message Block (SMB) 169
serverless computing
  container orchestrations 98
  containers, creating 97
  designing, Azure container instances used 97
Single Sign On (SSO) 150
site-to-site (S2S) VPN 123
SQL Service Stretch Database 194

standard Load Balancer
  reference 118
static IP addresses 110
storage area network (SAN) 170
StorSimple 170
StorSimple 8000 Series
  about 172
  reference 172
StorSimple Virtual Array
  about 171
  reference link 171
Subnet Mask Cheat Sheet
  reference 109

T

tools, Azure machine learning
  Azure AI gallery 289
  Azure machine learning workbench 289
  data science virtual machines 290
  machine learning modules 290
  machine learning studio 289
Transport Layer Security (TLS) 142

U

update domains 11, 12
User Defined Routes (UDRs)
  about 107, 132
  creating 133, 134, 136
user-defined functions (UDFs) 174

V

versions, Azure Load Balancer
  basic 118
  standard 118
virtual machine (VM)
  about 254
  adding, to managed domain 156
  joining, to domains 151
  series 9
  sizes 9
  solutions, designing for 8

Virtual Machine Scale Set (VMSS) 31
virtual network peering 108
virtual network service tunneling
  about 137
  reference 137
Visual Studio Team Services
  about 355
  continuous deployment 356
  continuous integration 356
  version control 356
VM scale sets
  about 21
  accessing 24
  creating, from Azure portal 22
  templates 24
VNet-to-VNet VPN 124

W

WCF Relays 144
web API
  Active Directory Federation Services 72
  API management 72
  Azure Active Directory (Azure AD) 72
  Azure Active Directory Business to Consumer 72
  designing 66, 67, 69, 70
  securing 66, 72
Web Application Firewall (WAF) 107, 138
web apps
  designing, for high availability 58
  designing, for performance 58
  designing, for scalability 58, 62
  for containers 53, 54
Windows PowerShell Desired State Configuration
  reference 348
Windows VM sizes
  reference 10
workflow-driven applications
  Logic Apps, used 87

Z

Zone Redundant Storage (ZRS) 161

CPSIA information can be obtained
at www.ICGtesting.com
Printed in the USA
BVHW06s1855280518
517560BV00013B/962/P